WESTERN CHALLENGE

THE PRESBYTERIAN CHURCH IN CANADA'S MISSION ON THE PRAIRIES AND NORTH, 1885-1925

WESTERN CHALLENGE

THE PRESBYTERIAN CHURCH IN CANADA'S MISSION
ON THE PRAIRIES AND NORTH, 1885-1925

PETER BUSH

Cover design by Doowah Design Inc.
Author photo by Mitchell Photographics and Solutions
Cover photo is Rev. James Robertson with other men at the opening of new church in Rossland, B.C., August 25 or 26, 1895.
Reproduced with permission of the United Church of Canada, 76.001 P/5568N
Printed and bound in Canada

We acknowledge the financial assistance of the Manitoba Arts Council and The Canada Council for the Arts for our publishing program.

Credits

A portion of Chapter 2 appeared as: "James Robertson: Presbyterian Bishop of the West," *Called to Witness:Profiles of Canadian Presbyterians*, vol. 4, pp. 38-51.

A section of Chapter 3 appeared as: "The Dakota Missionaries of The Presbyterian Church in Canada, 1877-1903," *Presbyterian History*, vol. 40, #2, October 1996, pp. 1-5.

An earlier and much shorter version of Chapter 4 appeared as: "Why Should the Church Confine Her Labours to Those Who May Show a Presbyterian Pedigree?: The Presbyterian Church Responds to Non-English-Speaking Immigrants in Western Canada, 1896-1925," *Canadian Society of Presbyterian History Papers*, 1997, pp. 2-12.

The copyright for each of these remains with the author, Peter Bush.

Canadian Cataloguing in Publication Data

Bush, Peter George, 1962-
   Western challenge: the Presbyterian Church in Canada's mission on the Prairies and North, 1885-1925

Includes bibliographical references and index.
ISBN 1-896239-73-0

   1. Presbyterian Church—Missions—Prairie Provinces—History. 2. Presbyterian Church—Missions—Canada, Northern—History. I. Title

BV2815.N6B88 2000   266'.5271   C00-901162-5

Dedicated to my wife
Deborah Ann Sutherland Bush
a woman who lives at the frontier of mission

Acknowledgements

This book had its genesis in the spring of 1987, when Professor John Moir suggested that I might write a paper on the Knox College Student Missionary Society. The Society's mission vision amazed me. Later I was to meet James Robertson, who has become one of my heroes.

But it was not until I had a discussion with the Rev. Dr. James Marnoch while we were standing in line for a meal at the 1995 Synod meeting held in Neepawa that I knew I had to write this book. I want to thank him for his kind invitation to write the second volume of the work he began with his *Western Witness*. I also wish to thank the History Committee of the Synod of Manitoba and Northwestern Ontario for their support of this project.

I wish to acknowledge the ways in which the late Professor George Rawlyk, Dr. Ian Rennie, Dr. John Moir, and Professor Phyllis Airhart have helped shape my historical understanding and to thank Dr. Marguerite van Die for her offhand question seven years ago, "So when are you writing your book?" At the time I just laughed.

I want to publicly thank the congregation of St. Andrew's Presbyterian Church in Flin Flon, Manitoba, who taught me much about not just ministry, but about mission at the frontier and who taught me to love the west. I also want to thank the congregation of Knox Presbyterian Church in Mitchell, Ontario who graciously and generously gave me a sabbatical so that I could write this book. Without the sabbatical it would never have come into being.

A special thanks to Gordon Shillingford for his work as publisher and to copy editor Rachel Donner.

Finally a word of thanks to my family—to Nathan for letting Daddy write his notebook even when you would have rather I was at home; and to my wife, Debbie, who has been a tower of strength, encouragement, and support. When I felt like giving up, she reminded me that historical writing is part of my mission frontier. And it is to her that I dedicate this book.

Table of Contents

INTRODUCTION

This book is about the history of the Presbyterian Church in Canada's mission in the west. It has been said, "The church exists for mission, as fire exists for burning." Between 1885 and 1925, the Presbyterian Church in Canada on the prairies burned with the fire of mission. This book explores how the Presbyterian Church became and remained the largest Christian denomination on the prairies through the first quarter of the twentieth century.

When one looks at the Presbyterian Church in Canada on the prairies at the end of the twentieth century, it is difficult to imagine that in 1921, nearly one in four people living on the prairies was a Presbyterian. In each of the three prairie provinces the Presbyterian Church was the largest denomination. Of the 13 urban centres on the prairies, which in 1921 had populations over 5,000 people, the Presbyterians were the largest religious group in nine, and the second largest in three of the other four. In fact, a higher percentage of westerners (including British Columbia) were Presbyterian than the percentage of Nova Scotians or Ontarians who were Presbyterian. Only Prince Edward Island had a higher concentration of Presbyterians than did the West. In 1921, 22.2 percent of Canada's population lived on the prairies; however, 30 percent of the Presbyterians in the country lived there. Even more remarkable these days, when Christian denominations feel happy if they do not have a declining membership, let alone being concerned about growing at the same rate as the population; between 1901 and 1921, the Presbyterian Church on the prairies grew by 450 percent almost exactly matching the growth of population.[1]

This book is about the mission vision that was widely held by Presbyterians between 1881 and 1912. The growth and expansion that will be described did not come without broad based support and a sacrificial commitment on the part of many ordinary Presbyterians. Ordinary Presbyterians were encouraged to become part of this mission and the vision was cast in such a way that they understood they had a role in the mission, a mission that was theirs if they would but join it.

In 1881, when James Robertson became the Superintendent of Missions for the West, there were 15 self-supporting congregations and 29 mission charges in the Presbyterian Church between Lake Superior and the Rockies. Twenty years later, at the time of Robertson's death in 1902, there were 141 self-supporting congregations and 258 mission charges, with 393 church buildings. And in 1924, on the eve of church union, the number of self-supporting charges had more than doubled to 321 and there were 287 charges receiving financial support from the national church. Together these charges had a total of 1,800 preaching points—places where groups of people gathered together to be a congregation in worshipping God and hearing the story of the Good News about Jesus preached. These congregations were ministered to by 479 ordained clergy and approximately 200 students and catechists. In addition to these congregations, there were 10 hospitals or nursing stations and 14 school homes on the prairies being operated by the women of the Presbyterian Church. There were three theological colleges for training ministers. The church also operated five Native residential schools and four day schools on the prairies. This remarkable growth in the space of 40 years was possible only because ordinary Presbyterians sitting in church pews in Ontario and Quebec and the Maritimes, along with Presbyterians in western Canada, caught the mission vision and gave financially. Some even gave themselves to serve in this mission adventure.

Dr. James Marnoch wrote the first volume of this history of the Presbyterian Church in the Northwest, taking the story up to the establishment of the Synod of Manitoba and the Northwest in 1885.[2] While recognizing 1885 to be its starting point, the present work begins with the appointment of James Robertson as Superintendent of Mission for the West in 1881 as a critical moment in the history of the church's mission on the prairie. The story is continued to 1925, when approximately three-quarters of the Presbyterians on the prairies entered the United Church of Canada. This too was a critical moment in the life of the church, for the Presbyterian Church after 1925 was fundamentally different than the church before 1925. The post-1925 history of the Presbyterian Church will have to wait for a further book. The story of the church in the west between 1885 and 1925 is an exciting one, and I hope that readers will catch some of the excitement of those times as they read this account.

The story of the Presbyterian Church in the west between 1885 and 1925 is a very large one, for it is made up of thousands of smaller stories of congregations and hospitals, of schools and inner city missions, and, most importantly, of women and men, children and youth. This book cannot hope to tell the story of every Presbyterian congregation during that time, or even to make mention of all the people who played important roles in the growth and development of the church on the prairies. The story will be told thematically, using mission as the primary organizing principle. Chapter 2 tells the story of the church being planted on the prairie among Anglo-Saxon settlers, many of whom were Presbyterians from Ontario.

This chapter opens with James Robertson being appointed Superintendent of Mission, and explores the methods used to start churches and the type of personnel needed to minister to the new arrivals. Following Robertson's death the church kept growing and expanding, and the story of this growth will be included.

Chapter 3 explores the mission of the Presbyterian Church among the Native people in Canada. Jim Marnoch had begun to tell that story in *Western Witness* and this chapter picks up the story in 1885. Of particular interest will be the work of the Dakota missionaries and other Native people who worked on behalf of the Presbyterian Church in reaching the Native people of Canada with the gospel. It is impossible to write about churches and Native people in Canada without making reference to the residential schools and the schools operated by the Presbyterian Church will be discussed. Chapter 4 tells of the church's work among the non-Anglo-Saxon immigrants, who by 1912, were quite consistently being called "new Canadians." The various cultural groups among whom the church had specific ministries will be touched on, by far the most significant group in terms of time and resources expended being the Ukrainian community. With Chapter 5 we look north to the Yukon, the Atlin Hospital, and the Peace River country. Here, as late as the 1920's pioneer life was being lived, and the church was faced with a new frontier. Chapter 6 asks how the church balanced evangelism and social service in its ministry. The discussion of these approaches to ministry within the Presbyterian Church had been in the wind since early the 1900's, but it was not until about 1910 when the challenge of the city was so evidently the new mission frontier that the discussion became more focused. Much of Chapter 6 explores how the church responded to the challenge of the city, but social service and evangelism also had an impact on the rural church. It is impossible to write about the Presbyterian church in the prairies between 1885 and 1925, without writing about the Church Union debate, and that is the story Chapter 7 tells. It tells the story from the perspective of those who remained Presbyterian, and asks the question, "Which denomination, the Presbyterian Church in Canada or the United Church of Canada, is heir to the mission vision that drove the church during the heady days of rapid growth on the prairies?"

Chapter 1 is different from the other chapters in that it tells in outline form the political, social, and economic history of the West between 1885 and 1925. It does so with a twist. A read through any standard history of the West will include somewhere a discussion of the religious groups that came to the prairies and will in thumbnail mention a few people and events, like Robertson and the temperance movement. Rarely, however, will a history tell you about the faith commitments of the politicians, community leaders, business people, and others who parade through its pages.

What Chapter 1 tries to do is respond to that imbalance. Here the reader will meet Presbyterian lay people and a few clergy who played roles in the social, political, and economic formation of the west. It will of necessity be an incomplete and skewed history. There will be Presbyterians whose impacts on the west should be recognized who will be missed. One of my concerns about much of the Canadian history I read is that it has been written as though people had no religious life, or that their religious life was separate from the rest of their lives. A single chapter in a book can not address this larger problem. If nothing else, I hope that readers find themselves surprised by some of the people of faith, in this case Presbyterians, that they will meet.

A number of themes emerge in this study of the mission of the church on the prairies.

First, the church was confronted by ever new challenges in the west as it sought to bear witness to its belief in Jesus Christ. In the beginning it was the land itself and how to establish the church in this new land. Just when that seemed to have been solved came the challenge of doing ministry in the Yukon with the Klondikers, which was followed almost immediately by the challenge of mass immigration and the arrival of non-Anglo-Saxon new Canadians. And then came the realization that while the focus had been on the new land and reaching the settlers regardless of their ethnic origin, another challenge had arisen while no one was looking—the problem of the city. All the while the Native community remained a challenge to the church. In the face of these challenges, which it had never faced before, the church developed new patterns of ministry. For example; creating the position superintendent of mission, establishing the Independent Greek Church, using mission techniques from the foreign mission field in Canada, and taking great risks in entrusting the mission of the church to people who were not ordained, who were not Anglo-Saxon, and who were not male. The Presbyterian Church in the west remade itself to advance the mission of the church.

Second, as the church confronted these challenges, it remained effective in dealing with them, as long as it remembered that its primary purpose was to proclaim the gospel of Jesus Christ in word and deed. When the church took its eyes off that purpose, and looked instead towards "Canadianization" or even humanitarian care as its primary goal, the church lost its way. That does not mean that the church was effective only when it was preaching the good news. Certainly the mission of the church was advanced through education, medical work, providing food and clothing to those in need and welcoming the stranger who was alone and afraid. But when it was no longer the gospel that was the motivation for doing those things, the primary purpose for the church's being was gone and it became simply a purveyor of the social mores of the dominant culture. This book will argue that in the years 1910 to 1916, a small number of key leaders within the Presbyterian church had already made an enormous shift in their thinking, making the gospel of "Canadian social religion" the primary mission of the church. And that after the war, their influence caused this transition to permeate much of the denomination. I am not sure that these leaders consciously made this change, or even understood the significance of what they had done. However, the effects of their shift in thinking were enormous. There were other Presbyterians who did not make the shift that I am talking about, they remained focused on the gospel as they went about doing the mission of the church. In part, this book tries to document the conflicting visions of these two groups.

A third theme is that mission generated at the congregational or presbytery level was more effective in addressing the mission challenges of the west than was the more structured approach of the church offices in Toronto. During the 40 years covered by this book, a major structural shift took place within the denomination. No longer was the work of the denomination overseen by clergy who were involved in full-time ministry; rather, the day of the church bureaucracy had arrived. And with the church bureaucrat came the use of efficient business methods in the operation of the church. The reader will see at times flashes of conflict between the church bureaucracy on the one hand and the missionary, congregation, or presbytery on the other. Usually it will be the group at the local level wanting to move quickly into some new aspect of ministry, and often going ahead and doing it, while church officials debate the policy that should guide such a move. The further one got from the church offices located in Toronto, the more likely was the presbytery, congregation, or missionary to just go ahead and enter into the ministry without consulting the appropriate church official. The Presbytery of Edmonton was a good example of this in launching its ministry into the Peace River country with little or no consultation outside of the presbytery, and then repeating the process when they sent the Rev. Duclos to Bonnyville, Alberta.

Finally, it will be hard to miss the figure of the Rev. James Robertson, for he strides as a giant through the history of the Presbyterian church in the west. Passionately committed to the mission of the gospel, Robertson's drive rubbed off on others who caught his vision and made it their own. Demanding and self-sacrificing, Robertson was able to recognize people who had the gifts needed to do ministry in the west.

All historical writing reveals as much about the author and the time the author is living in as it does about the period in history it is trying to describe. This book is no different. The Presbyterian Church in Canada at the dawn of the new millennium is not like the church described in this book. It is a church that has lost its mission vision, and to a large extent has lost the confidence and passion needed to carry out the church's mission, even if there were agreement on what that mission was. Among other things this book is an invitation to find in our time a mission vision that will burn within us with as much passion and clarity as did the vision held by the women and men whose stories this book recounts. I am not advocating a simple taking of the mission vision from the end of the nineteenth century and plopping it down in our time as our mission vision for today. The casting of a mission vision for the new millenium is more complex than that, although I would suggest that a contemporary mission vision needs to be in continuity with the visions of earlier in the church's history. A second question this study raises is: how is mission vision caught, nurtured, and passed on? How do the second or third generation of mission leaders keep the original vision authentic and alive for themselves? Or is it only possible for mission vision to last a single generation?

If all historical writing is in part about the author, it would be useful for the readers to know something about me. I am a minister in the Presbyterian Church in Canada. For seven years I ministered at St. Andrew's Presbyterian Church in Flin Flon, Manitoba. While I was there, the congregation moved from what would have been called augmentation in 1900 to become a self-supporting congregation. I presently minister in the rural/small town parish of Mitchell in Southwestern Ontario. In the process of researching this book, I discovered that my wife's grandfather, the Rev. Angus Sutherland, was an activist for the Presbyterian Church Association, the group that co-ordinated Presbyterian resistance to church union. Finally, I believe that the church is to be in the business of telling people about Jesus Christ; if that is not the primary thing the church is about, then the church is lost. There are many ways to proclaim the good news about Jesus, through caring for the outcast, seeking justice for the oppressed, feeding the hungry, along with bearing witness with one's words.

There are some things about how the Presbyterian Church in Canada operated that are useful for the reader to understand. The Presbyterian Church in Canada governs itself by a hierarchy of geographically based committees, which are called courts. At the congregational level there is the session, which at the time we will be discussing was made up of elders who were selected by the local congregation and were ordained to serve for life. The elders joined together with the minister to form the session, and the session was responsible for all aspects of the congregation's life and for the pastoral care of all households connected to the congregation.

In the west it was common for one minister to be responsible for three to six small congregations spread across the prairie; these would be lumped together in a pastoral charge. As the struggle to find enough ministers became more and more acute, a general pattern developed. Brand new congregations would be put together to make up a mission charge, which would be cared for by a student from one of the theological colleges during the summer, or there might be catechist, who was a non-ordained person who had been recognized as having the gifts to do ministry, who stayed in the charge for a longer time. In some exceptional cases an ordained minister would be placed in a mission charge. If the charge grew and became more financially secure a minister would be sent to assist the charge in moving towards becoming self-supporting. I have chosen to make little distinction between students, catechists, and ordained clergy, calling them all missionaries. There were also colporteurs who were people who travelled from town to town distributing Christian literature and talking to anyone who would listen about Jesus Christ. The colporteurs did not have responsibility for a pastoral charge; they were more like travelling personal evangelists.

A geographical cluster of congregations joined together to form a presbytery. The presbytery was made up of an equal number of ordained ministers and elders, essentially meaning one elder from each pastoral charge. Presbyteries varied in size, from being made up of 40 congregations and with as many as 100 voting members, as was the case with the Presbytery of Winnipeg in 1924, to being as small as six self-supporting congregations and the same number of mission charges and no more than 15 voting members, as was the case in Castor Presbytery in Alberta in 1924. It was the presbytery which oversaw the work of the missionary in a charge, ensuring that things were going as they should. Churches and other ministries were said to be "within the bounds" of a particular presbytery, and all ministries within the bounds were, in theory at least, responsible to the presbytery for their work. It was the presbytery who held the missionary to account, and it was to the presbytery's mission committee that the missionary reported. Each presbytery had a mission committee which played the largest role in oversight of these mission charges. The chairperson of the mission committee, called the convenor, had tremendous influence in deciding into which newly settled areas the church should move and in approving financial grant requests to be forwarded to the appropriate funding body. In theory these decisions were in the hands of the presbytery, but in reality the decision was often given over to the committee, who passed on the responsibility to the convenor.

One step up from the presbytery was the synod, which, after 1906, basically lined up with the provincial boundaries, except for Northwestern Ontario, which was joined with Manitoba in a synod. Prior to 1902, the Synod Missions Committee had made the final decision about which congregations would get the grants funds they had requested and which would not, and so the committee was important. But after 1902, the synod played a very insignificant role in the structural life of the denomination.

At the national level, there was the General Assembly, which met once a year to determine policy and to receive and debate reports and their recommendations. The Assembly had a series of boards and committees that carried out the work of the Assembly during the year. The Home Mission Committee (Western Section) oversaw all home mission work west of the Maritime provinces. Up until 1912, work among the Native people, the Jews, and the Chinese in Canada was overseen by the Foreign Mission Committee. In 1912, the name of the Home Mission Committee was changed to the Board of Home Missions (Western Section) and it became responsible for all the work that the Home Mission Committee had done plus Native ministry and ministry among Jews that took place in Canada. Ministry among the Chinese remained the responsibility of Foreign Mission Committee. In 1916, there was a further name change as the Board of Evangelism and Social Service was merged with the Board of Home Missions to create the Board of Home Missions and Social Service. Each year the reports of the various boards and committees of the church, along with the minutes of the General Assembly, were published in the *Acts and Proceedings of the General Assembly* for the given year. This resource is an absolute gold mine of material.

The women of the church had been interested and involved in mission ventures for many years, but their work in the Canadian west was limited to work among the Native people, primarily in the residential schools. In 1903, the small committee that had been overseeing the work of the hospital at Atlin in northern British Columbia, in responding to requests from across the country asking for hospitals to be built, was enlarged to become the Women's Home Missionary Society. This organization grew rapidly, building and operating hospitals and nursing stations, starting school homes, employing deaconesses, funding mission charges in Canada, and publishing a monthly magazine called *The Home Mission Pioneer*. In 1914, the Women's Home Missionary Society joined with the Women's Foreign Missionary Society to create the Women's Missionary Society (Western Division). The brackets were to prevent it being confused with the Eastern Division, which was the women's missionary society in the Maritimes.

Deaconesses were women who had received theological and ministry training at Ewart College, the college established in 1897 to prepare women for mission work overseas. In 1907, recognizing that there were opportunities for women to do missionary work in Canada, the church established the Order of Deaconesses. Trained and specially designated by the church, they were not ordained. They fulfilled a variety of roles within the church in the West ranging from preaching and visiting to teaching and running inner city missions.

Two stylistic comments need to be made. I have made the decision to not change the exclusive language used for people in the quotations that appear in this book, nor have I marked with the (sic), meaning "same in copy" to let the reader know that I understand the objectionable nature of such exclusive language. Most of the authors who will be quoted understood "man" as referring to all people, both women and men. When the authors gave special emphasis to the material they wrote, I have retained the emphasis by using italics and have noted that at the end of the quotation, [emphasis in original].

One of the things that I was taught in my graduate history courses is that it was important for an author to place his work in relationship to previous work on the same or similar topics. This is given the fancy name historiography. And so I feel I must at least briefly place the present work in relationship to the work that has gone before. Readers should feel free to skip this discussion and move immediately to chapter 1 while the historians go off in the corner to talk. That does not mean others are not welcome to come and join the discussion; the more the merrier. I leave it up to the reader.

In the first 40 years of the 20th century, there was a fair bit written about the development of the churches on the prairies, E.H. Oliver's massive unpublished multi-volume study of the religious development of Saskatchewan being the most ambitious. The equally detailed, nine-volume Canadian Frontiers of Settlement series recognized the importance of the churches when in the eighth volume of the series, C.A. Dawson and Eva R. Younge, outlined the pattern of congregational development on the prairie and the ways in which the churches became part of the life of the community. Looking more specifically for works about Presbyterianism, Charles Gordon's biography of James Robertson and Hugh McKellar's *Presbyterian Pioneer Missionaries* give in outline the lives of leading figures in the church's western development. McKellar is thorough in finding relatively unknown figures to include in his 1924 work.[3]

More recently, that being since World War 2, the religious history of the west has not been a major focus of Canadian historians. In fact, in his 1999 essay on historical writing about the Canadian prairie, Royden Loewen does not name a single book or article that explores the development of a mainline church on the prairies, or the role largest Christian denominations had in the development of the west. He notes studies that have explored the development of ethnic groups who had distinct religious commitments, his own study of the Mennonites being an example of this kind of work. The tragedy is that there were no less than three monographs and two collections of essays published in the decade 1985 to 1995, which explored the ways various denominations related to the prairie and the north. Loewen's omission is indicative of the insignificance that the scholarly community has attached to the role of the Methodist, Presbyterian, Anglican, United, Lutheran and Roman Catholic churches played in the development of the west and in the creation of a prairie identity.[4]

The story of the Anglican Church's growth is told by Frank Peake in the special 1989 issue of the *Journal of the Canadian Church Historical Society.* Peake outlines the expansion of the church in the 19th century, paying particular attention to the north and the work of William Bompas, the remarkable bishop of Mackenzie River and later Selkirk. But Peake's work says little about the development of the church in the southern part of the great northwest. Robert Choquette's study of the Roman Catholic brotherhood, the Oblates, while focusing generally on the northern part of the northwest, does help us to understand the alienation many Catholics felt in coming to a new land whose religious life was quickly dominated by the evangelical Protestantism of the Presbyterians and the Methodists. Both Peake and Choquette help us to understand just how fragile the existence of the church in the northwest was, as clergy were stretched at times to the breaking point and faced tremendous challenges. James Marnoch's study of the Presbyterian church in the west until 1885 fits into the work done by Peake and Choquette, helping round out the early history of the mainline churches in the northwest. But none of these three push their story into the early 20th century and the rapid population growth on the prairie. This leaves the student of Canadian church history with a solid understanding of the pioneer church, but with little to say about the church in the period from 1900 to 1925.[5]

Two collections of essays have been published in the last 15 years that have shed some light on the post-1900 development of the church in western Canada. *Prairie Spirit*, which was published to mark the 60th anniversary of the United Church in 1985, contains a number of articles about leading figures and organizations in the Presbyterian Church. Of particular interest for the present study is Catherine Macdonald's work on James Robertson, Raymond Smith's exploration of the churches' involvement with hospital and medical work in Manitoba, and N. Keith Clifford's remarkable work on church union in western Canada. But as with any essay collection, there is no attempt to draw these snapshots together into a more cohesive whole. The 1991 collection of essays on the Anglican Church in western Canada provides helpful context for the present study, but here again the majority of the studies explore the pre-1900 period. Only Trevor Powell's work on immigration into the Diocese of Qu'Appelle and Vera Fast's exploration of the caravan mission help push the understanding of the ways in which the mainline churches developed on the prairies in the early 20th century.[6]

Certainly for Presbyterians and to a much lesser extent for Methodists the first two and a half decades of the century were dominated by the debate about church union. An indication of the pivotal role church union has played in the history of the Presbyterian Church in Canada is that the 1975 edition of John Moir's *Enduring Witness*, which outlines more than 400 years of Presbyterianism in Canada, from 1541 to 1970, spent 10 percent of its text dealing with this "long crisis." Moir does deal with the mission outreach to the northwest, outlining in thumbnail form the developments of Presbyterianism on the prairies. He does this in a chapter appropriately entitled, "The Great Age of Missions." Neil Semple's 1996 history of Canadian Methodism discusses the involvement of the Methodist church in the northwest, providing a helpful foil against which to understand the work of the Presbyterian Church. Richard Morton's article on the American Presbyterian Church's experience with home mission at the end of the 19th century, provides some helpful parallels to the Canadian Presbyterian Church's experience: the use of foreign mission techniques to reach the Native people, the Mormons, and the Hispanics; and the shocking realization that the mission field was no longer the geographical frontier, but rather was the city. In the American case these adjustments were made about 15 years earlier than they were in the Canadian west.[7]

The one area of mainline church history on the prairies that has received the most study is the rise of what Richard Allen has called the "social passion." In seeking to bring about the kingdom of God, the moral and social reformers attracted not only the attention of the people of their day, but also the attention of late 20th century scholars: Michael Owen, Marilyn Barber, and Brian Fraser being but three researchers who have explored the thought of Presbyterian reformers. Owen and Barber hear a strongly anti-non-Anglo-Saxon bias in the Presbyterian church's reformist actions, whereas Fraser tries to place the reformers in their intellectual and theological milieu. None of these three has documented the progression in thought that the present study argues took place between 1890 and 1920, where some in the church surrendered its role as gospel proclaimer to become promoters of Canadianism. The present work would support the contention of Nancy Christie and Michael Gauvreau, who argue that the evangelical passion was alive in parts of the mainline church in Canada until at least 1925. The form that passion took had been modified, but it was still recognizably present.[8]

It is my hope that *Western Challenge* will be simply one small piece in a tide of research that will explore the growth and development of the mainline churches on the prairie after 1900, and that in the process the role played by the Christian churches and individual church members in the development of the west will be fully recognized.

"...there lies between the people and their goal a stretch and a struggle":[1] Prairie History as seen through some Presbyterians' eyes

A vast and diverse land stretches from the rocks and trees and muskeg of the country west of Lake Superior, to the three wide and open plateaus of the prairie cut by the great rivers like the Saskatchewan, to the foothills of the majestic Rockies. It is a land of lumber and mineral resources, a land of ranching and coal mining, a land where wheat would be king. The prairie is a place of open spaces and big skies, where the climate is harsh and distance is measured in hours and days. To this land, already inhabited by Native people, came fur-traders and then the first settlers, who sought to eke out an existence on the eastern edge of this vast land. A few brave souls launched themselves into the great undulating plain and staked their claim to field and farm, others ranched the great open spaces of the western plain. It was a land dominated by bachelors, and unmarried women had numerous suitors. The coming of the railroad opened the land to further development and the arrival of more homesteaders, people seeking a new life and a new opportunity. Towns and cities were born with their shops and livery stables. The new arrivals included families and there was a need for schools. The disorganized life of the pioneer community was developing the structures and systems of a settled community. And with the rise of the community came the development of social and literary societies, political organizations, and the growth of the church. Underneath this structure and organization lay the truth that this was still a pioneering land; these people had come from somewhere, had taken the risk to leave their home and start a new life in the great unknown. The blood of pioneers still pumped in their veins. These were independent thinkers who were used to breaking new ground, who knew the cost of marching to the beat of a drum they alone could hear, and their ideas were to create not just Prairie society. Those ideas would transform a nation. For they still lived on the vastness of the prairie, in the land of the big sky, a land that reminded its inhabitants on a regular basis that they were simply guests in an untamed land. Fire and drought, flood and blizzard, all bear witness to the truth; the prairie is still a harsh and beautiful land.

What follows in this chapter is an attempt to give an overview of the political, economic and social development of the prairies between 1880 and 1925. It will of necessity be a condensed telling, and will feel more like viewing a series of snapshots than watching a movie. The story will be told around two focuses: first, attention will be paid to Presbyterians who played roles in the development of Prairie society; and second, what impact did some of these large political, social and economic events have on individual Presbyterians and the Presbyterian Church generally.

THE NATIONAL POLICY

Sir John A. Macdonald, that pillar, albeit an "outside pillar" of the Presbyterian Church, had a problem: how to make a country out of what had been the colonies of British North America. The problem had become particularly acute in 1871, when British Columbia, 4,500 kilometers from Ottawa, had joined confederation on the promise of a rail link to the rest of the country. Macdonald's solution was the National Policy. An ambitious programme, it included among other things: the building of the Canadian Pacific Railroad through northwestern Ontario and across the prairies, the establishment of the North-West Mounted Police to ensure Canadian sovereignty of the prairies, and the building of a tariff wall to protect Ontario's infant manufacturing industries. Each of these were to become icons in western Canada, encrusted with all of the ambiguity that attaches itself to icons.

Construction of the railway was going slowly in 1880 and needed a boost if it were ever to be completed. That boost came in the form of "The Syndicate," as it was known by friends and foes. Among the leaders of the Syndicate was Donald Smith, Lord Strathcona, who had begun his career on the lowest rungs of the Hudson Bay Company and had risen to become its Governor. Through his business connections in Montreal, the Presbyterian Smith became interested in railway building, helping put together the consortium that would become the Canadian Pacific Railway Company. Smith was a shrewd business person, and he drove a hard bargain. To take over the construction of the railway, the CPR wanted to be given half of the sections in each surveyed township across the prairies, sections that they would either rent out, sell, or develop as they saw best. Macdonald, who was being pressured by British Columbia to keep his promise to have the railway completed, agreed to the terms, and the Syndicate took over the railway project.

In 1881, the railway came to Winnipeg, and people started to buy property around the outskirts of the town on the assumption that it was about to grow rapidly into a city. Land prices soared and a full scale land speculation boom was under way. In April 1882 the real estate boom ended as the Red River flooded, covering much of the land that was the subject of the land flipping. The mayor-elect Alexander McMicken and others on city council were convinced that the set-back was only temporary, and they made plans for major infrastructure developments: police and fire stations, bridge, and a city hall commensurate with the major urban centre Winnipeg was about to become. The Presbyterian McMicken headed to New York City to raise the necessary funds through the sale of city bonds. By the summer of 1883, it was clear that the boom was not going to return, and the city was burdened with large interest payments on its bond issue. In anger the electorate threw McMicken out of office late in 1883. Going through Winnipeg committed the CPR to crossing through the dry plains, rather than going further north to pass through the rich agricultural areas of the parkland. Where the rails went, shortly afterward came the settlers and homesteaders. The CPR chose the town sites, and in some cases the rail sidings had been laid and the grain elevator companies had erected their elevators along those sidings even before the settlers arrived. A number of communities across the west experienced, to a lesser degree, the challenges that Winnipeg faced as the rails arrived: land speculation, and determining what infrastructure would be needed and how to pay for it. In 1881 there was not a single house in Brandon; by 1883 there were 4,000 people in town. This almost overnight transformation happened in many places as the railway turned empty prairie into "ambitious town."[2]

If Smith and van Horne's business acumen created the CPR, it was Sir Sandford Fleming's engineering genius that oversaw the railway's construction. Fleming had drunk deeply of the Presbyterian belief that knowledge and learning were good things, and that scientific study brought glory to God. It was Fleming who created a system of standard time, so that people across the Prairies would know when the train was supposed to arrive in their community. Prior to the creation of standard time each town and hamlet had its own time, set by the movement of the sun. Fleming had pushed the CPR to put together a worship book containing orders of service that could be used by the survey and rail building crews as they planned and laid the rail line. Often these crews were miles from the closest church, but Fleming wanted to ensure they still had the opportunity to worship. It was Donald Smith who drove the last spike of the CPR line in November 1885.[3]

The completion of the coast-to-coast railway did not mean the end to railway building. A single rail line snaking across the prairies had created a long narrow band of settlement; not enough of the vast hinterland, which was owned in part by the CPR, was within easy reach of the rail lines and therefore could not be systematically settled. Sir William Whyte, a

Presbyterian, rose through the ranks of the Grand Trunk Railway to become its assistant superintendent for its central division. From there he jumped to the CPR, becoming superintendent of its western division in 1886. Fiercely loyal to the CPR, Whyte sought to defend the company from its greatest competitor in the west, the Northern Pacific and Manitoba Railway. At the time the CPR was doing little to expand branch lines, although in systematically settled areas like the Qu'Appelle valley, lines were built. The lines in the Qu'Appelle were engineered by the Presbyterian Donald Stewart. But it was clear by 1901 that the only way to beat the competition was to cut freight rates and aggressively enter a programme to construct branch lines, and this Whyte oversaw. By 1901, the mass immigration had begun, and branch lines could be profitable. The CPR built 4,000 miles of branch lines in a decade, experimented with more powerful locomotives and longer trains, and increased their rolling stock to ensure the more rapid movement of grain during harvest. Whyte also oversaw the development of 51 new townsites across the prairies and the development of the CPR's hotel chain across the west. Railroads were not just for the large companies like the CPR and the Northern Pacific; local entrepreneurs also got into the act. Local developer Donald MacLeod of Edmonton, a Presbyterian, joined a consortium in the construction of the Edmonton to Calgary line.[4]

It was with great joy that farmers hailed the arrival of the Northern Pacific railway. Farmers had never trusted the CPR and the Northern Pacific offered competition; and secondly, the Northern Pacific would pass through the rich agricultural land of the northern parklands giving these areas the benefits of being on a coast-to-coast rail line. The Northern Pacific faced financial difficulties from the very beginning. Even a new name, the Canadian Northern Railway, did not solve the problem. Twenty-five years after its arrival on the prairies, Arthur Meighan, Prime Minister Robert Borden's chief trouble-shooter and a committed Presbyterian from Portage la Prairie, steered the bills through the House of Commons that nationalized a series of bankrupt railroads, creating the Canadian National Railroad in late 1919.[5]

Railways were not the only way Macdonald hoped to hold the country together; he also needed some way to indicate Canadian sovereignty over the great vast lands of the west. The plan was to establish a police force that would maintain law and order and by its presence indicate that this land was Canadian, and not American. James Macleod of the North-West Mounted Police was a Presbyterian. He served first as a Superintendent, during which time he set up the garrison at Fort Macleod. He found allies in Blackfoot head chief, Crowfoot, and Blood head chief, Red Crow, in his struggle to stamp out the whiskey trade. In 1876 he became the Commissioner of the NWMP, a position he held until 1880. Resigning in 1880 to devote his time to being a magistrate, in 1887 he was appointed to the first

Supreme Court of the North-West Territories. Macleod had a vision of the west as "a place where newcomers and the native population might live together in peace and where disputes could be settled by reason." Other NWMP officers played important roles in the development of the Presbyterian Church in Calgary. Major James Walker, who was stationed in Calgary, had approached James Robertson, the Presbyterian Superintendent of Missions for the West, in early 1883, with a request that a mission charge be established at Calgary. Walker was to become a member of the first Board of Managers of the newly started congregation. In the 1910's Walker was to give the Presbytery of Calgary three building lots for the construction of new churches. Superintendent John Henry McIllree, who was in charge of the Calgary post, invited the Presbyterians to meet in the new constructed NWMP hospital until the church had a home of its own.[6]

The farmers in the west grew grain for export. That may seem blatantly obvious, but it indicates a mindset. The farmers always had their eyes on the world market, on the ability of the grain companies to get their product to market, and on the pricing structures used by the grain companies that either benefited farmers or hurt them. By the same token, the farmers needed materials and products that they could not produce themselves and that were not produced on the prairies. Prairie farmers believed in trade, in freer trade that was just.

The arrival of the railway put Winnipeg on the map, turning it into the commercial centre of the west. Goods would arrive from the east and be delivered to a wholesale warehouse, and from there distributed throughout the west. This merchandising trade made a number of Winnipeggers very wealthy, among them the Presbyterian John Mather whose most important eastern suppliers were Hiram Walker and Sons and the Halifax Sugar Refining Company. Mather was also an avid sports fan, serving as the first president of the Manitoba Curling Association, and overseeing its first annual bonspiel in 1889, a bonspiel which soon became "the largest and most important annual curling festival in the world." It was also in Winnipeg that grain was bought and sold, and in 1887 the Winnipeg Grain and Produce Exchange was created. Presbyterian Stephen Nairn was President of the Exchange in 1896. He was also a member of the Winnipeg Board of Trade; during his term as chair of the board of grain examiners the federal minister of inland revenue gave the Winnipeg Board of Trade the authority to collect samples and set standards for western grain.[7]

Macdonald's National Policy included a series of tariffs which were established to protect the newly forming manufacturing base of Ontario. The tariff wall ensured that Ontario manufacturers would have markets for their goods without fear of being undercut by the mature and more efficient American producers. But Macdonald seemed uninterested in imposing tariffs to protect western manufacturers as Stephen Nairn discovered.

Nairn opened an oatmeal mill in Winnipeg, with the hope of shipping this value-added product to the east. However, the tariff wall on oatmeal was half of the wall protecting oats, and millers in the northern United States, who did not face the shipping costs that Nairn faced, could easily undersell the Manitoba oatmeal. Numerous appeals to Macdonald fell on deaf ears, and Nairn finally sold the mill. The wholesale trade and the grain trade soon made Winnipeg the banking centre of the West as well, at times calling itself "the Chicago of the North." Following the massive population growth that would take place in the first decade of the twentieth century, Winnipeg would be a manufacturing centre as well.[8]

Farmers exported their grain, which was sold at the world price. They received no tariff wall protection on the sale of their produce, and this ensured that the factory workers in Ontario could buy food at reasonable prices. The Ontario manufacturers, however, did not have to sell their products at the world price; they could sell for higher prices, since they had the protection of the tariff wall. This seeming inequity led to screams of protest from western Canadians, who saw farm equipment being sold to their American counterparts at substantially lower prices than they as Canadians had to pay for the same equipment. The Liberals under Wilfrid Laurier had campaigned in 1896 on the promise to lower the tariff wall and therefore reduce the cost of many manufactured goods. Member of Parliament James Douglas was not pleased with the half-hearted way the newly elected Liberals went about reducing the duties on agricultural implements. In fact, opposition to the tariff walls and frustration over the CPR's monopoly became statements of faith for not just farmers, but for most westerners. Colin Campbell, who grew up in a well-established Presbyterian home in Burlington, Ontario, came west in 1882 convinced of the merits of Macdonald's National Policy. Within a couple of years of living in the west, he was advocating the absolute opposite. In many ways, the National Policy, whose purpose was to hold the country together, has been the source of much of the regional conflict which has dogged the Confederation's entire existence.

THE 1885 REBELLION

As the railroad brought settlers to the Prairies, the land surveyors moved ahead of them, which brought them face to face with the Métis at Batouche and other communities in Saskatchewan. The Métis' settlement pattern had been to divide the land into long strips with a portion of each strip having river access, the same pattern as had been used in Quebec and that the Métis has used in Manitoba. The surveyors had been instructed to survey the land into squares, a mile by a mile. Having been pushed out of Manitoba and now having their land taken from them by the surveyors was too much. The spring of 1885 was particularly difficult for farmers in the Prince Albert region; there had been a poor crop in 1884, and many farmers had been forced to eat their seed to make it through the winter. There was a widespread call for the government to provide farmers with seed wheat and oats to plant. Weighed down by debt and unable to feed their families, many farmers, both Métis and white, were in desperate circumstances.[9]

In addition there was the litany of complaints that the Native people had with the government. Hugh McKay, the Superintendent for all Presbyterian work among the Native peoples on the prairies and missionary among the Cree at Round Lake, Saskatchewan, wrote a private report to the Foreign Mission Committee of the church outlining six complaints which McKay considered reasonable. First, the treaty of 1874 had promised land which the government had not yet given to the Indians. Second, in the treaty the government had promised that every three years it would give blankets, guns, ammunition, tea, sugar, and tobacco to those covered by the treaty. The government had provided these materials once, but not since. In addition to these specifically listed items, the government had promised to provide $750 worth of other goods each year; this too was a promise on which the government had reneged. Fourth, the government had not provided the farm implements promised, and the other tools that had been promised had taken 10 years to deliver, and when they did arrive they were not what was needed. Fifth, instead of building and maintaining a school on each reserve as had been promised, the government simply provided an annual grant of $300 to be used towards schooling. If it cost more than that to educate all the children on the reserve, then not all the children could go to school. Finally, people were starving to death.[10]

As the Rebellion was beginning in the spring of 1885, the Manitoba correspondent for the *Record*, the semi-official voice of the denomination, laid the blame for the violence at the feet of federal government officials and some ministers of the crown. It was through "shocking neglect" that things had reached this point. James Robertson, who in his official reports to Assembly said little about the Rebellion, was more open with his wife, writing to her in May 1885, "To us the whole affair is a puzzle. There had been mismanagement from the outset... It is becoming clear that the men who are managing this whole affair are not equal to the task.... I fear more blood will be spilt yet." Robertson concluded with the prophetic words, "And blood spilt now may mean more hereafter." Malcolm Colin Cameron, Liberal Member of Parliament for West Huron in 1885, knew the west well from the trips he took each summer between 1880 and 1883. Trained at Knox College, the Presbyterian theological college in Toronto, but choosing the law over the ministry, Cameron was a harsh critic of the corruption and excessive administrative costs at Indian Affairs, a department under the ministerial responsibility of John A. Macdonald from 1878 to 1887. Cameron was aware in 1884 of the agitation in the northwest, and introduced a private member's bill to provide the Northwest Territories (present day Alberta, Saskatchewan, and more than half of Manitoba) with elected representation in the House of Commons. It was defeated, but he tried again in early 1885, again with no success. So biting was his criticism, that he was personally singled out during the 1887 campaign as a Liberal that the Conservatives wanted defeated.[11]

Although many Presbyterians held the government partially responsible for the situation that led up to the Rebellion, they had no trouble naming who was most responsible for the Rebellion and the bloodshed— Louis Riel. A correspondent to the *Record* wrote early in March, 1885, "As a former leader of rebellion, a plausible man, and of no mean capacity, he should not have been allowed full play in the Prince Albert region." Riel was to be respected as a charismatic and effective leader; he should have been arrested before things had come this far.[12]

On March 23, 1885 word reached Ottawa that Riel had seized hostages and set up a provisional government. And on March 27, General Middleton arrived in Winnipeg, heading immediately by train to Troy Station where the Carleton Wagon Trail intersected the CPR tracks. On March 30, two trains carrying 600 troops left Toronto. The railway was going to make this a very different rebellion than the 1870 Red River Rebellion. In 1870, the government in Ottawa had been unable to get troops to Manitoba in less than two months, and then only by having them travel through the United States. The government had had little option other than to negotiate with Riel and the provisional government. In 1885, there was an all-Canadian route available, albeit a route that was not quite complete, for there were still gaps in northern Ontario, and the first troops arrived on the Prairies in less than two weeks. This time there would be no negotiations with the provisional government.

The Rebellion impacted the lives of individual Presbyterians. In the spring of 1885, the Rev. J. H. Cameron and his wife, had planned to flee from North Battleford, Saskatchewan, to the safety of Prince Albert, Saskatchewan. But the fighting had cut off their escape route and they were stuck behind the Native lines. Prince Albert itself was crowded with settlers who were seeking safety, and the Rev. MacWilliam, minister in Prince Albert at the time, reported that the people cooped up in town were "waiting patiently for the arrival of troops sufficient to crush the rising." There were Presbyterians among the troops who came to "crush the rising," including a large number of present and former students from the Presbyterian-run Manitoba College. Mr. Ferguson, an undergraduate at the college, was one of the first Winnipeg volunteers killed in action. Presbyterian clergy were prominent among those chosen to be chaplains to the various units at the front. The Rev. W.S. Ball of London, Ontario; the Rev. C.B. Pitblado of

Halifax; and the Rev. James Barclay from Montreal, chaplain to the Royal School of Artillery "A" Battery were the non-Western chaplains. The Rev. D.M. Gordon, chaplain to the 90th Battalion, Winnipeg Rifles; Rev. Rowland, chaplain to the 92nd Battalion, Winnipeg Light Infantry; and Mr. McKenzie, a theology student at Manitoba College with Boulton's Scouts from Winnipeg were the western chaplains. The fighting was really over by mid-May 1885, although it was not until July 2 when Big Bear surrendered that the Rebellion was symbolically over. St. Paul's Presbyterian Church, Prince Albert, has a plaque on the front wall of the sanctuary commemorating those whites from the congregation who were killed in action or served with the army during the Rebellion.[13]

Riel was put on trial for treason in Regina. Daniel Clark (the Clark Institute in Toronto bears his name) was one of the foremost psychiatrists in Canada in the late nineteenth century. A regular worshipper at St. Andrew's Presbyterian Church in Toronto, Clark was asked by Riel's defense team to examine Riel and testify on his behalf. Clark believed that Riel actually did have visions, truly believed he had been called by God to save the Métis, and therefore was not legally liable to a human court of law for his actions. Clark's evidence was not persuasive for either judge or jury. Riel's conviction and death sentence were appealed to the Manitoba Court of Queen's Bench, where Justice Thomas Wardlaw Taylor, a Presbyterian, and his colleagues heard the appeal. It was Taylor who wrote the rejection of that appeal. Finally having exhausted all appeals, Riel was hanged on November 16, 1885. Malcolm Cameron strongly opposed the execution of Riel, arguing that it was nothing more than retribution for the execution of Thomas Scott 15 years earlier.

Robertson had remained remarkably quiet throughout 1885 about the whole situation. In early 1886, he sought to put the living conditions of the Native people in Canada on the national agenda. During a speech in Montreal, he accused the government of neglecting its responsibilities to the Native people, stating that many of the Native people were starving and that the Indian agents, who had been appointed by the government to look after the Native people's interests, were in many cases, "drunkards, gamblers, and rakes." Robertson went on to say,

> Mr. Andrews asks where are the Indians starving, searching refuse heaps and swill-barrels, and ravenously devouring crusts of bread and scraps of meat? At Minnedosa, Broadview, Birtle, Fort Qu'Appelle, Prince Albert, Battleford, Moosejaw [sic], Medicine Hat, and the rest, I have seen them doing this. It might have been because they were curious, and preferred dirty crusts and decaying meat to tender, well-bled beef, but I did not think of accounting for it in that way. I know the eager look, the shrunken form,

and wolfish face that speak of want in the adult, and the wan, pinched look that speaks of starvation in the child; and I have seen them near Fort Ellice, Fort Pelly, File Hills, and other places, and have had my sympathies drawn out to the owners.

These comments created quite a stir in the press, and on the floor of the House of Commons. There the above quote was read by the member from Brant, which then led to a number of Conservatives seeking to discredit Robertson and his observations about the situation among the Native people in the West.[14]

David Laird is another Presbyterian who played an important role in establishing Canada's relationship with the Native people of this country. He was involved in brokering Treaties 4, 6 and 7 with various Native peoples prior to 1880. In 1898, Laird was appointed Indian Commissioner by Prime Minister Wilfrid Laurier and returned to the west and Winnipeg. Two issues were to dominate his seven years as commissioner. First, many in the Department of Indian Affairs were convinced that the industrial and residential school system was not creating a permanent change in the lives of students; upon graduating students would return to their homes and would quickly be absorbed back into the Native culture, losing the behaviours they had been taught in the schools. W.M. Graham, Indian Agent at File Hills, Saskatchewan, made a proposal to Laird that a group of graduates from the residential schools in the area become an agricultural colony under the strict guidance of Indian Affairs; all influences that might tend to draw the colonists back into the native culture would be severely limited. Laird approved this experiment and the File Hills Colony was born.[15]

Second, no new treaties had been signed with the native people since 1878, nor had there been any need for new treaties. The Klondike Gold Rush in 1898 had had significant implications for the rights of Native people in the north, and Laird went in 1899 to negotiate a treaty with the Cree, Beaver, and Chipewyan peoples in the north. On June 21, 1899, Laird signed Treaty 8 on behalf of the Federal government. During his time as Indian Commissioner he also oversaw the negotiations leading to Treaty 9 in 1905 with the Ojibway and Cree in the District of Keewatin, south of Hudson Bay (present day northern Ontario); and to Treaty 10 in 1905-6 with the Chipewyan and Cree in Northern Saskatchewan. When Laird died in January 1914, those in the Native community who had known him mourned "the man-whose-tongue-is-not-forked." Laird was a regular attendee of the Presbyterian Church's annual General Assembly. He tried to live his life with integrity, seeking to improve the lot of the Native community.[16]

THE ROAD TO PROVINCIAL STATUS

In 1870, Manitoba became a province; but it was a postage stamp-sized province running from the United States border north to lakes Winnipeg and Winnipegosis, and extending from just west of Beausejour to just east of Carberry. In 1881, the boundaries were extended to include the full width of the present-day province and going north almost to Grand Rapids. It would take years of negotiations with the federal government, spearheaded in large part by the Presbyterian Attorney-General of Manitoba, Colin Campbell, until the present-day boundaries of the province were recognized in 1912. This expansion created a rush into the north, coinciding as it did with the start of construction on the Hudson Bay Railway.

In Saskatchewan and Alberta the road to responsible government and provincial status was more involved. Up until 1888, the North-West Territories were governed by a Lieutenant Governor and Territorial Council. But the real power lay with the lieutenant governor, who was appointed by Ottawa. The Council was dominated by non-elected officials, Supreme Court justices and appointees of the federal government, much to the disgust of uncompromising reformers like Frank Oliver. Lieutenant Governor Dewdney did not believe that the North-West Territories were ready to govern themselves, and often acted much more slowly than the handful of Council member who had been elected by the population of the Territories wished he would. Oliver, the Presbyterian editor of the Edmonton *Bulletin*, was a thorn in the side of the lieutenant governor; he had been elected to the Territorial Council, but was frustrated by the slow progress toward responsible government. In a scathing attack on Dewdney's policies in 1884, Oliver outlined the process by which other provinces had achieved responsible government, noting, "If history is to be taken as a guide, what could be plainer than that without rebellion the people of the North West need expect nothing, while with rebellion successful or otherwise they may reasonably expect to get their rights." The Prince Albert *Times* was supportive of the views expressed in Oliver's editorial. There is a prophetic ring to this piece, when it is recognized that it was written just over a year before the 1885 Rebellion. Much to Dewdney's relief, Oliver lost his seat on the Council in fall of 1885; defeated not because of his "fire-brand" stand on responsible government, but because of his temperance beliefs. This setback did not stop Oliver from tenaciously pursuing his vision of responsible government. But it was not until 12 years later, in 1897, when Oliver was a federal member of parliament, that full-fledged responsible government would come.[17]

In 1888, the Territorial Legislative Assembly replaced the Council. The Lieutenant Governor still held the power, but the body that advised him was an entirely elected body. Among those elected to the Assembly were Frank Oliver, a Liberal, and Thomas Tweed, a Conservative member from

Medicine Hat. Tweed joined forces with fellow Conservative Frederick William Gordon Haultain and others in struggling for responsible government and against the federally appointed Lieutenant Governor, Joseph Royal. Tweed, a Presbyterian, was a member of the executive of the Assembly and chair of the education committee. He believed that education should be in English-only, supporting the 1891 decision of the Assembly to erode minority educational rights. Tweed served as a member of the Assembly until his defeat in 1894.[18]

The election of the Liberal government in Ottawa, brought a new openness to western concerns, partly because a number of strong voices on the Liberal benches were from the west, including Frank Oliver. In 1897, responsible government came to the Territories as the power of the Lieutenant Governor was limited to an advisory one and the giving of royal ascent and the actual legislative and administrative power lay in the hands of the elected Assembly. But it was not until 1905 that the provinces of Alberta and Saskatchewan were created, giving to these two provinces the same constitutional authority that any province had. In Saskatchewan, William R. Motherwell joined the Saskatchewan cabinet as minister of agriculture and John Lamont was the first Attorney-General of the province. Both men were Presbyterians. In Alberta, David George McQueen, minister at First Presbyterian Church in Edmonton, began each day of the Legislative Assembly's sittings with prayer during the Assembly's first session. Attorney-General C.W. Cross was a member of First Presbyterian Church. In 1905, the attorney-general of each of the three prairie provinces was a Presbyterian.[19]

Immigration and Pattern of Settlement[20]

The boom of 1881-1882 in Winnipeg and the good crop years in the first part of the 1880's pointed to the rapid settlement of the west. But a series of events would delay that settlement by more than a decade. The 1885 Rebellion turned many prospective immigrants off; they were afraid of another uprising among the Native peoples. Then in the late 1880's there were a series of crop failures on the prairies, which caused people to wonder if the prairie could actually be farmed. But while there were crop failures in the west, in the rest of the world there was a glut of grain and prices were in free fall until the mid-1890's. These factors combined to dramatically reduce the number of settlers arriving on the prairies. The situation was so bad that in both 1895 and 1896 fewer than 20,000 people arrived in Canada, and it is estimated that more than that number of people left Canada to move to the United States in both of those years. The west was no longer regarded as a positive asset; rather it was a drain, having used up huge amounts of resources in the two rebellions, the establishment of the NWMP, and the development of the railroad. The economic boom was not happening. All of that is not to say that there was no population growth on the prairies; there was, but it was primarily the result of other Canadians, primarily Ontarians, choosing to move west. These newly minted westerners sought to make the west another Ontario; this explains in part why the struggle for responsible government was led primarily by transplanted Ontarians.

In 1896 things began to change for the west. The liberals under Sir Wilfrid Laurier won the federal election, and in the late summer Clifford Sifton was named Minister of the Interior, which included responsibility for immigration. Sifton was a westerner who understood how important the settling of the west was, and more importantly he still believed in the west. He aggressively pursued an open door immigration policy, particularly looking for farmers whom he believed would speed the advance of the west in a way that urban dwellers would not. It was during his time in the ministry that the Doukhobors and the Mennonites were able to not only settle as a block, but also acquired guaranteed protection to practice their religious faith. It was also while Sifton was the minister that the Ukrainians arrived in Canada. In recognition of his help, the Ukrainians chose to name one of the villages they built Sifton. Sifton had become the Minister of the Interior at a most fortunate time; grain prices made a turn around in 1896, climbing steadily for the next decade; the American frontier was declared closed; there was no more free land or even cheap land to be had and those with limited financial resources would need to look to Canada if they wished to homestead. All of these factors paid off, as new arrivals poured onto the prairies. The population of the three prairie provinces more than tripled between 1901 and 1911, growing by more than 900,000 people in the decade. Sifton resigned from the cabinet in 1905 and was replaced as Minister of the Interior by the Presbyterian Frank Oliver from Edmonton. Oliver tried to close the immigration doors somewhat, seeking to limit the number of non-Anglo-Saxons who were arriving in the west. But the flood of humanity continued, reaching its climax after the Laurier government had been defeated. In 1913 over 400,000 people arrived in Canada to set up new homes. Not all of these people came to the west but a large number did.

The West is not a monolithic block about which it is easy, or even safe, to make generalizations. And some of those differences across the west have to do with how settlement took place. Those differences relate not just to the ethnicity of the settlers who came to a given part of the prairies; they are also affected by when that part of the west was settled. These differences in settlement patterns caused the Presbyterian Church to develop in ways that were unique to that particular area of the prairies.

Rural Manitoba was basically settled by 1900. While the population of the province would rise by 200,000, nearly doubling, in the first decade of the century, two-thirds of those new arrivals were locating in urban centres, primarily Winnipeg. By 1911, over 40 percent of all Manitobans lived in what the census defined as an urban context. The mission edge, therefore, for the Presbyterian Church in Manitoba was not rural, rather it was urban. There was no need to appoint more than one district superintendent to the Synod of Manitoba and Northwestern Ontario in 1912; there was little Home Mission work to be done in the rural areas. The rise of urban concerns in Winnipeg coincides with the rise of the Social Gospel in Canadian Christian thought and the teaching of sociology to theological students at some of the denomination's theological colleges. Therefore those clergy arriving in this Synod during the first quarter of the 20th century were already primed to respond in radical ways to the social realities that they were about to experience in Winnipeg-dominated Manitoba. Adding calls for social change and the radical reform of the capitalistic structures to a clear gospel proclamation of salvation was an easy addition to make in the face of a quickly industrializing Winnipeg.

The region that became the province of Saskatchewan in 1905 saw 400,000 people arrive in the critical first decade of the century. The population in 1911 was more than five times larger than it had been in 1901. Three-quarters of new arrivals were settling in the rural areas; during the first 15 years of the century the number of farms in the province grew eight-fold. The newcomers were not settling in the cities but rather on the farm, or were farming part-time and working in the small towns that dotted the Saskatchewan countryside. There was still a need for the intentional starting of new congregations in the newly-settled areas of Saskatchewan. That is why in 1912 the Home Mission Committee of the Presbyterian Church decided to appoint three district superintendents for Saskatchewan; there was enough work to keep them all occupied. Saskatchewan, with two larger urban centres (Saskatoon and Regina) and two or three smaller ones (Moose Jaw, Prince Albert, and Swift Current), was not dominated by a single metropolis in the way that Manitoba was, giving it a very different psychological feel. By 1918, the rural areas of Saskatchewan were basically settled, and the Presbyterian Church reduced the number of district superintendents to two.

Alberta enjoyed the same five-fold growth in its population that Saskatchewan did in the first decade of the century, as 300,000 people flooded into the province. And as was done in Saskatchewan, the church appointed three district superintendents to oversee the mission of the church. Again the rise of the two metropolitan areas, Edmonton and Calgary, prevented one urban reality from dominating the province. Since Alberta was slower in being settled than the other provinces there was a pioneering feel to the mission of the church until well into the 1920's. In part this was because of the Peace River Country, where as late as 1925 the church was following the first settlers into virgin farm land. But a similar pioneer feeling could be found in the work being done in the Consort and Castor areas of eastern Alberta. The ethos created by this on-going mission of carrying the gospel to the frontier affected the way in which the Presbyterian Church in Alberta saw itself. It was a missionary church, called to proclaim the good news about Jesus Christ. The Presbytery of Edmonton responded to the growth of the city by aggressively planting new churches, not through the creation of city missions. When the Presbyterians did join with the Methodists in a city mission in Edmonton, communicating the gospel message remained the primary purpose of the mission. The church and its members affected the development of the west, but the ways in which the west was settled affected the ethos of the Presbyterian Church.

About a third of the new Canadians who arrived in the West between 1896 and 1914 were not English-speaking Anglo-Saxons; another 15 percent or so were from the United States; this meant that British-born Canadians (born in Great Britain or on British soil, i.e. in Canada) were the barest majority, and in some communities across the west were a minority. This confronted political and community leaders with a challenge: how to create one nation out of the diversity of ethnicities present on the prairies. Presbyterians were virtually unanimous that the public school should play a substantial role in this nation-forming exercise. In the 1890's Presbyterians were among the most vocal opponents of sectarian schools, that is separate Catholic and Protestant schools, believing that this would limit the nation's ability to create a unified identity. This opposition was led by such powerful voices as James Robertson and John Mark King, principal of Manitoba College. Colin Campbell, a pragmatic politician and the minister responsible for the education system in the Rodmond Roblin government in Manitoba, favoured mandatory school attendance for all children, but argued that it was financially impractical without financial assistance from the federal government, which was not forthcoming in the amount that Campbell believed was needed. In 1907, he introduced legislation requiring that schools fly the Union Jack during the school day, or lose their grant from the province. At the time this legislation passed it was common to see American flags and the flags of other countries flying on the flagpoles outside schools. In the provincial election held that year, Campbell, retained his seat by two votes; the riding of Morris, which he represented, had a large Mennonite population who were angered by the school flag issue.[21]

The role of the school in the creation of a single nation remained a point of concern on the prairies throughout the 40 years this book discusses. Colin Young, district superintendent in northern Saskatchewan in 1914, described a school event he attended. Part of the event was "a gathering of the nations." A student dressed in the custom of their homeland came up on stage and sang in English the national anthem of their country of origin. This continued until there were 13 students at the front, standing together under the Union Jack which hung at the back of the stage. Then together with the audience standing, they sang "O Canada" and "God Save the King."

Young concluded that the church should heartily support the work of all institutions that were helping non-Anglo-Saxons acquire "the Canadian British spirit."[22]

The population growth that began in the late 1890's changed the face of the prairies forever. The hopes and dreams of all those who had believed that the west could contribute much to the Canadian nation and that it could become an economic force in the confederation were finally realized.

FARMERS' MOVEMENTS

In the fall of 1897 the CPR announced that on much of its system the only grain that would be moved would be the grain of the elevator companies. No longer would individual farmers be provided with rail cars to fill on their own for shipment to the elevators at the Lakehead. Therefore farmers had to sell their grain to the elevator companies, for as we have seen, the farmers on the prairies lived by the export of their grain. Prairie farmers were furious; not only were their marketing options being limited, they did not trust the grain companies to act in the interest of the farmer. Most farmers believed that as long as they had the option of shipping their grain themselves directly to market, they had a tool to keep the grain companies honest.[23]

On February 14, 1898, James Moffatt Douglas, member for East Assiniboia, stood in the House of Commons to introduce a private member's bill that would regulate the storage and transit of grain in the west. Douglas was out to control the growing monopoly the elevator companies had over the grain trade. Douglas was a fascinating figure. Educated at Knox College, Toronto, and Princeton Theological Seminary in the United States, he had two pastorates in Ontario before being sent as a missionary to India in 1876. He returned to Canada in 1882, becoming the minister in Brandon and later moving to the Moosomin congregation. In 1896, he left the ministry to take up farming near Moosomin. He ran as an Independent Liberal in the 1896 election that saw Laurier become the Prime Minister. Douglas' bill created a great deal of debate, and in true Canadian fashion the whole issue was given over to a commission to study. The commission discovered that 301 of the 447 standard elevators, that is the vertical elevators, were in the hands of five companies. Over and over again the commission heard from farmers that they wanted the right to load their grain directly onto rail cars. On the commission's recommendation the 1900 Manitoba Grain Act, which covered the North-West Territories as well, was passed instructing the CPR to provide individual farmers with grain cars to load directly, and that grain cars were to be allocated on a first-come-first-served basis.

This should have solved the problem, but in 1901 a new problem arose. There was a bumper crop that year, the biggest the west had experienced to that point. Since shipping grain by boat is substantially cheaper than shipping it by rail, the grain shipping season was usually defined as the period from September 1 each year, the earliest that spring wheat could expect to be harvested, through to December 1, when shipping out of the elevators at the Lakehead closed for the winter. The bumper crop was late being harvested because of a wet September. The size of the crop and the lateness of the harvest jammed the rail and elevator system. The major roadblock was the CPR's lack of engines to pull the grain cars. By early November it was clear that only a fraction of the grain the farmers had grown would get into the elevators or be shipped to market. In the end farmers were left with half of their grain still in their hands, and although they built granaries to hold the abundance, it was clear that much of the crop was going to rot in the quickly constructed buildings.

Farmers in the area around Indian Head, Saskatchewan were particularly hard hit by this problem, which became known as the "wheat blockade," and began to hold meetings. On December 18, 1901, William Richard Motherwell and Peter Dayman, neighbouring farmers in the Abernethy area called together farmers to form an organization which would allow farmers to act in unison on these important issues. Motherwell, who started homesteading at Abernethy in 1883 and was an elder in the local Presbyterian Church, was elected the President of the Territorial Grain Growers' Association, which in early 1902 had 500 members. The Association condemned the CPR for its lack of engines and demanded the right to load rail cars direct from farmer's wagons at any station, regardless of the conveniences available for loading. The grain growers were also concerned about the elevator companies' practice of telling farmers that the only available room in the elevator was for lower quality grain, and that if the farmer wished to sell their grade "A" grain at below its value the elevator would be happy to take it, or the farmer could take it home. The farmers often did not believe the elevator operators were telling the truth, many were convinced that elevators took their grade "A" grain and mixed it with the poorer quality grade to raise the grade on the poorer grain and make a nice windfall for the elevator company. The difference between top quality grain and poor quality grain could be as much as nine cents a bushel. The grain growers wanted a clear standard for grading grain established that would be understood by all, and which would be fairer than the arbitrariness that existed at that time.

J.M. Douglas took up the Grain Growers' cause in the Commons and the Manitoba Grain Act was strengthened to ensure that rail cars could be loaded anywhere and that the rule that those whose requests for grain cars arrived first, would get cars first, was firmly enforced. In 1902, the Association was handed an opportunity to demonstrate that the CPR and the elevator companies were seeking to live above the law. Motherwell had travelled to Winnipeg at the start of the 1902 harvest season to politely remind the CPR of the new rules. He hoped to ensure that a repetition of the 1901 shipping problems did not take place, for the 1902 harvest was expected to be as big as the previous year's. A farmer at Sintaluta, Saskatchewan, W. W. Allen, had early in the harvest of 1902 asked for a railcar, had waited seven weeks for a car while 80 other cars came to Sintaluta and were allotted to other people. The case was brought before the panel of three magistrates, led by the Presbyterian Henry O. Partridge, who was also a farmer in the area. The CPR agent at Sintaluta was found guilty of violating the Grain Act. With this victory in the courts, the grain growers won not only the right, but also the actual practice, of being able to ship their grain directly to market.

As the head of the Territorial Grain Growers Association, Motherwell was a well known figure among the farmers of western Canada, and was an invited speaker at various farm gatherings. Elected to the Saskatchewan Legislature in 1905 as a Liberal, he became the province's first minister of agriculture, he remained Minister of Agriculture until 1918. In 1921, Motherwell tried his hand at federal politics, and after his election was appointed Minister of Agriculture by another Presbyterian, Prime Minister William Lyon Mackenzie King. In 1908, Motherwell married Catherine (Kate) Gillespie, the Principal of the Presbyterian-operated File Hills Native Residential School, located at Balcarres, near the Motherwell farm. The Motherwell homestead at Abernethy is now a National Historic Site.[24]

At the end of 1904, the Grain Growers were concerned about the seeming arbitrariness of the grading system, and they sent Edward A. Partridge to Winnipeg for four weeks to be their "scout" as he learned all he could about the grain grading and trading system. E.A. Partridge and, his brother, Henry O. Partridge, had arrived in the Sintaluta region in 1883 to homestead. Partridge returned from his Winnipeg experience convinced that the larger elevator companies and exporters were working as a syndicate to fix grain prices at the farm gate. In particular he was convinced that the inspection system placed too much emphasis on the colour and plumpness of the grain. Believing that it was the system itself that was the problem, the only answer in Partridge's mind was for the grain growers to establish their own co-operative grain company which would operate for the benefit of the growers who would receive the dividends. In January 1906, the Grain Growers Grain Company was born, and Partridge spent the summer selling shares at $25 a piece. By September 1906, in time for the 1906 harvest, the company had enough resources, both in grain they had been promised and in hard cash to buy a seat on the exchange in the name of E.A. Partridge. In November, 1906, Partridge and the Grain Growers got thrown off the exchange, because they promised to split their profits with the patrons of the Grain Growers Company. The Exchange saw this as the promise of a kickback to induce farmers to sell their grain through Partridge. Motherwell, in his role as Saskatchewan's Minister of Agriculture, put pressure on the Exchange to let the Grain Growers return. The seat was provisionally returned to the Grain Growers Company in the spring of 1907, but it was not until 1908 that the company would fully regain its seat on the Exchange, and it was no longer in Partridge's name. But by then it was the Exchange that was on the defensive, trying to defend its closed door policies and arcane rules. Recognizing the anger members of the Exchange held towards him, Partridge sought to resign as President of the Grain Growers Company in early 1907. He was convinced to stay on until the fall when he was replaced by T.A. Crerar. Having an established seat on the Exchange, it was only natural for the Grain Growers to begin to build farmer-owned elevators, to ensure that their grain could be easily loaded on cars and shipped to market, and it was the development of such an integrated system that the Grain Growers Company turned to in the second decade of the 20th century. This company was to evolve into the United Grain Growers, and UGG elevators dot the prairies today.

While the first generation of agrarian leaders had focused on the sale and shipping of grain, the next set of leaders was far more political. Radically committed to free trade and sensing that rapid urban growth was stripping farmers of their political power, the already politicized farm associations pushed forward candidates to run provincially and federally. The president of the Manitoba Grain Growers in 1915, the Presbyterian R.C. Henders, was nominated as an "independent, free trade" candidate. In his address to the annual convention in January 1916, Henders argued that the farmers did not achieve their political aims because they "as a class have not in the past, and do not even now readily develop the spirit of class consciousness." The independent spirit that the pioneering farmer needed to stay alive and to open up the west was not the approach that was needed in the increasing stratified and economically polarized Canadian society of the 1910's. The Rev. Thomas Beveridge, the Presbyterian minister from Deloraine, Manitoba, was nominated to run in the federal riding of Souris as an "independent progressive." Among Beveridge's policies was the introduction of prohibition across the country. Neither Henders nor Beveridge won seats in the 1917 election. The Progressive party, of which Henders and Beveridge were forerunners, was to sweep the west in the 1921 election. The Rev. William R. Wood, Presbyterian minister at Franklin and Glendale, Manitoba, fared better. Wood, who was the secretary of the Manitoba Grain Growers, ran provincially in 1916 and was elected as an independent committed to the farmers' policies of free trade, prohibition, and social justice. Wood lost his seat in 1919. In April 1919, as secretary of the Manitoba Grain Growers, Wood wrote to rural clergy in the province, urging them to support and join the broad-based coalition whose goal was "the promotion of better citizenship and of economic and political justice." Economically and politically the farmers had found ways to mobilize themselves to achieve many of their goals; they had become a force with which politicians and the business elite had to reckon in their decision making.[25]

The political strength of the farmers' movement would reach its climax in the 1920's, when the Progressive party would take 65 western seats in the 1921 federal election and both Alberta (1921) and Manitoba (1922) would elect farmer governments. These governments sought to bring together the interests of farmers with the concerns of town and city dwellers caught between radical labour and the capitalist elite. The rise of social gospel preaching in middle class urban churches and socially traditionalist town congregations would have encouraged church attendees to support political parties promising to solve many of the social ills of the day. It was the Progressives who openly campaigned on the temperance platform, and this would have drawn the large number of middle class voters who connected drink with the decline of morality.

The Progressive movement was not able to hold, and by 1930 was simply a small regional party with twelve seats in the House of Commons. More importantly, the agrarian revolt and the Progressive movement had laid the basis of the Co-operative Commonwealth Federation (the forerunner of the NDP), which under the leadership of individuals like Tommy Douglas would change the face of Canada forever.

Economic Development on the Prairies

Much of the economic development on the prairies was commercial. What Winnipeg became as the major trading centre for the west was repeated on a smaller scale by the newly arising smaller urban centres that provided the goods and services needed by their hinterlands. This commercial development was driven by locally based entrepreneurs; few large companies were involved in the delivery of goods and services in the small- and medium-sized towns of the prairies. Institutions like the Hudson Bay Company established stores in large urban centres expecting people to come to their stores. Eaton's, which sent its catalogue to thousands of households across the west, did not have face to face contact with its catalogue customers, relying instead on the mail. If there were to be personalized direct service in the medium-sized communities and in the small towns of the prairies it would be delivered by local entrepreneurs. A number of people saw the opportunities and slid in to meet the need. They were risk takers, making fortunes and losing them almost as fast as they had earned them: investing in schemes that never panned out, speculating on where the CPR would put a townsite, sometimes being right and at other times wrong. The prairie brought out the risk-taker and the dreamer in those who were building the economy of the west. These entrepreneurs also recognized they had a role to play in the growth of the community, becoming leaders in the development of hospitals, fraternal organizations, community groups and churches.

George Murdoch, a harness maker, arrived in Calgary in the spring of 1883 when it was still a cluster of tents on both sides of the Elbow River. He did well in this new land, charging "like mischief" for his services, as he admitted later. Among his best customers were the NWMP and the Blackfoot, whose language he learned to speak. As one of the first permanent business people in Calgary, he took a leading role in its political and social development. A founding member of the Presbyterian Church, he was also active in the volunteer fire brigade, the agricultural association, and the literary and history societies.[26]

Thomas Tweed and his partner, James Lougheed, set up a general store in Medicine Hat in 1883, just before the steel arrived. They started out in a tent, Lougheed soon moved on to Calgary, but Tweed remained in Medicine Hat and in 1885 added a second store in Lethbridge. Tweed quickly became a wealthy man. He, along with many of the first generation of the western entrepreneurs, was not satisfied to stay in just one field of economic endeavour. In 1886 he joined with William Finlay and two other partners to establish the Medicine Hat Ranch Company, one of the first large scale ranching operations in the district. Tweed was instrumental in the establishment of St. John's Presbyterian Church in 1883, and in the 1890's he helped establish a hockey club (forerunners of the Medicine Hat Tigers) and a drama society. William Finlay was also a member at St. John's. Finlay had arrived in Medicine Hat in 1883 as a sales agent for the Northwest Lumber Company. Recognizing Medicine Hat's potential he had set up an agency of the company there and in Lethbridge. The lumber business was one of the few businesses in which larger commercial systems had been developed on the prairies. Since there was virtually no wood on the prairie, it all had to be shipped in, and sales agents from various lumber companies who had cutting rights west of Lake Superior were dispatched across the west to market their products. Shortly after arriving in Medicine Hat, Finlay decided he too wanted to diversify his business opportunities and joined with Tweed in the ranching enterprise. In 1888, Finlay, a Liberal, and Tweed, a Conservative, ran against each other for a seat in the North-West Territories legislature. It was, not surprisingly given the close connections between the two men, a bitter campaign, which Tweed won. Finlay focused his attention on the ranching business and community development, becoming a leader in the cattlemen's associations and serving for eight years on the Medicine Hat hospital board. He was elected mayor in 1900, serving for two years, during which time the water-supply system was built.[27]

Wellington White arrived in Prince Albert in 1893, having come from Pennsylvania by way of Owen Sound, Ontario. He was a brick maker by trade. Business was slow in Prince Albert, whose glory days were past, but it was in Prince Albert that White met Olive Brooks and they were married. In 1898, White was looking to expand his brick business, and hearing about a heavy clay quarter section of land near Moose Jaw, he went to investigate. The Whites moved to Moose Jaw where they became influential members of St. Andrew's Presbyterian Church. By 1902, White had built a state-of-the-art brick making works at Moose Jaw, and was providing brick to a number of major developments in the area, including the three-storey Maple Leaf Hotel, the City Hall, and the "Union Bank and White Block." White expanded his brick making business to Irvine, Alberta, but this turned into a business failure. The coming of the war meant the end to most large building projects and the brick business collapsed. White turned his hand to farming, with which he quickly became bored. He transformed his brick making business into a construction company and was poised after the war to take advantage of the various community infrastructure projects that were being built in southern Saskatchewan.[28]

Although grain was certainly the dominant product of the prairies, it was not the only thing produced on the prairies. Sir Alexander Galt, who had been at the Charlottetown Conference in 1864, recognized the potential of the vast coal deposits on the western fringe of the Canadian prairies. Coal was a valuable commodity used to run the steam engines that plied back and forth across the prairies, and it was a source to heat homes on the treeless prairie. Galt, a deeply committed Presbyterian who did not make a major business decision without praying about it first, formed the North Western Coal and Navigation Company in 1882 with financial backing from investors in Winnipeg, Montreal, and London. The decision was to begin mining at present day Lethbridge, 160 kilometers from the proposed CPR rail line. It was necessary therefore to find some way to transport the coal to the mainline. In 1883 and 1884 Galt tried moving the coal by barge to Medicine Hat. This proved virtually impossible, and so he began exploring the possibility of a railroad, a costly proposition. Federal authorities were so excited about getting coal for prairie residents that they offered Galt six sections of land for the cost of the survey for every mile of track built. As well, the government sold 10,000 acres of coal lands for ten dollars an acre. The operation had now grown dramatically; no longer was it a simple coal mining proposition, there was the capital cost of the tracks and rolling stock, and the company was the proud owner of 600 hundred sections of prairie, room for 2,400 homesteading households. This was now a complex business operation. The rail line was completed in the summer of 1885, and coal began to be shipped.[29]

The town of Lethbridge quickly grew, made up of miners and their families, and the shopkeepers, hotel owners, and other service personnel who made up a growing community on the prairies. Among the miners were a large number of Hungarians who came to Lethbridge by way of Pennsylvania, where Galt had found them in the coal mines and offered them jobs in his mine. Lethbridge, as a mining community, was a rough town with gambling, drinking, and prostitution. The Presbyterian and Methodist clergy in town sought to have the town council rid Lethbridge of the prostitutes, but the chief of police responded that if the ministers "would turn their attention to the juvenile depravity and promiscuous fornication that is going on under their own eyes and in their own congregations, they would be kept so busy that they would have no time to think of the professional ladies."[30]

The North Western Coal and Navigation Company had 600 sections of farm land which it needed to have settled if the company was going to realize the financial value of the subsidy the federal government had given it. The problem was that the land was on the edge of the Palliser Triangle, the northern edge of the Great American Desert; the only way to farm it was through irrigation. But the Deputy Minister of the Interior, the Presbyterian Alexander M. Burgess, was opposed to any irrigation. He, along with John A. Macdonald, believed that if reports about irrigation being used in the west became widely known, people would stop moving to the region, scared off by the implication that the land was a desert. In 1893, Burgess changed his mind and began to advocate for a system of irrigation. The area needing irrigation was very small so it would not be a large factor in dissuading immigration. More importantly, the Americans had already made plans to divert and dam the Milk and St. Mary's Rivers for their irrigation plans, and therefore it was necessary for the Canadian government to assert its water rights. Finally, those who would be directly affected by irrigation were in favour of it. This change in direction allowed the diversion of rivers and streams to irrigate the land around Lethbridge, making it viable for settlement just in time for the more aggressively open door immigration policy of the Laurier government. Alexander Galt and his son, Elliott. had anticipated a very simple coal operation, which grew into a multi-faceted business enterprise on the prairies.[31]

Coal was also found near Edmonton. As that city began to grow rapidly in the early 1880's, Presbyterian Donald McLeod developed a coalmine in the valley of Whitemud Creek. This was the least expensive source of domestic coal for the Edmonton market. McLeod also shipped coal to Calgary. Shortly after Rev. D. G. McQueen's arrival in Edmonton, family members in the east invested in the Clover Bar coal mine near Edmonton.

The mine did well and shares were placed in a trust fund, with the dividends to be used by the Presbytery of Edmonton for its mission work.[32]

The rapid population growth that took place on the prairies in the first decade of the 20th century created a ready market for manufactured goods. The development of Winnipeg into an urban centre at this same time meant that a pool of useable labour had been drawn together in one place. It was not surprising that the number of factory workers in Winnipeg grew by six times between 1901 and 1914, with more than 18,000 Winnipeggers working in factories and producing 50 million dollars worth of product in 1914.[33]

SOCIAL DEVELOPMENT

As this chapter has unfolded there has been mention of school policies, the establishment of hospitals, and the building of community infrastructure. It was often women who led the developments in these areas. The three women whose stories are told in thumbnail sketch below are but a sample of the hundreds of women who transformed the west by their lives and visions.

Charlotte Ross (nee Whitehead), with the support of her husband and the family's physician, enrolled in the Woman's Medical College in Philadelphia, there being no medical school in Canada that would accept women in 1870. She graduated in 1875, and began to practice medicine in Montreal in 1876. In 1881, she and her children joined her husband David in the frontier community of Whitemouth, Manitoba, where David operated the sawmill. The only doctor for 160 kilometers, her practice began the night she arrived in town. Much of her practice was made up of the men from the lumber camps and railway, an unusual circumstance for the few women doctors in Canada in those days. She was never licensed by the College of Physicians and Surgeons of Manitoba, but continued to provide medical care because the need was there. The Ross family were committed Presbyterians, donating the land and materials to build a school-cum-church in Whitemouth. Their door was open to all clergy, including Father Albert Lacombe, who became a friend and who Charlotte treated for pleurisy in her home.[34]

Jessie McEwen (nee Turnbull), in 1895 met Lady Aberdeen, wife of the Governor General. Lady Aberdeen was a leading force in the Presbyterian Church during her time in Canada and the founder of the National Council of Women of Canada. Before coming west with her husband in 1884, McEwen had been a leading advocate for women's rights in Ontario. This meeting with Lady Aberdeen seemed to trigger McEwen's commitment to again become active in the community. McEwen became the president of the Local Council of Women in Brandon, a position she would hold until 1916. The Brandon chapter established the public library and other reading rooms in the district, introduced vocational training courses to the Brandon schools, pushed for the election of women school board trustees, and furnished and equipped a ward of the Brandon General Hospital. McEwen was instrumentally involved with the start of the Brandon Red Cross Society, the first such society in Manitoba. In 1907, she spearheaded the formation of the Young Women's Christian Association in Brandon. McEwen was also active in the Presbyterian church, helping organize no fewer than four Women's Foreign Missionary Society auxiliaries in the Brandon area. McEwen was a small, erect woman with "the frailty of a steel girder."[35]

Olive White (nee Brooks), wife of the Moose Jaw brick-maker, was no less active in charitable causes then McEwen. White was involved in virtually every charitable cause in the city of Moose Jaw, and used her social position and organizational ability to do fundraising on a grand scale. Committed to the Children's Aid Society, she was constantly developing new ways to help fund its operation. In 1921, she organized the opening gala of the Temple Tea Gardens and Dance Hall because it was to be a benefit concert for the Children's Aid Society. White was for a decade the president of the St. Andrew's Presbyterian Ladies Auxiliary, entertaining missionaries, hosting teas, and getting down on hands and knees to scrub the church floor.[36]

The social transformation of the west was not led just by women. At times political figures like Colin Campbell, Manitoba's attorney general, acted to bring improvements to society. Campbell was becoming increasing aware by 1907 of the problems surrounding the trial and incarceration of juvenile delinquents. In 1909, the changes he guided through the legislature established the first juvenile court in Canada, including the establishment of a special detention facility for children. Campbell regarded this as his most lasting achievement as a politician.[37]

Many westerners dreamed of a better society, and much of the radicalism of those visions can be attributed to a growing frustration among some westerners at the fact that much of prairie culture was dominated by the same societal forces that had formed Ontario. There was at the heart of the west a struggle between those who wanted to transplant Ontario onto the prairies and those who wanted something different to happen in this new great land, something as open and exhilarating as the sky and the land themselves.

THE WAR

The coming of world war had a dramatic effect on the prairies. First, immigration dried up almost instantly. Many of the countries from which the new Canadians had been coming, particularly the Austro-Hungarian Empire, were now enemies of Canada. It also meant that many of the new

Canadians who had once lived in an enemy nation were now looked upon with suspicion. Second, thousands of new Canadians who had come from Great Britain immediately volunteered to return to the homeland to defend the great British institutions. It became a time of flag waving and jingoism. Many Presbyterians heard the call to arms to "Defeat the Kaiser," and others helped proclaim the message, the Rev. Dr. C.W. Gordon (Ralph Connor) being among them. In one of his speeches in support of the war effort, he said, "Rather must Canada, with calm, deliberate, clear-eyed purpose, make resolve that she is committed to this world conflict to her last man and her last dollar, not for the Empire's sake alone, but for her own sake and for the sake of her national ideals, for the sake of human rights."[38] When the war started, Saskatoon College, the Presbyterian theological college in that city, was anticipating an enrollment of twenty-eight for the fall of 1914. By the spring of 1915, fourteen of the students had enlisted. And by 1916 the Principal himself, E.H. Oliver, had enlisted.

The western provinces sent more than their share of young men to the front. One of out every nine soldiers in the Canadian Expeditionary Force, or 11 percent, were Manitobans. At the time Manitoba made up just more than 6 percent of Canada's population. There were a couple of reasons for this. First, as noted above, many of the new arrivals in the west were from Great Britain and they were returning to defend the motherland. Second, an economic downturn hit the prairies in late 1913 and a number of young men were out of work. Joining up was not only a great opportunity for adventure, it was a job.

One-fifth of the military chaplains were Presbyterian. Of these 117, 28 had some connection with the West, either having joined up from a western pastorate or entering a western pastorate after the war. The move of 28 clergy into the chaplancy did not create a personnel crisis for the Presbyterian Church in the west; there were 434 Presbyterian clergy in active ministry in the west in 1914. Of the 28, only seven returned to the congregation or ministry they had been in when they went to become a chaplain. It is a little surprising that that more Presbyterian clergy from the west did not become chaplains. In January 1917, of the 788 doctors registered in Saskatchewan, 74, or nearly 10 percent were on active military service; only just more than six percent of Presbyterian clergy on the prairies enlisted. The chaplains were often substantially older than the men to whom they were ministering: Charles Gordon, E.H. Oliver, and A.D. Reid were all in their forties when they enlisted. John Hood Selkirk was 39 when he enlisted on March 10, 1916. Selkirk had been born in Scotland and by enlisting he was returning to help the motherland. He never got to the front, staying in England for the duration of his chaplancy.[39]

The war did have another impact on the west, many young men were killed in action or were so badly wounded they would not go back to the lives they had once led. E.A. and Mary Partridge of Sintuluta, Saskatchewan, had both of their sons killed in the war. Frank Mantle came to Canada at the age of 16, an orphan. He homesteaded and wrote on agricultural topics for the Belmont (Alberta) *Star*, in 1908 he became the agricultural editor for the *Manitoba Morning Free Press*. His ability was recognized by many, and in 1910 he became the deputy minister of agriculture in Saskatchewan. In Regina, he became an active member at Westminster Presbyterian Church. In August 1915, he enlisted, and on September 26, 1916, after only two days on the Somme front, he was killed by a sniper's bullet. He was 34. W.R. Motherwell, the minister of agriculture, voiced aloud what many thought: "such indispensible men as Frank Mantle in a new land like Saskatchewan should not be permitted to enlist." The war meant the deaths of some of the brightest and most gifted young men the west had to offer. Their loss would leave gaping holes not just in the hearts and souls of their families but in the political, social and economic spheres as well. The war left many broken and wounded hearts and communities across the west; the impact of this psychological and spiritual pain on the post-war era is only gradually being realized. The pain associated with World War I, for most Canadians, was much greater that the pain that accompanied World War II.[40]

THE FLU

The so-called "Spanish" influenza arrived in Canada aboard the troop ships and spread to the prairies on the transcontinental trains. Between the fall of 1918 and early 1920, at least 50,000 Canadians died from the flu, 5,000 of them in Saskatchewan. The flu was just a familiar disease run wild, and the medical profession was unable to stop it. The onset was sudden; there was sudden weakness, pains, chills; then coughing including coughing up blood; in the worst cases this led to a blueness of the fingers and face that spread to the whole body, delirium, and in the most extreme cases death from respiratory failure. The flu was indiscriminate in who it killed; young and old, men and women. One of the brightest stars in the Ukrainian-speaking Presbyterian Church in Winnipeg, the Rev. C. T. Othen, who had just graduated from Princeton Theological Seminary, died from the flu. The principal of the Cecilia Jeffrey Residential School near Kenora, Ontario, also died from the flu, yet none of the students at the school did.[41]

The prairies were left reeling from the body blow delivered by the flu. As the Rev. Willie C. Clark of Knox Presbyterian Church in Saskatoon said, "During the past year large demands have been made on our courage. Our heart's strength has been tested. The end is not yet. We have had war, partial crop failure and today we are in the middle of pestilence." Finally in the late fall of 1918 the government began to dramatic action to stem the spread. Alberta banned all gatherings of more than seven people who were not related to one another. That meant the end of school, church services, community sports, the legislative assembly, and a host of other things. Saskatchewan banned all public gatherings. Clergy became creative and had their sermons published in the Saturday papers to be read on Sunday in homes during family worship. Clergy also became involved in nursing the sick. A Presbyterian missionary,

> hearing of the case of a smitten family living in a shack, some fifteen miles away, rode over. He found the father just able to crawl about, the mother in bed with the corpse of a six-year-old girl beside her, and one or two younger children crying on the floor. Sending word to his family not to expect him home for a few days, he remained at the shack until the worst was over, and then returned to his home himself a victim.

The flu disrupted lives and wiped out entire families, and in this chaos the church sought to minister.[42]

Within the first 48 hours, 22 people in Moose Jaw died of the flu. There were homes in which everyone was ill, so that no one could care for the sick. A state of emergency was declared and Olive White was one of the lead figures on the Citizens' Health Committee. She set up a soup kitchen in the basement of St. Andrew's Presbyterian Church and organized a car pool to get soup and medical supplied to the sick. She arranged for the distribution of 15,000 cotton masks, which every resident of Medicine Hat was required to wear, and she developed a system for linking calls for medical help with the available doctors and nurses. Later she estimated that she had slept about ten hours in the two weeks that the epidemic was at its height in Moose Jaw. The local newspaper commented, "Mrs. White's genius as an organizer has been given full scope and her untiring devotion to duty has had a wonderful effect upon the general situation."[43]

THE STRIKE

The 1919 Winnipeg General Strike stands as a significant event in the life not just of Winnipeg and the west, but in the life of the country as a whole. The Communist Revolution in Russia, the rhetoric used by leaders of the One Big Union, and the generally recognized tension between labour and capital, which was at a boiling point, all increased the unease with which the strike was viewed. On May 1, 1919, workers in the building and metal trades in Winnipeg went on strike to back their demands for better wages and the recognition of their union. The membership of the Winnipeg Trades and Labour Council voted in favour of a sympathy strike, supporting the workers already on strike, and on May 15, 30,000 employees joined in the General Strike. This included some 12,000 workers who were not even union members. The city of Winnipeg ground to a halt. A Strike Committee was established by the Labour Council, which took over many of the responsibilities of the municipal government. The committee issued placards "By Permission of the Strike Committee" to milk delivery wagons proving that the drivers were not strike-breakers; and the committee instructed the city police who had voted to strike to remain on the job.[44]

The anti-strike forces established a Citizens Committee that created a "citizens militia" and urged the federal government to send in troops to maintain order. Arthur Meighan, who was Acting Minister of Justice in the federal cabinet, arrived in Winnipeg on May 22, with the primary purpose of getting the postal workers, who were federal government employees, back to work. Meighan, in conjunction with his cabinet colleague, Senator Gideon Robertson, Minister of Labour, issued an ultimatum to the postal workers in Winnipeg: they were to be back at work on May 26 or they would lose their jobs. Only a quarter of postal employees returned to work and Meighan supported the decision of the post office to begin hiring new workers.

With the mail moving again, Meighan and Robertson turned to the general strike itself. They were convinced that the provincial government was too afraid to do anything about ending the strike, and so they returned to Ottawa convinced that if something were to happen, the federal cabinet would have to respond. The response came in three forms. First, legislation was introduced allowing for the arrest and automatic deportation of individuals who were threatening the state; second, military patrols were established in Winnipeg; and third, on June 17, strike leaders were arrested. On June 21, there was violence as mounted police charged marching strikers, and one man was killed. This was the beginning of the end of the strike, and by July 3 it was over. Meighan believed in the right of workers to strike, but he opposed general strikes because by their very nature they undermined the authority of duly elected officials to maintain social, political, and economic stability. In one of the great ironies of Canadian political history, at the very time that Meighan was being the hard-nosed advocate of law and order and a supporter of the capitalists, he was actively moving the government towards the nationalization of the railways, a socialist approach to economic policy.[45]

C.W. Gordon (Ralph Connor), in his novel *To Him that Hath*, took a different approach. The novel is about the Winnipeg strike. The town where the action takes place is Blackwater; Winnipeg translated into English means "muddy water." He believed that as long as all parties in a labour-capital dispute were willing to talk to each other with respect and honesty, a way of conciliation could be found. In the novel, Gordon draws the portrait of a progressive minister who has close connections with both labour leaders and capitalists, urging the two sides to talk with each other in the presence of a mediator. This again is a thin disguise, for the book's protagonist, Murdo Matheson, is a former military chaplain, just as Gordon was. Being a mediator was a role that Gordon was to play in real life as the provincially appointed chair of the Council of Industry for Manitoba. The purpose of the council was to function as a conciliator between the two sides in labour-capital conflicts.[46]

CONCLUSION

The chapter has tried to give readers a feeling for the ebbs and flows of western Canadian history, by telling the story through the eyes and lives of Presbyterians. The almost single-minded focus on Presbyterians has skewed the telling of the story of the west in at least one important way. The denominational lines that were so significant in Ontario and the eastern part of the country were largely ignored in the west. It was not unusual for a Presbyterian minister to lead worship in a congregation made up of Presbyterians, Methodists, Anglicans, Roman Catholics, Lutherans, and even Seventh Day Adventists, Christian Scientists, Jews, and Mormons. The Roman Catholic priest, Father Charles Cahill experienced the same thing, reporting that at Rat Portage (Kenora), Ontario, his bilingual evening prayer was well attended by English-speaking Protestants. The union Sunday school was the most obvious place where the denominational lines faded. All across the west there were union Sunday schools; in these Sunday schools children of many different denominational backgrounds were brought together and taught the same curriculum, usually the International Sunday School material. In the rural areas and in pioneer country there were not enough children or teachers for each denomination to have their own Sunday school programme. In Saskatchewan no one did more to promote the religious education of children than did W.R. "Sunday School" Sutherland. For more than 20 years he travelled through rural Saskatchewan developing Sunday schools, encouraging teachers, and quizzing children on their lessons. He worked with everyone and anyone. So well known and respected was he, that Presbyterians, Anglicans, Methodists, and others mourned his passing.[47]

The west was a new land for those who were just arriving on the prairie, and in this new land there was an openness to new ideas, new models, new ways of doing things. That openness to risk, to experiment, to try out radical ideas affected the church as well, preparing it to take bold steps to live on the frontier of mission.

"...to give them the gospel...":
Planting the Presbyterian Church on the Prairies

The prairies were nothing like what anyone from Eastern Canada or "the Old Country" had ever seen or experienced. Charles Gordon (later writing under the pen-name Ralph Connor) spent the summer of 1885 on the Killarney, Manitoba, mission field and tried to describe the prairie to his eastern Canadian readers,

> One September evening, driving home, I could not but stop and look at the sunset, as I kept looking the beauty grew upon me, till it filled me with a kind of pain, down somewhere in my heart— and this is what I saw. High up the clouds were piled in dark heaps, but below, near the prairie, they were little and only a few, in a sea of golden light—and all so quiet, so very still, like the sea at times. It made one think of the rest of Heaven.... How can the new earth show us more? but then we, too, shall be changed.[1]

The west was a new world, so magnificent it was painful to observe. Gordon felt he was standing on the edge of the new heaven and the new earth. He, like the apostle John in the book of Revelation, struggled to express in mere words what he had seen and experienced. But the west defied any attempt to define it, or describe it. Not only was it a new world, it also made people new. B. A. Barron, who had also spent a summer in a mission charge on the prairies, said, "as soon as one enters the country he feels as though a new element has entered his being, making him walk with a more buoyant step and think with a clearer head."[2] It was in this new world of the prairie that the Presbyterian Church in Canada sought to plant itself. This new world challenged the church to have new visions, to adopt new methods, and to create new patterns of ministry, as it sought to carry out its mission.

As we noted in the last chapter the vast majority of the settlers coming to the west between 1885 and 1896 were English speakers who had lived for a while in Ontario. They brought with them the expectation that the west would be simply a new Ontario with all of the institutions, including the church, that they had become accustomed to in Ontario. Even after Clifford Sifton and the Laurier government opened the doors to a wide variety of immigrants, the majority of the new arrivals on the prairies were English speaking and shared a common Anglo-Saxon heritage, be it from the United States, Great Britain, or from English-speaking Canada. This chapter explores how the Presbyterian Church in Canada planted itself among these English-speaking immigrants.

Church leaders assumed that if gifted ministers were sent into the recently opened areas where the new arrivals were homesteading and developing communities, congregations would grow up naturally. By ensuring that "the ordinances" of preaching, baptism, and communion were available, the church would have done its part and the "children" of the church who had moved west would be reminded of their faith heritage and could then be drawn together into self-supporting, viable Presbyterian congregations. For the most part the leadership was correct in their assumptions; but they were to discover that pastoral visiting and the missionary's clear identification with the settlers were far more important in the west than they were in Ontario. Given that the essential patterns of ministry were to be the same as those used in eastern Canada, the challenge confronting the church was to provide the personnel and financial resources needed to securely plant the Presbyterian Church on the prairies. The provision of those resources meant organisational re-thinking and the adoption of models for delivering them that made sense to the west. In the discussion of the ways the church re-organised itself to meet the needs of the west, it is important to remember that the bottom line for the church was how to most effectively give "the ordinances" of the faith to western Canadians who were wanting and needing the ministry and spiritual centre of the church.

THE SUPERINTENDENT OF MISSION

As the trickle of settlers to the west became a steady stream in the late 1870's and early 1880's, Presbyterians in the west developed an ambitious two-part plan to respond. First, the Presbytery of Manitoba would ensure that there was a Presbyterian clergy person in place at each townsite within a year of the town being established. The goal was neatly expressed, "The gambler, the rum-seller, and the strange woman travel by fast express—the Church by slow stage. When the Church arrives she finds saloons, gambling hells and worse places in full blast, and largely controlled by bilks.... The missionary should accompany the settler, not follow [them] afar off." The Presbyterian Church wanted to be part of the life of these fledgling communities from their earliest days. The missionary on the charge was to develop four or five preaching points with a total of about 60 Presbyterian households, on a circuit that was no more than 60 kilometres round trip; the distance which could be reasonably ridden by horse on a Sunday. Sometimes the charge would be in two parts, with two or three preaching points being covered this week and the other two or three next week. Second, to make this vision live, there had to be someone to implement the plan and oversee the development of hundreds of new churches that would be needed across the prairies. In a word, the Presbytery of Manitoba was asking for a Presbyterian bishop. Since that is a concept anathema to Presbyterians, they asked the denomination to create a new position, a superintendent of missions. The Assembly was being asked to create a unique position, for in Presbyterianism, built as it is on a collegial model of collective responsibility, virtually all decision-making power resides with the presbyteries. Having an individual in this supervisory role meant devolving much of that power from the presbyteries to a single individual. Although the position of Superintendent was new in the Canadian Presbyterian Church it had historical precedent in the annals of Presbyterianism. The First Book of Discipline of 1560, the earliest codification of the rules governing Presbyterian churches, allowed for the appointment of Superintendents at critical moments in the life of the church, who were given the power to establish congregations and appoint ministers without reference to a presbytery so "that Christ Jesus be universally preached throughout the realm." In June 1881, the General Assembly agreed to the request from Manitoba, largely because it saw the unique challenges of the west required a unique response. The record of the Assembly's debate about the appointment of a superintendent does not indicate if anyone made reference to the First Book of Discipline. General Assembly appointed the Rev. James Robertson of Winnipeg superintendent of missions. His territory would be from Lake Superior west to the Pacific Ocean. And so the die was cast, for it is impossible to tell the story of the Presbyterian Church's mission on the Prairies and in the North without recognising the central role played by James Robertson.[3]

James Robertson was born in Dull, Scotland in 1839. In 1855 his family emigrated to Canada, settling in that hotbed of Presbyterianism, Zorra Township, Upper Canada. Through the influence of the local Presbyterian minister, Robertson decided to enter the ministry and took his university education at University College, Toronto, graduating in 1866. During his last year at University College, he saw military action with the Queen's Own Rifles who repelled a Fenian-sponsored invasion of Canada at Ridgetown, Ontario. Robertson was deeply shaken by the fighting, and saw his survival as a further confirmation of God's call on his life. In the fall of 1866, Robertson enrolled at Princeton Theological Seminary in New Jersey. Under the leadership of Charles Hodge, Princeton had become one of the foremost missionary sending theological colleges in the world. Hodge's deep commitment to prayer and his spiritual passion created a crucible in which the lives of students were refined. Robertson remained at Princeton for two years, his second year (1867-1868) overlapping with George Leslie Mackay's (another Zorra Township product) first year at Princeton. The fall of 1868 found Robertson completing his theological training at Union Theological Seminary in New York City. While studying there, he worked parttime in an inner city mission. Upon graduation he was offered the leadership of the mission on a full-time basis, but he chose instead to re-turn to Canada. On Sept. 23, 1869, after a 10 year courtship, James Robertson and Mary Ann Cowing were married. They were to have five children. On Nov. 18, 1869, Robertson was ordained and inducted into the pastoral charge in Norwich, Ontario.[4]

The evening of Dec. 30, 1873, found James Robertson in Union Sta-tion, Toronto preparing to journey to Winnipeg in response to an urgent request from Knox Presbyterian Church for a minister to fill their pulpit for six months. The journey took 10 days and involved travelling through the United States to the end of the rail line and then north by boat and horse-drawn sleigh. On Jan. 9, 1874, Robertson arrived in Winnipeg and was immediately hooked by the west. Because of a communication mix up, there was already a Presbyterian minister preaching at Knox. Robertson was left free to travel extensively outside of Winnipeg, witnessing the chal-lenges faced by the settlers, as well as marvelling at their optimism. At the end of the six months Robertson returned to his family and ministry in Norwich. Almost immediately Knox, Winnipeg issued a call to Robertson, which he accepted, moving his family and beginning a fruitful seven-year ministry. He developed a rapport with newcomers to the west who stopped in Winnipeg on the way to their homesteads, providing them with advice, help, and often a place to stay while they got together the goods needed to begin farming the harsh beauty of the prairie.[5]

When the 1881 General Assembly met, Robertson was in Winnipeg and his wife and children were travelling in Ontario. The Clerks of Assem-bly sent a telegram to Robertson informing him of the Assembly's unani-mous decision that he be the new Superintendent of Missions. Without consulting his wife or children, Robertson replied that he would be hon-oured to accept the new position. In a letter to his wife he said, "I would like to have communicated with you ere taking the final step but the As-sembly's call was urgent and there was no time to write."[6]

Robertson's new responsibilities included: determining where to start new congregations; meeting with the prospective congregation members; recruiting missionaries, both clergy and theology students, to minister on the prairies; providing oversight to all mission stations and congregations receiving grants from the Home Missions Committee; and doing regular fund-raising speaking tours to encourage eastern Presbyterians to give generously to the cause of Home Missions. Robertson was to report his activities twice a year to the Home Missions Committee of the General Assembly, and was to consult with the various presbyteries as they were established. This job description carried with it an enormous administrative component. There were hundreds of details to be noted and remembered. There were letters to be written to supporters and church officials back east, letters to recruit students, and letters to ministers in the field answering their questions, which ranged from complex pastoral problems to practical insurance and maintenance issues. Robertson wrote thousands of letters in his expansive scrawling longhand over the 20 years he was superintendent of missions.[7]

Robertson had a public relations role to play, raising the profile of the vast mission field of the west through his speeches and sermons given both in eastern Canada and on his two tours of Britain and the European Continent. His sermon notes on Matthew 20:1-16, Jesus' parable of the workers in the vineyard, illustrates the way Robertson expounded on Biblical texts to advance the mission of the church. Using the vineyard as a metaphor for the mission field, Robertson stated that God still asks human beings to enter into the vineyard of mission. God does not force anyone to labour in the mission, but once we have entered the vineyard we are called to work, working with our best effort until God calls us at the end of the day. There is a reward that is given to all who work in the vineyard, but it is not a reward that is earned by our labour; rather the reward is a gift from God purchased by the blood of Christ, and labourers will not receive their reward until the work is done. There is no advantage to be achieved in putting off entry into the vineyard and the beginning of work. Those who previously had decided that they did not want to enter the vineyard could change their minds and enter now. Robertson ended his sermon with the challenge, "Have we entered into the vineyard?" It was Robertson's preaching pattern to fill a general sermon outline like this with examples of mission work taking place in the west, and of missionaries who had entered into the vineyard. Robertson hoped that sermons like this would encourage people to enter into the work of western mission either through their financial contributions or by having young people volunteer to become missionaries to the west.[8]

While the Assembly had been unanimous in its choice of Robertson and the Presbytery of Winnipeg was happy with the choice, not everyone was pleased with his appointment. In March 1883, a vicious letter signed "A Blue Presbyterian" was published in the Toronto *Mail*,

Another matter that demands immediate attention is the abolition of that nondescript office of superintendent now paraded in Winnipeg. For pity sake, if we are to have a bishop let him be a

man of education and culture, of enlarged mind and entire devotion to his work and not a man of very little education, or wretched
pulpit ability, of abnormal sectarian views, of little judiciousness,
and of less sense.[9]

Robertson and the Home Missions Committee weathered the storm, ob-
taining an apology from the *Mail* for printing the almost libellous letter.[10]

A challenge that threatened the very existence of the superintendent's
role within the church came before the General Assembly in 1886. The
Presbyteries of Brandon and of Rock Lake believed that the power that
had been entrusted to Robertson conflicted "with the undoubted rights
and privileges of Presbytery." The presbyteries asked the Assembly to limit
Robertson's power. The problem had arisen because it was the Synod's
Home Mission Committee that decided which mission fields would get
financial grants and which would not, thus controlling which congregations would have a future and which would not. Since Robertson had the
ear of the Committee it was his wishes, and not the wishes of the presbyteries
within whose bounds the congregations were located that generally won
the day. The fact that Robertson's views won out over the wishes of the
presbytery in question was viewed as a violation of the power presbyteries
were supposed to have in the establishment and closure of congregations
within their bounds. The matter received lengthy debate on the floor of
Assembly before being referred to a committee that was called upon to
investigate the complaints. Here Robertson was at his masterful best, fully
in command of the relevant data and in his own self-deprecating style gave
evidence of times when he had in fact overstepped his mandate. In the
process he so won over the committee that their report to the Assembly
stated, "it is undesirable to effect any change in the regulations affecting the
duties of the superintendent or his relationship to the Synod or the
Presbyteries within its bounds." Robertson had not only been named Superintendent, but now after five years in that role, his ability to act as largely
a free agent in the prosecution of the mission of the church had been
affirmed.[11] The level of conflict and rhetoric that swirled around the position of Superintendent of Mission indicates just how out-of-step with the
normal practice of the Presbyterian Church this model of ministry was.

Robertson threw himself fully into the task of being superintendent.
Boldly he stated the vision of what the church could do, in fact should do,

Half a continent is now thrown open for settlement. Thousands
are coming in every year to people its fertile plains. The pressing
work of our church is to give them the gospel…If we neglect this
work, and the people lapse, we are guilty…. God gives us this
work to do, and let us in his name do it with our might.[12]

The west was the great challenge facing the church and the time to act was now, for the west would soon be filled with settlers. Bringing the gospel to the settlers on the prairie was as important as the foreign mission work of the church. He wrote an annual report to the General Assembly detailing the past year's activities and painting powerful pictures of the developing west. At times, he painted broad sweeping pictures of the land and its inhabitants; at other times his reports looked at specific communities and the development of the Presbyterian church in those communities. Robertson had his finger on the economic pulse of the west and was capable of interpreting the statistics generated by the various government agencies for his readers. At times he described in detail the geography of the land and its sheer vastness; at other times he wrote of the mineral and timber wealth that stood on the edge of the prairie. He understood that the fortunes of the church in the west were intimately tied to the economic well-being of the west. If the economy of the west was solid, then congregations would move quickly from being grant-receiving to self-supporting congregations. As well, a growing western economy would attract immigrants to the Canadian west, providing a larger population for congregations to build upon. In the late 1880's it was said of Robertson, "No man living knows more about the Canadian Northwest, its resources, its development, its social, moral and religious conditions and necessities." Robertson's reports to the Assembly provide snapshots of the west and the life and thinking of western Canadians in the last two decades of the nineteenth century.[13]

In the early 1880's Robertson's prediction of thousands of immigrants coming west each year seemed reasonable. Western farmers were enjoying bumper crops and land was still plentiful. Most important of all, the railway was coming. In his first six months as superintendent, Robertson reported that, "I travelled in all by buggy 2,000 miles, preached on 96 different occasions, and delivered about 400 addresses." He had seen the number of families receiving pastoral care from a Presbyterian Church double to nearly 2,000 in just six months. That growth continued as in each of the first four years of the decade, between 40,000 and 50,000 immigrants arrived in the west. But by the late 1880's, Robertson was aware that his earlier predictions for the rapid economic development of the west were not going to be fulfilled. In 1887 he reported,

> The last few years have made it manifest that the progress of the country is not to be as rapid as was at one time anticipated. Church and State must consequently be prepared to make sacrifices for a few years longer, that the moral and material well-being of the people may be secured. The ultimate result does not seem to be doubtful, but evidently there lies between the people and their goal a stretch and a struggle.

The runaway exuberance of the early vision of the west had been tempered by the unrest of the 1885 Riel Rebellion, the drought of the late 1880's, and the high cost of living on the prairies. Yet to be added to the gloomy economic picture was the flat population growth of the late 1880's and early 1890's and the poor rate of return to farmers for their crops and livestock. By the mid-1890's the slower-than-expected economic growth and slow population growth prompted some contributors to the Church's home mission venture to complain that they were not seeing the results they had been promised. Why should they continue to support a project whose goals seemed to be so unattainable? By 1896, the momentum of the home mission enterprise had slowed, and Robertson feared there would be a reduction in the money given to the various Home Missions schemes. However, the twin events of the mass immigration to the prairies, which began in 1896, and the discovery of gold in the Klondike in 1897, fired again the imagination of the average Presbyterian in the pew to support the home mission cause.

Establishing the church in this new land required money and missionaries. One of Robertson's ongoing struggles was convincing people in eastern Canada and Scotland that the home mission work of the Presbyterian Church in Canada was as deserving of their financial contributions as was the foreign mission work. There were three "schemes," or funds, of the church that related to the home mission endeavour on the prairies. First, there was the Home Mission Fund, which provided grants for starting new congregations. Primarily it paid the salaries of the missionary, be that a minister, a catechist, or a student, who was going into a new area to begin the work of the church from scratch. These missionaries were supported not only by individuals and congregations giving to the Home Mission Fund; missionaries were also sent by and directly supported by organisations like Knox College (Toronto), Presbyterian College (Montreal), and Queen's (Kingston) Student Missionary Societies who raised funds to send theological students to the west to do six months of summer ministering in the break between school years. After 1903, the Women's Home Missionary Society (Western Division) also directly funded missionaries in home mission charges. When a pastoral charge, usually a congregation in a town with three to five preaching points located in the surrounding countryside, was paying 60 percent of the missionaries' stipend and had provided either a manse or rented accommodation for the missionary, the congregation could apply to come off of the Home Mission Fund and move to the Augmentation Fund. There were substantial advantages to both congregation and minister in moving from the Home Mission Fund to the Augmentation Fund. Stipend levels for clergy in congregations on the Augmentation Fund were 10 to 15 percent higher than for those in congregations receiving grants from the Home Mission Fund. As well, once congregations were put on the Augmentation Fund they were able to issue a regular gospel call to their minister. This lessened the fear that the minister might suddenly be moved by the Home Mission Committee to a more important mission field. Receiving a grant from the Augmentation Fund brought a stability that was not present for congregations receiving Home Mission Fund grants. Both the Home Mission Fund and the Augmentation Fund had been used in the development of congregations in northern Ontario and their application to the west was a natural progression of these mission schemes of the church.[14]

As a result of how these two funds worked, a pattern developed for the starting of Presbyterian congregations in the west. A clergyperson would scout out a district, meeting as many potential church attendees as possible and seeking to determine the potential for creating a new mission field. As part of the survey the minister would lead a few worship services in the area, usually in the evening. The area being scouted could have come to the attention of the superintendent or the presbytery either through a request from homesteaders in the area asking that a minister be sent, or, it might have been that church leaders heard of the new district being settled. Once it was decided that a new mission field would be opened, a student would be sent in during the summer months to begin gathering together small congregations. The reason for sending a student was two-fold: first, there were more students available than there were ordained clergy; and second, students were substantially cheaper, allowing the Home Missions Committee to stretch its funds further. As the mission field developed, it would move from having only summer ministry, to getting year-round ministry still using students or catechists. Once the mission field had achieved a critical mass, an ordained missionary would be appointed in the anticipation that the charge would quickly move from being a mission field to an augmented charge. From there the now-called minister of the charge was responsible for encouraging the congregations being served to become self-supporting.

There were three great challenges that accompanied these first two funds. First, how long should a pastoral charge remain a mission field before it should have moved into being a augmented charge? While Robertson did not believe what people gave to the church was the only indication of their faith or the value of a given pastoral charge, the truth remained that congregations could not remain on the dole forever. Robertson was generally pleased with how people in the mission fields gave to the ministry of their local congregations and to the mission schemes of the broader church. He noted on a number of occasions that on a per capita basis communicants in the west were more generous than communicants in the eastern part of the country. This data would have been skewed by the fact that a number of those who attended and supported Presbyterian congregations in the west were not members, because they had not been Presbyterian in their original communities and were not prepared to become Presbyterians in the west, although they faithfully supported the local congregation. Despite this positive overview of congregational stewardship, there were pastoral charges that Robertson did not feel were not taking their financial responsibilities seriously and he was prepared to cut these charges off if that became necessary. A second problem was that there was often not enough money in the Augmentation Fund to pay the grants to which it was committed. A number of times during Robertson's 20 years as Superintendent the Augmentation grants were cut by 25, and even in one year, 50 percent. This meant that clergy often received substantially less than had been promised. As Robertson said of the stipends received by the clergy in the west, they "are not large in promise and too frequently they are less in fulfilment." This leads directly to the third problem; throughout the period under discussion, the stipends received by clergy in augmented charges on the Prairies were higher than those received by their colleagues in similar situations in northern Ontario. This was a very hard sell back east, where clergy, who were making less than their western colleagues, were being encouraged to raise funds from within their congregations to pay those more highly paid western colleagues. The primary reason for the discrepancy was the cost of living in Manitoba and the northwest which was anywhere from 25 to 50 percent higher than the cost of living in Ontario or Quebec.[15]

The third fund in support of the home mission work of the church was the Church and Manse Building Fund. Its sole purpose was giving grants and making loans to congregations seeking to build either church buildings or manses. This fund was Robertson's brainchild. He had seen a similar fund at work in the United States as a theological student. Through this fund not only were congregations able to get the monies they needed to build, the committee also made available building plans for simple church buildings and manses, and even combined manse/churches drawn up by professional architects. Robertson was able to find building material suppliers who would sell material at below market prices to congregations building a church or manse, and he also convinced the CPR to ship these building materials at half the ordinary freight rate.[16] At times the construction of a church building was an essential part of helping a congregation grow numerically. For settlers used to the institutions of eastern Canada or Great Britain, attending worship services in a neighbour's living room seemed strange. A church building gave "visibility and permanence" to the Christian faith within a community, standing as a witness to religion's importance in the life of individuals and the community as a whole. A missionary wrote of the change the construction of a church building meant to his community,

Before the church was built in this village only the decidedly religious people could be got to attend service. The store was open,
the bar was full, the ordinary business of the week went on as
usual. But the very day the church was opened all this was changed.
The store closed up, the bar was empty of all except a few recognized and well-seasoned 'tough,' the ordinary work of the week
stopped, and many came to *church* who would not think of coming to the *service* in the shack. The silent appeal of that building
with the Gothic windows was a more powerful sermon than any
I had ever preached. [Emphasis in original][17]

A church building could transform a community, reminding people of the
faith of their parents, giving them a spiritual anchor as they lived far from
home.

But money and church buildings would not plant the church. If the
vision of the Presbytery of Manitoba to have clergy at each townsite within
a year of its founding was to be fulfilled, there had to be missionaries to
preach and visit people, nurturing the new arrivals spiritual lives. Robertson
knew the kind of people who had what it took to be a minister in the west.
They had to be able to ride a horse, since clergy often travelled 60 kilometres a Sunday on horseback covering three or four preaching points in
their immense charges. Robertson "would far rather have a man know less
Latin and more Horse" for without "some knowledge of horse" a missionary was useless in the West. That did not mean that clergy were to be
uneducated. Robertson noted that a number of the settlers were univer-
sity-educated and well versed in the latest philosophical theories and scientific debates. Clergy needed to be able to participate in those discussions.
Robertson in his trips east described the type of clergy he sought. First,
they were men (at this time only men were ordained as clergy within the
Presbyterian Church in Canada).

[T]he man needed should be every inch a man; one who could
eat anything and sleep anywhere…he should be a man for whom
Divine grace has done much and not one of the boys who had
always been good; "the good boys at school" would be no use,
they wanted a man who when a boy at school had had many
fights and always came out best, a man full of vigour and force of
character who would be respected and listened to.

In a word, clergy were to be muscular Christians, able to adopt the lifestyle
of the settlers to whom they ministered, which included the hard-rock
miners of the eastern Rockies and the lumber workers of the northern
prairie. This muscular Christianity should not affect their ability to provide

spiritual nurture and guidance to the flock under their care. Spiritual vitality and quality preaching and worship leading were as important in Western Canada as they were back east. The settlers should not get second class preaching or spiritual direction. Robertson hoped that by clearly painting the challenge of ministry in Western Canada the best clergy would apply to come west. On the whole Robertson was pleased with the clergy who came. Often in his reports to the General Assembly, he bore "testimony…to the zeal, energy and efficiency of the missionary staff."

Robertson's greatest personnel problem, generally, was not that the clergy who came were not up to the task; rather it was finding enough personnel for the constantly burgeoning congregations in the west. Filling pulpits was not difficult in the summer time when theological students were on holiday and looking for summer employment that would prepare them for their future ministry. In fact, through much of the 1890's there were too many students applying for summer appointments, and some of them were going to work in the Dakotas or other northern states. Robertson feared that they would develop strong ties south of the border and be lost from Canadian Presbyterianism. It was the adventure and novelty of the West that drew these students to summer ministry. The students were appointed either directly by the Home Missions Committee or by the various student missionary societies of the theological colleges that supported and sent student ministers in Western Canada each year.[18]

Robertson's, and therefore the Presbyterian church's, greater difficulty was finding students to fill pulpits in the winter. As Robertson said, "The people do not hibernate nor should the church." It was very difficult to see healthy church development on the mission field when ministry only took place during the six summer months from April to September. Robertson, a member of the Board of Manitoba College, the Presbyterian theological college in Winnipeg, was able to convince the College to reverse its academic year. Theological students attended Manitoba College in the summer and were free in the winter to take up the charges that had been vacated as the other theological students headed back to school in the east. This shift to a summer school session meant that instead of a third of mission fields being vacant during the winter months, just over one fifth of them were. Robertson suggested this same model to the eastern colleges, but none of them were willing to take up his suggestion. In fact, in the summer of 1903, just when there was an increased demand for students to work in the winter because of the population growth on the prairies, Manitoba College ended the summer session.[19]

Much more frustrating to Robertson was his sense that many recent graduates of the theological colleges were not willing to go wherever Christ might call. In a letter to student who was not willing to take up his appointment, Robertson, frustration in full flight, wrote,

You are preparing for the ministry and you think this kind [of refusal] in good taste and perfect keeping with your views of the ministry. Were I to make public your conduct here—were I to give your letter to the committee you would likely find that you would ask in vain for an appointment for some time to come.... I wish to find out...why you refuse to go to your field?[20]

His struggles led Robertson to suggest that all graduates of the theological colleges be compelled to spend a year on a mission field prior to their accepting a call to a congregation. Robertson was remembering the impact his own six month interim ministry in Winnipeg in 1874 had had on him. Pushing his point, he noted that the student's education was paid for by the denomination and that taking the gospel to the settlers in the West was the great task of the church, therefore the students owed it to the denomination to make this sacrifice. This suggestion too fell on deaf ears, and Robertson spent much of his time struggling to find enough personnel for the charges he was responsible for, as well as creatively stretching the personnel he did have available.

Many did apply to go west, but not enough. By 1898 the church was confronted with a paradox. There were about fifty charges in the west which would not have any missionary to supply them during the winter months; at the same time there were 90 individuals who were either ordained or who had just graduated and were awaiting ordination in Ontario who were not willing to come to the West. This situation drove Robertson wild and in his report to the Assembly he accused parents, relatives, and even pastors of actively discouraging these recent graduates from accepting appointments in the west. In the *Record* Robertson wrote,

...you have studied that you might preach the Gospel, why not go where there is an opportunity, where men and women and children need you, where missions and settlements must suffer unless the Gospel is preached? What would your Lord do? What would He have you do in the circumstances of our Church? I feel certain He would not have you go competing with two or three score other licentiates for choice vacancies in Ontario, while wide fields in the West were lying untilled.[21]

Robertson was tough and demanding, and could at times, as has been noted, be very acid in his response to people with whom he disagreed or who, in his opinion, were not committed to the all-important task of carrying the gospel message to every corner of the prairie. Under the "strong, rugged exterior" was "a warm heart." Missionaries who came to the west loved him because he cared about them and understood the challenges and joys of ministry on the prairies in a way that no else did. Robertson never asked any of them to do something he himself would not do. He led by example, living the "devotion and self-sacrifice which he expected to see manifested by the servants of the church whose work he was appointed to superintend." After Robertson's death a clergy spouse wrote,

> He gave the impression that we were all fellow-workers in one great work. One cannot forget the human kindliness in the home. He possessed that unique trait "Easy to get on with."...He was never too busy to enjoy a good story, or laugh at a joke. But his good opinion would be forfeited by indifference to the great Home Mission cause, or laziness in the great work laid to the hand.[22]

Robertson showed his caring by knowing the names of the wives and children of the missionaries whose work he oversaw. On one occasion while travelling to a very important meeting about the future of a congregation, he asked G. S. Wood the ages of the three Wood children by name, saying, "Only a mother can remember ages." Then only a week or two later a parcel arrived from one of the Ladies' Auxiliaries in the east which included age-appropriate gifts for each child. Another minister remembered that just over a week after the death of his and his wife's "little baby" they received a letter from Robertson "which showed what a tender, sympathetic heart he had."[23] Robertson never lost his passion to care for the people of the west nor his ability to relate to them. In 1892, having been superintendent of missions for 11 years, Robertson was on one of his many trips through the west, when,

> A man frantically came on board the train and shouted if Dr. Robertson was on board—I assured him he was...[The man insisted I would] have to come off and marry a couple...—I told the conductor the situation and got him to stop the train till I could marry these poor people and the conductor went with me to the hotel. But the bride was in the kitchen working, ignorant of what was coming. She was taken away hurriedly washed and dressed and ushered into my presence. She belonged to the Crofters, and I had to marry partly in Gaelic and partly in English, but finally got them made one.[24]

Robertson willingly got off the train to perform a wedding for a couple he had never met, but who were left without a minister to perform the wedding due to circumstances beyond their control. The minister with whom the couple had made their wedding arrangements had been prevented by a November blizzard from getting to the hotel. Robertson's name was so well-known across the prairies that a complete stranger could ask for him by name, and the train crew was prepared to hold the train.

During 1896, the year he was Moderator of the General Assembly, the Robertsons travelled to Scotland. While there Robertson was diagnosed with diabetes. While still trying to maintain his usual gruelling schedule, he began to have periods of illness during which he could not work. Realising that his life was short, Robertson began to reflect on his years as superintendent. Showing his personal side, he wrote to C.W. Gordon, "We are all a band of brothers working with our Father and Elder Brother to establish truth and righteousness in the west." He wanted to be allowed a few more years to see what he hoped would happen in his beloved west come into being. During a bout of illness in 1897, he wrote, "I want to live a few years longer to see the development that I feel I see is coming one day and I think is drawing near."[25] His words were prophetic, for the growth he anticipated as being just around the corner for Western Canada and which he longed to see began with the changes and decisions made in 1896. Although Robertson did not see the rapid expansion he dreamed of, he would have seen the start of that development.

James Robertson died at his home in Toronto with his wife by his side on January 4, 1902, of complications from diabetes. He had been working on correspondence right up to the day of his death. Fittingly he was buried in the west, in Kildonan Cemetery, Winnipeg.

When Robertson died, the Presbyterian Church in Canada was the largest denomination on the prairies, making up just over 22 percent of the population. The Presbyterian Church had 141 self-supporting congregations and 226 mission charges for a total of 1,120 preaching points, a far cry from the four congregations and eighteen preaching points that had been the Presbyterian presence on the prairies in 1881 when he had become superintendent.

In a letter to his eldest child, Tina, on her 15th birthday, Robertson shed light on his personal motivation in life and in ministry, a motivation that he hoped and prayed would become the centrepiece of his daughter's life. He wrote, "Christ loves us and gave himself for us and we ought to love Him and honour Him all through our life." Loving Christ meant keeping his commands, which "is the surest and best way of being happy—healthy and useful in life. To keep his commands means that we show His disposition in our thinking, speaking and acting." Finally Robertson wished for his daughter to "Be decided—firm about things—...many a person has been lost by being undecided."[26] Robertson knew that he was loved by Jesus Christ, and in response to that love; Robertson loved Jesus. He knew only one way to show that love, hearing the call of Christ he decided to give his total person to the service of Jesus Christ and His church. At the end of his life, Robertson again articulated his motivation in mission, "I would like to do a little more to express my love to Him who is all my salvation and my desire."[27]

THE HOME MISSION ORGANIZATION AFTER ROBERTSON

The death of James Robertson left a huge hole in the home mission work of the church. But his death also provided an opportunity for some re-organisation of the superintendent's portfolio. Robertson's style of person-ally surveying prospective mission fields and knowing each missionary and their family by name would not have worked for long in the years of rapid western expansion between 1900 and the start of World War I in 1914. For example, in the year between March 1902 and March 1903, twenty new mission fields were opened on the prairies. The next year there was an additional 40 new mission fields. It was impossible for one person to look after the administrative tasks related to that kind of expansion and at the same time be looking for new places to start congregations, while simulta-neously overseeing the work of the already existing mission fields and build-ing relationships with the missionaries who were in place in those fields. The General Assembly divided the superintendent's role into three posi-tions. There was a Field Secretary, whose title quickly became General Secretary, located in Toronto who was responsible for distributing the grants to congregations, overseeing applications from congregations seeking to move onto the Augmentation Fund's roll, approving grants and loans from the Church and Manse Building Fund, and screening application forms from prospective missionaries. There were two superintendents, one to cover British Columbia and present-day Alberta, and another to look after work in Manitoba and present-day Saskatchewan. The work of the Superintend-ent for Northern Ontario, a position which had been created in 1884 in light of the success of the experiment on the prairies, was also brought into the mix. Thus there was a General Secretary who had the overall picture of what was happening in Home Mission, and there were three Superintend-ents who knew their regions of responsibility in greater detail. In the proc-ess, individual superintendents were stripped of much of the decision-mak-ing power that Robertson had enjoyed. Much of that power either de-volved to the General Secretary or to the Home Missions Committee, which met as a whole committee twice a year. As the organizational struc-ture became more complex, a need arose for written policies and clearly established lines of communication; no longer would one person know everything that was happening in the Presbyterian Church's mission on the prairies.[28]

E.D. McLaren was appointed General Secretary of the Home Mission Committee. McLaren had been ordained in 1873, and had been the second minister at the Presbyterian church in Brampton until 1888, when he had accepted a call to St. Andrew's Church in Vancouver. In his 12 years in

British Columbia, he been the Convenor of the Home Mission Committee of the Synod of British Columbia. In that role he would have worked closely with Robertson during Robertson's trips to the Synod. McLaren was a diplomat, whereas Robertson was not, and this would have stood McLaren in good stead in his challenging role. McLaren seems to have been a better administrator than Robertson had been, he certainly had more details of which to keep track during the rapid population growth on the prairies during his tenure. McLaren's word style, both spoken or written, was more literary than Robertson's blunt passion. In describing the needs of the church, McLaren wrote, "The great desideratum now is an adequate supply of the right kind of men [sic], men of practical sagacity and fervent piety; men of wide outlook and large, generous instincts, and yet, withal, men of faith and prayer and whole-hearted consecration." The same organizational challenges that had faced Robertson faced McLaren; where to find enough bodies to carry on this important mission and how to raise enough funds to make the appointment of the missionaries possible.[29]

J.A. Carmichael, who had been helping Robertson as a kind of assistant superintendent since 1896, the year of Robertson's first extended trip to Britain and Europe and the start of his health problems, was appointed Superintendent for the Synod of Manitoba and Saskatchewan. This was a wise choice, since he was already known by the missionaries in the field and he knew the situation on the prairies intimately. J.C. Herdman, who had ministered at Knox Church in Calgary for 16 years was appointed Superintendent for British Columbia and Alberta. This too was a wise choice since much of the new mission work in the far western part of the country was among the hard rock miners and ranchers of the foothills and British Columbia interior, situations that Herdman would have been familiar with because of his vantage point from Calgary. In 1907, Herdman became ill and by 1909 it was clear that he would need to be replaced. Early in 1910, W.D. Reid, who had been ministering in Montreal, took over Herdman's responsibilities for Alberta only.

The Women's Home Missionary Society (Western Division) was born while McLaren was general secretary of the Home Mission Committee in 1903 in response to the call for the expansion of the medical work being undertaken at Atlin, British Columbia. The story of the medical work and the Women's Home Missionary Society will be discussed in detail later in this book. It is raised now because McLaren was particularly pleased to have had a role in the birth of this organization.

The Home Mission Committee, in response to the huge numbers of people coming to Canada, appointed full time Immigration Chaplains in 1907. At first they were located at Halifax and Quebec City, the major entry points into Canada. Their primary job was to find those new arrivals who were Presbyterians, discover where these new Canadians were hoping to settle down, and then let the Presbyterian Church that would be closest to these new arrivals know that there were potential new church members in the neighbourhood. By 1912, there were five Immigration Chaplains at work. One in Britain asked people their denominational affiliation as they got on the ships carrying them to a new land. This chaplain also provided those leaving Britain with addresses and phone numbers of Presbyterians in Canada who could help them in acclimatizing to Canada. Added to the Halifax and Quebec City chaplains were chaplains in Montreal and Winnipeg. The Winnipeg chaplain and Immigration Hall, the facility out of which he worked, functioned as part referral centre and part city mission. The chaplain would make connections between new arrivals and Presbyterian congregations in the west. He also provided immigrants who had few resources with clothing to withstand the prairie winter and a short-term place to stay as people got their feet on the ground. He would also stock the cupboard and fill the coal hopper of families who were staying in Winnipeg and were struggling to keep body and soul together in their first couple of months in Canada. Immigration Hall was also the stopping point for those who were being refused entry into Canada and in 1913, 600 people being deported from the country spent at least one night in the hall. The chaplain held Sunday evening services each week for those who wished to attend, and he also baptized babies who were born en route to Winnipeg. He performed marriages for couples where one of the partners had gone ahead to set up a home and the other, usually the wife, was now joining her fiance. The war changed the chaplancy programme; it became focused on the soldiers who were leaving for Great Britain or who were returned to the west and being de-mobilized. Through the chaplancy the church sought to respond to the needs of these soldiers at this critical transition time. The regular programme of the Immigration Chaplains was resumed after the war, but immigration had peaked and the programme was not as effective as it had been before the Great War.[30]

A second organizational shift in the Presbyterian home mission enterprise took place in 1912. In June 1911, McLaren resigned as general secretary of the Home Mission Committee and in the early summer of 1911 Carmichael became seriously ill and died in the fall. During the nine years that Carmichael was superintendent of missions in Manitoba and Saskatchewan, the number of mission fields had increased from 154 to 353, and the total number of charges in the two synods had risen from 261 to 552. This was truly remarkable growth, even more rapid than that which occurred during Robertson's 20 years as superintendent.[31]

The 1912 Assembly, like the 1902 Assembly, was confronted with the decks being cleared and an opportunity to reorganise. A Board of Home Missions was established, which assumed responsibility for all mission work in Canada. The change, it was reported, "tended greatly to simplify the work" since there was now one overall Board supervising both the mission to the Native people and to the homesteader. At places like the Birdtail Reserve in Manitoba, this allowed the missionary at Birdtail to also do ministry at Beulah, the white settlement right on the edge of the Reserve. Psychologically it recognised that the Native people were not foreigners but part of the Canadian reality.

A second major change was that there would now be 10 district superintendents spread across the region that had previously had three. There would be one each in northern Ontario and Manitoba, three each in Saskatchewan and Alberta, and two in British Columbia. This change did two things. First, it turned the superintendents into middle managers, who oversaw mission work in their district and provided pastoral care to the missionaries in the field, becoming a pastor to pastors. They were able to make day-to-day decisions, but they could not enter into bold new mission ventures without approval from the administrative levels of the newly minted Board. Second, it did an end run around the role of the Presbytery Mission Convenors. During the rapid prairie population growth during the first decade of the 20th century, the presbyteries had taken back some of the decision-making role that they had lost with the creation of the superintendent 20 years earlier. Carmichael could not personally oversee the establishment and nurturing of more than 250 new pastoral charges; it was the convenors of the missions committees of the local presbyteries who assumed many of the tasks involved in opening and nurturing mission fields. Therefore, by 1912 much of the actual home mission work of the church was being guided by the presbytery convenors. But the creation of the 10 district superintendents severely limited the convenors' role in the ongoing mission of the church. After only a year with this restructured system the Board of Home Mission was very positive about this change,

> …it has greatly increased the efficiency of the work done in these fields. The District Superintendents have brought the fields up to a higher standard or self-support—thus the fund has been relieved and at the same time there have been secured a better organisation of the fields and a closer supervision of the [missionaries].[32]

Efficiency had become the new watchword for the increasingly bureaucratic structures of the church. A cartoon shown at the 1913 Pre-Assembly Congress, a major Presbyterian mission conference held at Massey Hall in Toronto, depicted a man dressed in late 19th century clothing riding a rocking horse named "Antiquated Methods" and another man dressed in the businessman's attire of 1913 driving a car named "Business Methods in Church Finance." The caption, which was the car driver speaking to the horse rider, read "Get in, brother, and make some progress." The goal of the

re-organisation of home missions was to ensure that the best possible align-
ment and oversight of the work was accomplished, so that the valuable
mission funds could be stretched as far as possible. The importation of
organisational business language and style into the mission activity of the
church is a subject that demands further study.[33]

The third fundamental change that took place in 1912 was the unified
Budget Plan of the church. Instead of there being a variety of "Schemes of
the Church" from among which donors could choose which they wished
to support, there was now a single fund into which all contributions for
the mission work of the church, foreign or home, went. The funds were
then distributed to the various mission projects of the church by a committee made up of mission administrators. The benefit to mission administrators was that the competition that had arisen between the various mission schemes was eliminated, and the change had "greatly helped to unify
the work of the Church at home and abroad." The problem was that groups
like the Student Missionary Societies at the various theological colleges
were now not allowed to raise money from congregations to send fellow
students to the west to do summer ministry. For example, in 1911, the
Knox College Student Missionary Society raised more than $11,000 to
send 40 students to summer mission fields, 24 of them in the west. In 1912,
they sent no missionaries. Unable to raise money and unable to decide
whom they would send, the missionary vision and passion of the Society
was squelched. While the Budget plan made things easier for mission administrators, the question remains was the change good for the mission
vision of the church as a whole? It will not be possible to answer that
question in full until further work has been done on the actual giving
patterns and mission commitment of the individual Presbyterians who sat
in the pews and gave their offerings Sunday by Sunday. But the initial
indications are that the unified Budget plan was not good for some aspects
of the church's mission.[34]

The first convenor of the new Board and General Superintendent of
Home Missions was the Rev. Andrew S. Grant. He was responsible for
leading the organisation. Grant had made his name as a creative and effective missionary through his work in the Yukon. He conceived of holding
the Pre-Assembly Congress in 1913 as a means of raising the church's
awareness about mission both in Canada and internationally. He went on
to become the chief financial officer of the church. The General Secretary
of the new Board was J.H. Edmison. Edmison, who inherited the day-to-
day administrative responsibility, had been ordained in 1901. After serving
in Cheltenham, Ontario, for eight years, he had accepted a call to Kincar-
dine in 1909, and from there he had moved to the Board of Home Mission
in 1911.

By 1914, a good portion of the work overseen by the Home Mission

Board was in the area of social service: the redemption houses for women, the inner city missions, the immigration chaplancies, the educational work done among various groups, and the medical services offered in a variety of settings. As well there were the Board's involvement with the temperance movement, the struggle for Sabbath observance, and the anti-gambling lobby. Given all of this it was agreed to change the name to the Board of Home Mission and Social Service.

THE MORMON CHALLENGE

As noted earlier, the leaders of the Presbyterian Church assumed that if they had the resources to provide "Gospel ordinances" to the English-speaking settlers, these settlers would be drawn together naturally into communities of faith under the Presbyterian banner. And on the whole the plan succeeded. There was one group of English-speaking immigrants, however, that presented the Presbyterian Church with a unique challenge: the Mormons. While the correct name is The Church of Jesus Christ of Latter Day Saints, every Presbyterian reference to this group between 1893 and 1925 calls them Mormons. To maintain historical continuity this discussion will do the same.

The Mormons, who came to Canada in 1887, first appeared on Canadian Presbyterian consciousness in 1893, when James Robertson reported to the General Assembly that a group of 700 Mormons had settled north of the American border and just east of the Rocky Mountains. They were "thrifty and industrious" and this would make them good settlers, but there was "the matter of marriage." Assurances had been given that they would comply with Canadian law, but Robertson reported that "observing men who have visited the colony have their doubts." It was the responsibility of the Presbyterian Church, Robertson argued, "to give the gospel to the Mormons" even though it would be an expensive proposition. In 1894 the Home Missions Committee sent a missionary to work among this group.[35]

The tightly-knit nature of the Mormon community meant that it was extremely difficult for the Presbyterian missionaries to make much headway. In 1906, there were the first signs that the more than a decade of mission effort was beginning to pay off, as a few individuals renounced "the tenets of Mormonism" and became joined to the Presbyterian mission in the Cardston area of Alberta. But the work was hard and bore little fruit; in fact, there was no other home mission endeavour "which shows so little impression made upon the community as we have been able to make there." In order to maintain the mission for the long haul, the Presbyterian church began to intentionally draw together the small groups of non-Mormons in the area between Cardston and Raymond. Out of these groups had been formed, by 1909, a two-point mission charge and a three-point mission charge, and in the process the church had "secured a series of evangelical ports extending through the very heart of the Mormon district." As the number of Mormons in Alberta grew, not just through immigration from the United States but also from Scandinavia and even Scotland, their political power became evident. The Assembly was warned, "We cannot afford to relax our efforts to win them to a loyal acceptance of the teaching of Scripture in regard to marriage and all other questions." If the Mormons were ever to "become a great power," it was argued, "it would be a sad day for vital religion and morality." An article published in *The Home Mission Pioneer* with the ominous title, "The Menace of Mormonism," contended that the only way to reach these people with the gospel was by placing in the midst of the Mormon community to live among them Christian men and women who showed "their fellowship with their Master in their daily lives." The transformation would not be accomplished "by railing or pleading, by accusation or argument." The difference the gospel made needed to be seen in the lives of those people who claimed to follow Jesus Christ. The Presbyterian Church was never to be successful in its mission to the Mormons, even though often reminded that it was "the duty of the Church to spare no pains" in proclaiming the gospel to "the followers of the wondrous Joseph."[36]

Mission Models of Ministry

It would be easy to assume that all the Presbyterian missionaries were male clergy who were in full time ministry. And that assumption would be wrong. We have already made mention of the students who did summer ministry and that Manitoba College for nearly a decade reversed its academic year to provide a crop of students in the winter. There were other students who took a year out of their schooling to minister in the west, either for the adventure or to acquire the funds needed to return to school for another year. Some of the students who came for a year were from Scotland, and after their graduation from their Scottish college, returned to the Canadian west. Canada was considered a foreign mission field by a number of Scottish Presbyterians. Not all of the student missionaries were in theological college; some were third and fourth year undergraduates. How much theological training students were expected to have was a function of how desperate the Home Mission Committee was for students.

There were minister-evangelists who did not have a set mission field, but rather travelled from charge to charge doing week-long or sometimes two-week-long preaching missions. The evangelists would visit both places where there was a missionary in place as well as places where no missionary was located. In the latter case, the evangelists provided short-term ministry and drew the members of the congregation together in the time when there was no minister present. The role these itinerant evangelists played within the denomination has not been fully explored.

There were some homesteading missionaries. In fact there were nine such people in Central Alberta alone in 1913, doing ministry while at the same time homesteading. These bi-vocational ordained ministers were working in mission fields that could not afford to pay the stipend of a full-time minister, but through the work of the homesteading missionary were able to have ministry in their midst. While doing two jobs would have been a challenge for the ministers in question, they benefited from having two sources of income, making them a little less susceptible to the financial vagaries of the small rural churches they served. As ordained individuals, they would have been able to administer the sacraments. William Shearer, the district superintendent for Central Alberta, was not a fan of this model, noting, "This is not an ideal way of carrying on home mission work." This same model was used in Saskatchewan where in 1911-12, the Rev. James Bews had homesteaded and ministered south of Kindersley, Saskatchewan. Homesteading was not the only second vocation that Presbyterian clergy mixed with ministry. The Rev. Charles B. Kerr taught school while ministering at Hutton, near Redvers in south-eastern Saskatchewan, in 1911. While these bi-vocational ministers had "rendered good and faithful service" by 1914 the time had come when they had to choose "either to give all their time to the work of the church, or else make way for regular missionaries." The openness to experimentation that had been a hallmark of the church on the prairies was slowly being systematized and regularized.[37]

There were also catechists who were non-ordained preachers. As the need for missionaries was rising dramatically, the General Assembly authorized, in 1902, the development of a course for the training of catechists. Ministers were encouraged to be on the look out for individuals who would be "capable of doing effective work as catechists." The certification process, which was approved by the Assembly in 1906, had a number of steps. Prospective catechists were to be evaluated by an examining committee of their presbytery as to their spiritual fitness for ministry and theological knowledge before they were given a mission field. They needed a letter from their pastor indicating they were a member in good standing of the local congregation and had taken an active interest in and had been involved in the work of the Sunday School, Young People's Society, and prayer meeting. In addition, at least two other clergy needed to vouch to their character and ability to lead a worship service "fittingly and to the edification of the people." They had to know the main points of Biblical history and be aware of the general content of each of the books of the Bible and be able give the answer to any question from the Shorter Catechism. They were also to "be fully acquainted" with the rules in the Book of Forms which governed the workings of congregations, sessions, boards of managers, and presbyteries. Finally, prospective catechists had to prepare a sermon on a subject given them by the examining committee. Having successfully passed through this process, the candidate was given a certificate indicating that they were a catechist. At that point they would be appointed to a mission field.[38]

On average catechists were paid about 75 percent of the stipend that ordained clergy received. As non-ordained persons, catechists were not able to administer the sacraments. Catechists stood as a hybrid between clergy, and lay people, really belonging in neither category. The creation of this role within the church met two fundamental needs; first, it allowed the church to find additional missionaries in the midst of a personnel shortfall that was becoming acute by 1905; second, it allowed gifted lay people to find a way of serving the church without their needing to leave their homes and families for an extended period while they received their education. Many within the church saw the catechist position as simply a stepping stone to regular ordained ministry. W.S. Brooker, who was working at Airdrie, was a catechist who "might well be considered for special ordination." And an unnamed catechist who had been a plumber in his first career was "pressing forward to ordination."[39]

By the end of World War I the Presbyterian Church was using "lady missionaries" to advance its mission on the prairies. These women came in two categories. Most were students at the deaconess training school in Toronto, and therefore were like their male counterparts from the theological colleges who were looking for summer employment that would enhance their ministry. There were however two women, Miss Rose who served in the mining community of Nordegg, in the Alberta foothills west of Red Deer, and Miss Kirk, who worked the three point Pollockville, Alberta, field, who were not in the deaconess training programme. It is not clear how Rose and Kirk came to work in the Presbyterian Church in Alberta. Catherine Goodchild ministered to a large prairie mission field and during her tenure "had by far the largest attendance at her services of any of her [male] predecessors." Among the other women missionaries who had summer charges in 1918 were: Agnes Staples, Luella Crockett, Jennie Mills, Bessie Bentley, W. Maude Achison, Marion A. Cruikshank, and Anna M. Keith. In each of these cases the woman named was the minister of the charge, being responsible for the pastoral care and Sunday worship leading and sermon preaching. Having women missionaries had "passed the experimental stage" for they had "proved themselves to be faithful and successful preachers and pastors." The Sunday School programmes were well organized. In fact, a woman home missionary had certain advantages over her male counterparts. As a woman, it was argued, she would be able to relate more quickly to the women and children of "the humble isolated shack." A woman's "sympathetic nature" would stand her in good stead when dealing with the pastoral care crises. Only one concern was raised regarding the use of women as home missionaries: "only

ladies who can handle horses should be sent to widely spread prairie fields."
Robertson had said essentially the same thing about male missionaries 30
years earlier. Peter Strang, District Superintendent for southern
Saskatechwan, where four of the deaconess students had worked, concluded
that the church could "with profit" continue to use women in its home
mission enterprise.[40]

As the opportunities for women to receive theological education expanded in the first quarter of the 20th century, the Presbyterian Church
was confronted with two realities. First, there were not enough men to fill
all the mission positions that needed to be filled, and second, there were
theologically trained and highly gifted women who were willing to give
themselves to the mission of the church. Lydia Gruchy graduated from the
Presbyterian College in Saskatoon in 1923, standing first in her class. In "a
departure, new in the traditions of the Presbyterian Church in Canada" she
was appointed the missionary at Veregin, Saskatchewan. There she taught
in the Presbyterian day school and led worship on Sundays in the church,
ministering to a mixed Ukrainian and Doukhobour community. It was not
new, as we have seen, to have a woman preaching and leading worship;
what was new was that she was listed as the minister of the charge. Up until
this point women who had been involved in ministry had been seen as the
equivalent of students or catechists, simply forerunners of the minister. But
in Gruchy's case, she was the minister, but with limitations. Her name
appears in brackets in the column listing the name of the minister, and her
name was not included on the roll of the Presbytery and she was not
permitted to perform the sacraments. While Gruchy was the first, a year
behind her at Saskatoon was Jessie Elliott, also top of her class and who had
indicated "her intention of giving her life to this work" of ministry. The
doors to women were opening, but they had not been flung wide open by
any stretch of the imagination.[41]

In 1902, the General Assembly authorized the publication of a worship
book entitled, *Aids for Social Worship*, it had the longer sub-title, "Being
short services of Prayer and Praise for the Use of Christians." It was a
collection of five different orders of service, with calls to worship, almost
60 different prayers, hymns, and both prose and metrical psalms. Also included
was a funeral service. The book ended with "Instructions for Conducting
Divine Services." The book was designed to be used by lay people who
wished to have regular worship but who were "for the time, cut off from
the ordinary ministrations of the Church." This was a radical statement that
the church expected people to hold worship services without the presence
of a minister or missionary. In the fall of 1922 it was clear that there was
going to be a severe shortage of missionaries over the winter months in
Southern Alberta and in the Kootenays. W.G. Brown and A.C. Wishart,
both clergy who were deeply involved with home missions, devised a plan

to help congregations while they were without a missionary. They produced a series of printed sermons which were circulated to those congregations that had no missionary. The sermons were read by an assigned reader within the local congregation and the rest of the service, the hymns, prayers, and scripture readings were all done by other members of the congregation. In this way the worship life of the congregation stayed alive through the winter, parents had something to do when they brought their children to Sunday School which increased Sunday School attendance, and lay people were given the resources to lead worship services themselves. The results of the experiment had "been encouraging" and there were plans to repeat the experiment in the fall of 1923, only this time with earlier preparation which would mean being able to have more congregations involved.[42]

Since the opening and development of new mission fields was in the hands of individuals who had not received much theological training and who were not ordained, there was some concern about how this absolutely essential work was being supervised and its quality being evaluated. In 1912, W.D. Reid, the mission superintendent for Alberta, argued that a group of ordained clergy who had experience in the planting of new congregations should be appointed mentors to the missionaries in 15 to 20 mission fields. The mentors would visit each field for a week or two each year, providing a trained and somewhat objective eye and a listening ear to help the missionary who was seeking to see the field grow numerically, financially, and spiritually. Between these annual visits, the mentors would be available to provide advice and support to the missionary and the mission field. Reid argued it was only through this close one-on-one mentoring that missionaries would develop the gifts needed see their mission fields develop quickly into the self-supporting charges they could become. Picking up on the idioms of the day, he remarked, "this is only business," for this effective model would lead to a doubling of the membership on these mission fields. The Presbyterian Church did not adopt his mentoring model.[43]

In a variety of ways, the Presbyterian Church sought to respond to the shortage of missionaries on the prairies and in the process they pushed the limits of who could do the mission work of the church. In meeting the mission challenge of the West, the church developed new models of ministry which called into question many of the previously held assumptions about ministry within the church.

THE LIFE OF A MISSIONARY ON THE PRAIRIE

Without the work of the missionaries in the local mission fields and augmented charges, the Presbyterian Church would not have grown to become the largest church on the prairies, nor would it have been able to keep pace, as it did, with the population growth that occurred between

1896 and 1913. Robertson and his successors paid frequent tribute to these people as a class. From this group "little complaint" was heard, even though no group in the church deserved "better treatment." The missionaries came to the west and they were "buried," disappearing from the consciousness of the church. "The advanced position of the Church in Western Canada to-day is largely due to the self-sacrificing spirit of her missionaries."[44]

Being a minister on the prairie meant facing the same day-to-day challenges that the settlers faced: not losing their way on the trackless prairie, getting something to eat each day, and finding adequate shelter being top of the list. The students or newly ordained clergy, who had never seen the prairie before in their lives, would step off the train in a prairie town and go in search of the Presbyterian minister who would give them the next two things they needed: a horse and the directions to their mission field. From their carefully packed trunk the missionary would take the items they could get into a grain bag tied on the back of the horse and head off, often alone, to a place they had never been before to meet people who sometimes did not know they were coming. Once they arrived at the field, they needed to find a place to stay. Sometimes arrangements had been made ahead of time, sometimes they had not and the student had to go out and make the arrangements.[45] In the early days the vast majority of the students and even many of the ordained ministers were bachelors, and they were coming to a land where there were few manses. Those bachelors who were lucky boarded with a family taking care of the problems of meal preparation, laundry and cleaning. But not everything about boarding was positive. It was hard to find privacy and the opportunity to study and prepare for sermons. As well, the houses were small, and adding another body to the already cramped quarters made things even more challenging. Other missionaries were forced to fend for themselves, which was for many of them an eye-opening experience, as a student from Knox College who spent a year on a mission field in the west testified to,

> I will not enter into any lengthy scientific explanation of how we cooked our meals, washed the dishes (the bête-noir of bachelordom), or kept the floor clean and the house tidy. Suffice it to say, that nine months of such an experience ought to convince anyone, even though he were not a divinity student, that it is not good for man to be alone.[46]

Having found a place to stay and call home was not the end of the practical challenges facing the missionary. Many of the fields were huge and it was not possible to return to the security of a known bed each night. Instead it was necessary to spend the night "almost wherever it overtakes one." W.A. Cameron told of sharing a bed with two English brothers, a bed built for

two with Cameron in the middle. James Robertson told a student missionary who was complaining about "what he considered hardships in the way
of uncomfortable beds in which there were crawling things, and irregular
meals not always prepared in the most tasty form" of one of his experi-
ences while out surveying a mission field. A settler put Robertson up for
the night in his sod shack. Shortly after lying down for the night in his bed
roll on the floor, Robertson felt something brush across his face, wiping at
it with his hand, he rolled over, only to feel the same thing a couple of
moments later. This kept up most of the night. When Robertson got up in
the morning he discovered that lizards had been walking over him all night,
attracted by the heat of the stove in the kitchen portion of the shack.[47]

Those missionaries and their families who were lucky enough to have
manses provided for them faced challenges as well. In March 1909, F.A.
Clare visited the Rev. C.W. Bryden and his family. Clare, in the letter he
wrote to R.P. Mackay in Toronto, described the conditions under which
the Rev. C.W. Bryden and his family lived,

> It was so cold that with three stoves in the house and one in a
> kitchen, water would freeze a few feet from the stove on cold days
> this winter.... In the summer when the floor settles again after the
> frost is out there is a hole at the bottom of the door through
> which snakes and even small gophers could enter. When it is windy,
> the draught is sufficient in the dining room to blow out a candle
> on the table.[48]

For the married missionary their spouse and children, if they had children,
faced these day-to-day challenges as well. Robertson also paid tribute to
the spouses of the missionaries, "These ladies can get no help in their
household duties, and it may be truly said that their work is never done."[49]
This was a time when many of the spouses of Presbyterian ministers in
eastern Canada were able to employ some domestic help because the household income was high enough to allow for it.

An article in *The Home Mission Pioneer* by an unnamed "Missionary's
Wife" described her role. She wrote, "The West demands men and women
who can work,...And the missionary's wife is not the only woman who
has to work hard. Our lot is easy compared to many." She outlined some of
the work she had to do. A student missionary appointed to an outlying
mission field had been offered the use of a shack for the summer where he
could "batch," but it was entirely unfurnished, and so he had arrived back
looking for bedding, dishes, table and chair, and the like. It had been the
task of the minister's spouse to find these necessary things from among her
neighbours and members of the local congregation. New settlers from the
Old Country came by the manse asking about how to put up preserves for

the winter in this strange land, or why their bread would not rise. There was an open door policy at the manse towards all visitors, which included feeding additional mouths at meal times without prior notice that there would be more mouths to feed. And then there was the actual church work itself. The unnamed writer of the letter was superintendent of the Sunday School and taught one of the classes; she was also the president of the Ladies' Aid. This woman, her minister husband and their three daughters lived in a two-room shack in a newly-started town, where shacks were "the order of the day." She eloquently summed up the attitude of most clergy spouses when she wrote, "if others can bear discomforts and inconveniences for ultimate material gain, surely, if we have the pioneer spirit, we can bear them also for the ultimate victory of the Cross of Jesus Christ."[50]

The missionary's stipend was also a source of challenge. The salaries that congregations promised to pay the missionary were "not large" and frequently they were "less in fulfilment." As well, it was not unprecedented for the Home Missions Committee to declare that it did not have enough money to pay all its obligations and therefore every missionary receiving financial support from the committee's funds would get 20 percent less than they had been promised. This level of financial uncertainty led many missionary families to live a hand-to-mouth existence, much the same as the situations faced by the settlers among whom they lived.[51]

Once the missionary had a place to stay and a sense of where their meals would be coming from, it was time to start pulling together a congregation. To do that the missionary needed a great deal of skill and patience. Each family and person connected with the mission field was to be visited as frequently as possible and other families and households were to be visited, encouraging those people to also attend. The missionary had to organize a Sunday School and begin a Bible Class. There were administrative responsibilities as well; at each preaching point there was supposed to be a Managing Committee of at least three people, who were to meet at least once every three months to discuss the financial situation of the church and to develop ways to encourage people "to contribute as liberally as possible." Twice a year there was to be a joint meeting of all the managing committees on a mission field. There were reports to be sent to the Presbytery's Home Mission Committee and the Synod's committee and to the superintendent. The missionary was, not surprisingly, also to lead worship and preach at the various preaching points on the charge. When the congregation reached a sufficient size the missionary was to lead the congregation through the process of erecting a church building. On top of that, they were to be the moral guide to the community, leading those around them "to fear God and love their fellow [human]." The Rev. A.T. Murray, who delivered the sermon at an ordination service in Minnedosa, Manitoba, in 1898, made the role of the minister clear,

> The minister's stand upon all questions of public morals must al-
> ways be decided, and always against the evil. Abraham was a sol-
> dier ready to do battle on the right side. So we are on a battlefield.
> We have much evil to contend against. With God we may be
> more than conquerors. Abraham, by erecting his altar, claimed the
> land for God. So we must claim our land for Christ, place mis-
> sionaries in every district, and not stop until we have won our
> community, our province, our Dominion of our Captain.

Just as Abraham had set up an altar to show that the land belonged to God,
so the church needed to erect a church as a sign that the prairie belonged
to Christ. It was a battle, a battle in which the minister was on the side of
good, on the right side. The church was the conveyor of morality as well as
the nurturer of spiritual life.[52]

The minister had to be present for the people of the parish in their
joys and in their sorrows, and therefore "systematic pastoral visitation" was
imperative.

> Many of the people are strangers, and some are homesick. A visit
> from a minister is to them particularly welcome.…When frost has
> blighted prospects; when prairie fires have swept through the coun-
> try side, wiping our wheat stacks and dwelling,…when sickness
> has visited the home, or death has robbed the family of some
> loved one, the Missionary finds opportunity to sympathize, to
> encourage and to lead the stricken heart to Him who has prom-
> ised to be the Refuge and Strength of His people and a Present
> Help in their time of need.[53]

Effective pastoral care was absolutely essential if a missionary was going to
build a congregation. Given the size of some of the mission fields, this
pastoral visiting means that the missionary spent an inordinate amount of
time travelling by horseback.

One of the challenges in pulling together a congregation was finding
a place for the services to be held. Since most of the houses were small
there was little room for a gathering of more than a handful of people. This
made the schoolhouse a natural meeting spot, but in a land full of bachelors
there were few families with children, and schoolhouses were sparse in
many parts of the prairies. A group of bachelors and men who had come
west without their families, all from Glengarry were homesteading in the
Eagle Lake district west of Saskatoon in 1906. The arrival of a student
missionary allowed them to have regular services. The first worship service
was held in James McCrimmon's 6-foot by 10-foot lean-to with nine men
and the missionary present. McCrimmon had taken everything out of the

lean-to and put a 10-foot board inside down one side and a six foot board across the end to act as benches. W.A. Cameron, the missionary, wrote years later, "These boys were fine but they would not sing. When the time came to sing Mr. McCrimmon and I sang a duet. He sang one note all the time." Music and singing were a challenge for those ministering to these small gatherings of people on the prairies. Without musical instruments of any kind and few people who had the ability to read music and who could help in leading the singing, hymn singing became a painful, rather than a joyful, part of the worship service. For Presbyterians for whom singing the psalms was part of their heritage this was a particularly bitter pill to swallow.[54]

In other locations, it was possible to meet in people's homes without completely re-arranging their meagre furnishings. Near Wiggins, Saskatchewan, the services were held in the home of the Moffats, settlers from Manitoba who had some furniture. A gentleman in his fifties, old by pioneer prairie standards, would sit in the Moffats rocking chair slowly rocking back and forth during the service. After the first service at Moffats, he told the student missionary, "Well, parson, that's the best sermon I have heard in two years." And then he added, "But parson, it is the only one I've heard." The church services also became an opportunity for community to be built among the settlers. At Glengarry Plains near Ruthilda, Saskatchewan, the woman of the house where the service was held every second week, had everyone stay after service for Sunday dinner. This would have been the highlight of the week for the bachelors who made up the majority of the congregation.[55]

The missionary may have visited faithfully during the week and people may have promised to attend the worship service, but there was "nothing more nerve wrecking than to stand in a Western schoolhouse, as the advertised time for service draws near, and await the arrival, or non-arrival, of those who have faithfully promised to be there." Missionaries needed to learn that the time set for the service was "purely nominal." It was common for the hour of worship to arrive and no one except the preacher be present. R.F. Thompson at Frog Lake, Alberta, had the experience of people dropping into the service after it had already begun 15 minutes later than advertised. So many of them arrived after the service had started that part way through the service, Thompson had to stop and go in search of another board to turn into a pew so the late arrivals could sit. All manner of things prevented people from actually making it to the worship service, the largest of those being the distance needed to travel to get to the service and the lack of transportation. The rain would also prevent people from attending worship services. Since few of the homesteaders had buggies those who wanted to attend church on a rainy Sunday would have been soaking wet by the time they arrived at the church, and therefore would have decided not to attend. A further factor that kept people from church was the highly mobile nature of people on the prairies in the early days of settlement. People were constantly moving in and out of areas, homesteading for a while and then leaving it without finishing the claim or selling out before the claim was completed. Therefore it was very difficult for missionaries to get a handle on how many church attendees there were in a given area and who exactly they were and where they lived. A final challenge to gathering a congregation was the great mixture of denominational linkages present on the prairies. R.F. Thompson reported that in the three point Presbyterian charge at Frog Lake, half those who attended services were Lutheran and that three families were originally Presbyterian, the rest being Anglican, Methodist, or Baptist. Therefore the arrival of a Lutheran minister in the area would seriously impact the Presbyterian charge. Those homesteaders who had roots in some form of Protestantism were quite flexible, being willing to attend any church that was present in their area until a congregation of their particular denomination was started. The erratic attendance and the late start of services were sources of great frustration to the missionaries. Most prairie preachers had more than one service on a Sunday, and if the first one started late that meant that they would be running late all day, and would not have time to collect their thoughts between arriving from one preaching point, and needing to begin the service at the place where they had just arrived.[56]

Ministry in the west was difficult. In the early 1910's the church sponsored a series of one-week retreats across the west aimed at encouraging and uplifting western Presbyterian clergy. The leadership for these gatherings came almost entirely from eastern Canada, who were overwhelmed by the challenges their western colleagues faced. "All the visitors returned from these gatherings with a new regard for the toilers in the great West." But recognizing the problem did not mean the church had figured out how to help clergy deal with the discouragements of "the lonely prairie missionary." In eight months in the fall and winter of 1917-18, one quarter of the ministers in the Presbytery of Vermilion in Alberta resigned their charges. All those who resigned had been in ministry for less than three years, and 60 percent of them left the ministry entirely. The district superintendent for northern Alberta, William Simons, saw this as a warning sign of something deeper and was concerned that the church assist, "the younger ministers of the church, who in the first years of their ministry are discouraged in their work and its results." William Shearer summed up the challenges this way,

> The work is hard....Very often the people are unsympathetic, and the congregations much smaller than they should be. But over against all that is the animating consciousness that this is the Lord's work and that we are doing our best to carry out the Master's last

command, which applies to Alberta as well as to China, "Go ye into all the world and preach the gospel to every creature."

With the Great Commission to preach the good news about Jesus clearly ringing in their heads and hearts, the missionaries sought to be faithful to their calling in the midst of their discouragements and challenges.[57]

The pioneering settlers had expectations of the preachers who came to minister among them. They expected the same self-reliance in the missionaries as was expected of the settlers. As bachelor clergy were willing to wash, cook, mend their own shoes and clothes they gained respect from the other bachelors in the area. As they took on the tasks of homesteading life; clearing the land, breaking the sod, and even putting in a crop, their stock in the community went up, for they were showing that they were one with the settler and could understand the struggles of the homesteaders life. A number of Presbyterian clergy actually took out claims on their own quarter section of land, further tying them to the land and to the community. One young minister in central Alberta was struggling with church attendance problems until he made an appearance at the local rodeo. There were only four young men signed up for the bull-riding competition and there were five bulls. The cry went up, "Let the preacher ride him." Which the preacher did, and never having done this before in his life walked off with the first prize. "From that time on he had good congregations." While having preachers enter the bull-riding competition may not have been the answer to church attendance problems everywhere, the missionary did need to find ways of becoming identifiably one with the community.[58]

Despite these great challenges most missionaries felt it was an enormous privilege to carry the message of the gospel and of a caring church to these pioneers on the prairies. Robert Campbell on a trip into the lumber camps north of Grandview, Manitoba, discovered two families living on the edge of one of the camps. Both families had babes-in-arms who had not been baptized. And so at nine o'clock at night, at his third service of that Sunday, "two little boys, Douglas H. and Eric R., were added to the church visible." In his second service that day, Campbell had led a worship service in the camp bunkhouse for 75 loggers, "all at attention, and we prayed, and sang, and we read." There was no higher reward for these missionaries than to preach the gospel and to see the kingdom of God expand. The missionaries also understood that there was a public role for the church. Communities where there was a church presence were more attractive to settlers than were communities where there was no church visible. The simple presence of the church called people's thoughts to "something higher than the mere bread, which perishes." The church was a moral stablizing force, and over and over again church leaders pointed to the presence of the church in the Canadian west as one of the major factors in stopping a repeat of the American west's experience with lawlessness and vigilante justice. At its most basic level the presence of the missionary gave the message, "You may be hundreds of miles from your former home. You are 100 miles from your Post Office but you are not one hundred miles from God nor from the church." To live this message in word and deed was a great honour.[59]

The Presbyterian Church in Canada recognized the prairie provinces as a mission field, and developed ways to ensure that the ministry of the church was available to the homesteaders and other pioneers who were "the children" of the church. In this new land, the church tried out new models of ministry. Through the creation of the office of Superintendent of Missions, through the system for the opening and nurturing of mission fields, through the fund for the building of churches and manses, and through an openness to using non-ordained individuals as missionaries, the Presbyterian Church in Canada had sought to plant congregations throughout the Canadian west. Understanding that the people of western Canada needed and wanted the church as part of their newly founded communities, the Presbyterian Church did everything in their power to meet the spiritual needs of western Canadians. By meeting those spiritual needs they sought to mould a Christian society on the prairies.

Verberg School House, Alberta,
where unknown photographer held services in 1919.
(United Church of Canada/Victoria University Archives, 93.049P/2652)

Main St., Wintecourt, Alberta, the building marked with X is hotel
where Presbyterian Church and Sunday School were held, 1920.
(United Church of Canada/Victoria University Archives, 93.049P/4241)

"...also our own people"[1]:
Presbyterian Native Ministry on the Prairies

The west presented the Presbyterian Church in Canada with a new geography to adapt to. It was a vast territory that was already inhabited by the Native peoples of the prairies and the northern woodlands. The plan that the Church had developed for addressing the spiritual and religious needs of the new settlers who were coming west was predicated on the fact that the settlers were strangers in a strange land. For the Native people this was not a strange land; it was the settlers and the churches who were the strangers. The Presbyterian Church in Canada was very late in seeking to minister to the Native peoples of the west. John Webster Grant in his 1984 study outlined the ways in which Christian missionaries as early as 1534 sought to proclaim the message of the gospel to the Native people's of Canada. Robert Choquette and Frank Peake have outlined the work of the Catholic Oblate brothers and the Anglican Church respectively among the Native peoples of the west and north, ministry that dates back to the late 1700's. As James Marnoch wrote in the first volume of this history of Presbyterianism on the prairies, it was not until 1866 that the first Presbyterian missionary to the Native peoples in the west was appointed when the Rev. James Nisbet went to what became Prince Albert, Saskatchewan. It was not until the 1870's that Presbyterians would expand their Native mission beyond that small outpost.[2]

A striking feature of the work of the churches among the Native peoples is the use that was made of Native missionaries. Native people were not simply translators and guides, domestic help and providers of food; there were Native people who were missionaries in their own right and they were recognized as such by the white missionaries with whom they worked, and by the mission boards who oversaw the mission. The Presbyterian Church was not an exception to this pattern. In her doctoral dissertation, Darcee McLaren argues that Native Presbyterian missionaries lived in a middle ground between the Native culture of their upbringing and ethnicity on the one hand, and the white culture of the church and the increasingly dominant society on the other. The Native missionaries were forced to negotiate the size and shape of this middle ground on a continual basis. McLaren explores the question of finding a middle ground from only the Native missionaries' perspective. The exploration of how white Presbyterian missionaries found a middle ground is also an important question. To be a missionary to the Native people on the prairies required a willingness on the part of both white and Native missionaries to find a middle ground between the dominant British-Canadian culture and the Native culture of the reserves and Indian bands. As McLaren notes, the Foreign Mission Committee was "fully aware that the qualities essential to success in a mission field were not necessarily the same as the qualities essential to success in Toronto or Winnipeg."[3]

The Rev. Hugh McKay, one of the most gifted and committed of the white Presbyterians to work among the Native people wrote,

> ...my labours are among a people that is becoming extinct, a poor people suffering for want of the necessaries of life and dying without any sure hope for the life to come. They are also our own people living in our own country, living in our midst. Have they not for these reasons the first claim upon us as a church. When I see their need and see how little the church has done for them I wonder.

Here McKay stands with a foot in both camps. He can stand outside the situation and objectively predict the future for the Native people, acting as the white outsider. But quickly the Native people are not a nameless "they"; instead the Native people are "our own people." McKay had moved to the middle ground. And from that middle ground position, he was able to turn and confront the church with how little it had done to address the desperate needs of the Native people. It is from this position that McKay can say, "I feel thankful to the Lord that I have been privileged to engage in this work."[4]

White missionaries who were not able to negotiate some middle ground remained firmly entrenched in the dominant culture, and therefore their ministry and their attitude towards their ministry was effected by their finding no middle ground. The Women's Missionary Society gave its analysis of the "Indian problem" in 1916:

> The Indian is beginning to realize the benefits of tilling the soil and the great necessity of an education for his children. There are discouragements; as many of the older people are shiftless and idle, and have learned to take literally our Lord's words regarding the folly and uselessness of over anxiety.... It will take another quarter of a century to develop a more manly reliance.[5]

The Native people were "shiftless and idle," not showing the self-reliance that real people had. There was no middle ground here—nothing in the native culture was worthy of being retained, it needed to be changed completely. McKay's understanding that the Native people were his neighbours, were part of his "own people," was gone. This chapter seeks to explore ways in which this middle ground between the predominantly white Presbyterian Church and the Native peoples the church ministered to was slowly eroded, and finally eliminated.

The extent of the Presbyterian Church's work among the Native people of the prairies was outlined annually in reports to the General Assembly. By the 1910's, the church was operating the Cecilia Jeffrey Residential School near Kenora, Ontario, along with a small struggling congregation that was ministered to by the principal from the school. In Manitoba, there were day schools at Swan Lake (south of Portage la Prairie) and Okanase (near Elphinstone). The school at Portage la Prairie had been started by women from the Presbyterian Church in town as a day school, but over time facilities had been added to allow students to board at the school, making it a hybrid day-boarding school. The Native Residential School at Birtle, begun in 1888, had been started as solely a residential school. Church communities had been drawn together at Lizard Point (near Rossburn), Rolling River (near Minnedosa), Birdtail (near Birtle), Pipestone/Oak Lake (near Virden), and at Okanase and Keeseekoosee (near Elphinstone). In Saskatchewan, there was a day school at Moose Mountain (near Carlyle), and a combined day school/residential school at Crowstand (near Kamsack). There were also residential schools at File Hills (near Balcarres) and Round Lake (near Whitewood). Church communities had been drawn together at File Hills and Muscowpetung, as well as at Mistawasis, Makoce Waste (near Prince Albert), Hurricane Hills (near Sintaluta), Round Lake, and Moose Mountain. There was no Native ministry listed as taking place in Alberta. In 1911, the Foreign Mission Committee, which at the time was responsible for overseeing the ministry to Native people on the prairies, listed 44 people employed by the Committee in 18 different ministries.[6] In Manitoba, the work was primarily among Dakota people, while in Saskatchewan the church worked with Cree and Chippewa peoples and a small number of Dakota people.

The Foreign Missions Committee was responsible for all Native ministry in Canada until 1912, when that work became the responsibility of the Home Mission Committee. Both committees gave responsibility for educational work with women and children to the Women's Foreign Missionary Society and its successor, the Women's Missionary Society. Evangelistic work among the Native people remained the responsibility of the Assembly's mission committee. At times it was difficult to know where educational ministry ended and evangelistic work began. The simplest way of thinking about it was, if it was a school the women of the church were funding it and therefore providing a significant administrative role; if it was a church, the responsibility was entirely in the hands of the missions committee.[7]

THE CHURCH RESPONDS TO THE 1885 REBELLION

As noted in the first chapter, the 1885 Riel Rebellion was a cataclysmic event on the prairies, an event that impacted the mission of all churches working among the Native people. The Rebellion confronted Hugh McKay, Presbyterian missionary at Round Lake, Saskatchewan, with a difficult choice. Early in April 1885, a group of Native elders from the nearby reserve came to visit McKay with a warning: if "the Riel party" came toward Round Lake, the elders said they would be forced to kill all the whites, including McKay, even though he was a friend. The elders urged McKay to flee. Following a couple of "fearful nights" worrying about what might happen and what he should do, McKay resolved to stay with the people to whom he had been ministering. Three days after receiving the ominous warning, McKay visited a Native village near his mission station, where he:

> ...found the women and children gathered in one house crying afraid they would never see again those about to leave. The men were all busy fixing up their guns and knives and clubs and much excited. I said don't go. They said the soldiers were coming and will take us prisoner and we would rather fight and die on the battlefield than to go away as a prisoner. I said if you put away your guns and remain at home there is no danger from the soldiers. If they take you they will take me. I shall go with you. I was not a little astonished to see them take my advice and remain at home.[8]

By choosing to stay in Round Lake, McKay had proved his commitment to the Native people around him. Therefore when he told the men that he was willing to be taken prisoner along with them, if the soldiers came to do that, he was believed because he had proven he was committed to the Native people. McKay promised to stand in the gap for the people in this village, to be the mediator between the government and his friends in the Native community. Through his commitment to incarnational living, McKay had defused a potentially explosive situation. He had learned to live in the middle ground between his own culture and the culture of the native people; learning what it was to live in both but to not feel a part of either.

The Foreign Mission Committee from the safety of Toronto saw the Rebellion, not surprisingly, in very different terms than McKay did. The Committee gave to it a very particular meaning,

> Even amid the strife and bloodshed, it may be seen that the Gospel of peace has prevented what might have been even more widespread disaffection, for the Indians who have been under the care of our own missionaries, or of those of other Churches, have proved themselves loyal and law-abiding, not withstanding many temptations to fall in with the insurgents. And your Committee believe that, the sad events which we now deplore, the Lord is calling is to greater diligence and greater fidelity in imparting to those poor benighted tribes the knowledge which alone can lead them in the way of peace and everlasting life.[9]

The work and witness of the Christian churches had prevented the Rebellion from becoming much more serious. It was implied that the Native people might have some grounds for dissatisfaction, but they had valiantly resisted the "many temptations" to join the rebels. The Committee believed that such incidents of rebellion could only be avoided in the future by the church whole-heartedly committing itself to the evangelization of the Native peoples. It was through the proclamation of the "Gospel of peace" to the Native community that the antagonism between the Native people and the whites could be eliminated.

There were Presbyterians who much more intentionally sought to address the material needs and political frustrations of the Native people, which the Rebellion had highlighted. At the 1886 General Assembly, William Caven, Principal of Knox College and one of the most widely respected clergy in the denomination, brought a motion to the floor of the Assembly which condemned some government officials working with the Native people as "tyrannical, unjust, or immoral." Caven asked that a standing vote be taken on this motion as a public sign of the denomination's commitment to seek "the social improvement and the temporal well-being" of the Native peoples of Canada. The motion, which was carried by the standing vote that Caven requested, said in part,

> ...it seems to be established by irresistible evidence that in too many instances a people who are wards of the Government are being wronged and defrauded by those who are specially appointed to care for them and promote their interests, whilst flagrant immorality is too often chargeable upon public servants, as well as upon traders and other whites who come much in contact with the Indian population.

The leadership of the church had no problem being the conscience of the government when the church saw that the government was acting in ways that brought "many sufferings" upon the Native peoples. But the leadership was unable to think of the "Indians" as anything other than the wards of the state. The criticism that was being leveled against the government was not about policy; it was about the implementation and delivery of that policy. There is no call here for a change in the status of Native people; rather it was a call for the government to provide better care to the Native people. The resolution also pledged the Presbyterian Church in Canada to work co-operatively with any and all people who were seeking to bring the Native people "under the holy influence of the Christian religion."[10] The leadership intentionally sought to balance the material and the spiritual in their response to the 1885 Rebellion.

THE NATIVE MISSION PERSONNEL

In order for the Presbyterian Church to bring the Native people into contact with Christianity's "holy influence" they needed to have personnel willing to carry out the church's mission. Many of the techniques used in this mission were those used in foreign mission work, for even up until the 1920's the Native people of Canada were seen as a foreign people. Like most foreign mission work, the church's ministry relied heavily on help from the Native people themselves. The roles fulfilled by these Native workers included: translators and guides, cooks and other support staff in the schools and support workers at the mission stations. In these roles, Native peoples on the prairies fulfilled roles very similar to those done by indigenous people working with Canadian missionaries in Taiwan (Formosa), the New Hebrides, or India. Remarkably by 1887, four out of the 10 ordained missionaries working among the Native people on the prairie, were themselves Native or Country-born. Country-born is a term referring to individuals whose mother was Native and whose father was British (usually Scottish or English.) In the late 1880's and early 1890's, Country-born and Métis (French-speaking father and Native mother) were two distinct groups on the prairies. Members of the Foreign Mission Committee seem not to have drawn a distinction between Country-born and Native personnel, referring to both groups as "Indians." The four Native missionaries working among the Native people on the prairies are listed as regular ordained missionaries, with no reference to their ethnicity, whereas the two indigenous church workers involved in the mission on Formosa are listed as "Native pastors," and the one working with the Trinidad mission is called "Assistant Missionary." Of the 28 ordained missionaries listed in 1887 as being supported by the Mission Committee (this does not include missionaries supported by the Women's Missionary Society), 10 were working with the Native people on the Canadian Prairies.[11] This made this group of missionaries the largest team of missionaries working under the Foreign Mission Committee.

One of the early Country-born, Presbyterian clergy was the Rev.

George Flett, a former Hudson's Bay Company postmaster, who had joined the Rev. James Nisbet as Nisbet took up his mission in Prince Albert, Saskatchewan in 1866. Flett became disillusioned with the tasks he was assigned at Prince Albert and soon left the mission. Beginning in 1873, Flett was appointed to a series of reserve ministries based out of Okanase in western Manitoba. Flett was ordained a minister in the Presbyterian Church in Canada in 1875. On his deathbed Chief Okanase predicted that a great religious leader would soon come to his people, and he urged his band members to listen to this leader. It was shortly after Okanase's death that Flett arrived, and he was hailed by many as the great religious leader who had been predicted, and many on the reserve converted to Presbyterianism. One of the last to covert was Keeseekoowenin, the son of Okanase and chief of the Saulteux band; he was baptized Moses Burns. This made the Keeseekoowenin an almost entirely Presbyterian reserve. Flett and Burns mixed native traditions such as the pow-wow ceremonies and respect for wildlife with orthodox Christianity, walking in a middle ground.[12]

By 1885, Flett was responsible for mission work on five reserves in the area. Flett was by now a member of the Synod's Foreign Mission Committee, the regional group that oversaw the work among Native people. But Flett was, McLaren argues, never fully accepted by this group, "from their point of view Flett was "Indian" first, and only incidentally was he Canadian." The path was not open for a Native person, or even a Country-born missionary, to become part of the senior leadership group of the Presbyterian Church. Through the first half of the 1880's, at Presbytery meetings and when speaking at Mission Committee meetings, Flett was very critical of the Government officials and Indian Agents who worked on the reserves, but he was unwilling to make such critical statements before the Government inquiry into the Riel Rebellion. His area of responsibility was reduced to the three reserves of Okanase, Rossburn, and Rolling River in 1887. Flett retired in 1895, after 23 years as a missionary with the Presbyterian Church. Flett died in 1897. He was 81 years of age.[13]

A second Country-born Presbyterian missionary was John McKay. McKay was 31 when he joined Nisbet and his team to establish the mission at Prince Albert. McKay was originally hired as a general labourer, but when Flett left the mission, McKay took over the evangelization of the Indians living at some distance from the mission station. Nisbet needed a translator if he was to do this work, but both Nisbet and McKay could not be away from the mission at the same time, since that would leave the women and children alone. McKay was more than willing to spend two months a year traveling with the Native bands. In 1880, two years after his ordination, McKay moved his family to the Mistawasis Reserve about 100 kilometers from Prince Albert, at the invitation of Chief Mistawasis. McKay consistently kept at a distance from British-Canadian culture, immersing himself in the Native world. In fact, the only criticism ever directed at McKay came from missionaries sent to minister to the incoming settlers, missionaries sent to Prince Albert to minister to the native community had nothing but praise for McKay's ability and commitment to the mission. McKay worked on the Mistawasis reserve for a decade; he became ill in the summer of 1888 and retired from Mistawasis at the end of 1890. McKay died in Prince Albert on March 22, 1891. The McKays' daughter, Christina, remained at the reserve following her father's death as the school teacher in the employ of the church; the rest of her family moved back to Manitoba. Twenty-four years after his death, McKay's fame was still alive, "as the finest specimen of physical manhood of his time, as the most eloquent of Cree preachers, and as the most daring and successful of all Buffalo hunters; a combination of qualities surely worthy of enduring memory."[14]

There were other Native people who were involved in the Presbyterian mission work. Jacob Bear was a Cree, who was the assistant missionary at Round Lake, Saskatchewan for maybe as long as 20 years, from about 1903 through the early 1920's. Little is known about Bear. In 1909, W.W. McLaren believed that Bear should be ordained. The 1920 WMS report to the Assembly described him as Hugh McKay's "co-worker." A name that appears but which has been impossible to track down is the Rev. Donald MacVicar, who is identified as a "pure Cree Indian." In 1907, the white missionary to Okanase resigned, and the Foreign Missions Committee turned to Chief Boyer, appointing him "to take the spiritual oversight of his band." This was a new approach to mission work among the Native people—finding a Native person who was already in place to take on the ministry. The committee noted that it was "earnestly watching the results." There is no record of how this experiment went. In 1911, the Rev. J.A. Donaghy was appointed missionary to Okanase without any reference being made to the work of Boyer. There was, however, enough work on the Okanase reserve to require a full time missionary and a full-time teacher. When Boyer had taken over in 1907, the missionary at Okanase had been responsible for Lizard Point as well. Other Native people involved in the work were: Agnes Thomson who, in 1909, was assisting Miss E.A. Armstrong, the teacher and missionary at Moose Mountain, near Carlyle, Saskatchewan; and Earnest Goforth, educated at the Hampton Industrial and Agricultural Institute in Hampton, Virginia, a school specializing in the training of Blacks and Natives. Goforth's education was financed through a scholarship supplied by Church of Scotland supporters and administered by the Rev. W.W. McLaren of Birtle. Upon graduating Goforth ended up working with the Anglicans.[15]

In the years leading up to World War I, the Presbyterian Church showed its willingness to negotiate a middle ground in which Native people could do ministry among their own people. In fact, the church actively encouraged the development of such leadership, at times willingly taking risks in entrusting this ministry into the hands of Native people. Nowhere was that openness more evident than in the churches work among the Dakota people.

THE DAKOTA MISSION[16]

In May 1876, the Presbytery of Manitoba, passed the following:

> That the presbytery would strongly recommend the establishment of a mission among the Sioux Indians, that the Foreign Mission Committee be instructed to correspond with Dr. Williamson, Clerk of the Dakota Presbytery, to ascertain whether the service of Mr. Solomon Tunkasuiciye or any other competent missionary can be secured permanently for that mission.[17]

1876 had been a momentous year for the Northern Plains. General Custer took his last stand against the forces led by Sitting Bull. In the wake of that victory, Sitting Bull had led his forces across the Medicine Line (the Canadian border) into the safety and protection of British rule. Sioux had been living in western Canada since 1862, refugees from the last major conflict between the Dakota people (as the vast majority of the Sioux living in Canada are properly called) and the American cavalry. These earlier arrivals from Minnesota came bearing evidence that their forebearers had fought on the side of the British crown in the War of 1812. This evidence, combined with the fact that sending the Dakota back across the border would mean summary execution for many, caused the Governor in Winnipeg to allow the Dakota to stay in Canada, and he provided them with the bare essentials for survival.[18]

The Dakota had a serious problem. Canada was not their usual territory so they had no ancestral land claims and no treaty rights; they were not regular Native people. But neither were they regarded as regular immigrants to the new land, for they were governed by the Indian Act. Without a land base they became workers on the farms of the settlers who were starting to flow on to the prairie. As immigrants continued to pour in, the government decided that the Dakota needed to be placed on reserves, essentially as a way to control them. Two reserves were established in 1875: one at Oak River (now the Sioux Valley Reserve), and, a second, where Birdtail Creek joins the Assiniboine (the Birdtail Reserve). A third reserve was added in 1877 at Oak Lake. During the negotiations to establish the reserves, the citizens of Portage la Prairie sent a petition to Ottawa asking that a reserve be established in their area. This petition was supported by the local Presbyterian congregation. Eventually the Portage area got its reserve, as Dakota Tipi was added in 1898. An additional Dakota reserve was established near Prince Albert in 1894, and was expanded in 1908.[19]

The Presbytery of Manitoba, seeing no Christian ministry being done among the Sioux and recognizing that the Presbyterian Church had been late in getting involved with the Native peoples on the prairie, saw an opportunity for mission among the Dakota. There was an unofficial agreement among the Canadian Protestant churches to not compete with one another in doing ministry among Native people. Being late to the field meant that the Presbyterian Church was largely locked out of Native ministry. The Dakota chief at Birdtail, Enoch Mahpiyahdinape, was in contact with the leading Presbyterians in Manitoba, and had a relative who was an ordained minister in the American Presbyterian Church. In fact, the Rev. Solomon Tunkasiuciye had visited Fort Ellice in June 1875, and was familiar with the situation of the Dakota in Canada.[20] With an ordained Presbyterian Dakota minister who was also a relative of the chief at Birdtail living just south of the border, the Presbytery of Manitoba in May 1876, knew exactly who they wanted to be doing this ministry among the Dakota people.

Tunkasuiciye began his ministry at Birdtail in November 1877. It is difficult to determine much about him or his ministry style. The printed reports of the church Native ministry make little reference to the work at Birdtail, largely because Tunkasuiciye spoke no English and could not write. Whenever he attended presbytery meetings he was accompanied by a translator. In 1880, the General Assembly was told that he enjoyed "the full confidence of the Presbytery of Manitoba and of Christians who reside in the neighbourhood in which he labours." This was high praise from a committee who was very business-like in its relationship with missionaries on the field, and was not much given to paying compliments to any of its missionaries. In 1881, James Robertson visited the Birdtail area and was able to speak "in the highest terms of the missionary and his work." In early 1882, Tunkasuiciye attended a Presbytery meeting, reporting 41 communicants on the Birdtail reserve, 20 were in Sunday School, and two Bible Studies: one on Wednesday with 10 men in attendance, and one on Thursdays with 10 women in attendance. This was on a reserve with a total of 80 resident households. The presbytery was able to report to the Mission Committee that: "The whole band is making satisfactory progress in religious knowledge and in material comfort. They are becoming successful farmers."[21]

Despite these positive signs, economically things were challenging on the reserve. In 1887, the band leadership asked W. Hodnett, a settler in the Birtle area, to write to the convenor of the Foreign Mission Committee, the Rev. T. Wardrope of Guelph, Ontario. The heart of the letter was: "the Sioux (sic) of the Birdtail or Beulah Reserve, anxious to tell that they are not "Treaty" Indians that is they do not receive regular support from the government. They say they are badly in need of clothes." In response to this letter, a number of Women's Missionary Society groups began collecting clothes to be sent to the Birdtail Reserve. With the establishment of the Native residential school at Birtle in 1888, less than 15 kilometers from Birdtail, a natural distribution centre for these clothing packages was created.[22]

Problems began to develop in the church community on the Birdtail Reserve. The Rev. Hugh MacKay toured the Birdtail Reserve in early 1885 and reported that Tunkasuiciye had hired some members of the congregation to do some work on his house, there had been a misunderstanding about the rate of pay for the work, "and this lead over from one thing to another until a faction had been formed in the church." The division had become so severe that a petition had gone from the congregation to the Presbytery of Brandon asking that Tunkasuiciye be replaced. The Foreign Mission Committee, who was responsible for the appointment and removal of missionaries among the native people in Canada, agreed to find Tunkasuiciye another appointment, but the committee took a long time to figure out where that appointment would be. In fact, 18 months after agreeing that a change was necessary, the Committee was still looking for an appropriate place for Tunkasuiciye to minister. In 1888, the Committee reported that Tunkasuiciye was on a leave of absence since "he has been in ill health for the last year or two." It is easy to understand that the stress of having his congregation asking for his removal, the slowness of the Foreign Mission Committee in finding him a new placement, the need to communicate with the Committee via translator, and his distance from family and friends south of the border, would all have taken a major toll on Tunkasiuciye's health. Tunkasuiciye returned to the United States for a leave of absence, and the last word about him in the record of the Presbyterian Church in Canada is the 1888 report of the Foreign Mission Committee, "the reports received from him [regarding his health] are not encouraging. It is our earnest prayer that he may soon be restored to health and usefulness." Tunkasuiciye's problems with the Birdtail church and his subsequent return home did not mean that the Presbyterian Church in Canada was prepared to give up on using indigenous missionaries to reach the Native peoples of Canada with the gospel message.[23]

In 1877, the federal government established a small reserve for the Dakota living at Oak Lake, southwest of Virden, Manitoba. In 1892, the Young People's Society of Christian Endeavour from the Presbyterian Church in Virden, recognizing the need for Christian ministry on the reserve, employed Thomas Shield, an unordained Dakota from the United States. Shield had apprenticed under the Rev. John Williamson, the legendary missionary to the American Sioux. The support of a full-time missionary was too much for the Young People's Society and they turned to the Foreign Missions Committee for help. The Committee gave the help, taking over the funding and supervision of the ministry. Shield's ministry was short-lived; he developed a hemorrhage in his lungs and was forced to stop working in late 1893.[24]

In the late 1880's and early 1890's, three young men who had grown up under the ministry of Tunkasuiciye on the Birdtail Reserve presented themselves as willing and able to serve the church: Peter Hunter, Jason Ben, and John Thunder. All three were educated at the Shingwauk Home in Sault Ste. Marie, Ontario, and the Santee Missionary Training School in Nebraska.

Peter Hunter went to Nebraska on a scholarship from Knox Presbyterian Church, Winnipeg, in the hope that he would return to be a missionary among the native people. Hunter returned in 1892 and in 1894 he became the missionary at the Pipestone Reserve. Hunter quickly got himself in trouble with the two white authorities in the area: the Indian Agent J.A. Markle and the government-employed Farm Instructor Scott. Hunter was accused of campaigning against the permit system, which allowed government agents to control how much of their produce Native peoples were allowed to sell on the open market. The government's goal was to teach Native people "to husband their resources," but in fact it prevented Native people from becoming integrated into the market economy because they were not free agents in buying, selling, or transacting business. To protest this control, Hunter was holding meetings among the Dakota at Pipestone and Oak River, as well as writing to Markle's superiors in Brandon. Markle, in response, complained to the Rev. Prof. Hart, who was joint convenor of the foreign mission committee of the Synod of Manitoba and the North-West Territories, about Hunter's actions. By January 1895, Hart reprimanded Hunter, who promised to confine his energies to mission work. It will remain an open question as to whether Hunter would have limited his ministry in this way for the long term, because Hunter died suddenly on May 22, 1895.[25]

The Rev. A.B. Baird, the other joint convenor of the foreign mission committee of the Synod of Manitoba and the North-West Territories, wrote of Hunter, "He was a young man of considerable energy and he wielded a great influence among the Indians." Over the course of his year-long ministry, Hunter had drawn together a congregation of 23 in worship and was teaching five boys in a day school setting. Although Hunter had created headaches for Baird and other members of the Committee, Baird was genuinely "very much grieved" by Hunter's death.[26]

This was not the only blow that the Presbyterian Church's ministry among the Dakota was to suffer. In 1897, the Foreign Mission Committee reported that the Birdtail Reserve was mourning "the loss of Jason Ben, one of the main helpers to the missionary." Ben had been the assistant to the missionary responsible for the Birdtail Reserve and the Home Mission charge at Beulah, five kilometers from Birdtail. Due to Ben's health problems, which plagued the last three years of his life, he was not named the missionary to the Birdtail Reserve. Instead he translated the worship service led by the minister from the Beulah charge into Dakota, and interpreted Dakota culture and worldview to the missionary. He was remembered as one "who has left behind him a life example of great influence."[27]

The third of the trio from Birdtail was John Thunder. In late 1887, the Portage la Prairie day school run by the local Presbyterian Women's Missionary Society, which taught children from the Sioux village just outside Portage, was desperately seeking an assistant for its overworked teacher. They were pleased in May 1888, to announce that "such a person has for a few weeks been connected with the school. His name is John Thunder."[28] He had become indispensable to the work of the school. In 1889, Thunder was at the school at Indian Head, Saskatchewan working as a translator and teaching a group of "young men" how to read and write the Dakota language. The Foreign Mission Committee applauded this teaching of the Dakota people how to read and write their native tongue.

It would appear that someone seeing substantial gifts in Thunder encouraged him to seek further training, for his name does not appear again in the records of the church until 1894 when he was named as one of the three missionaries who grew up on the Birdtail Reserve, and who had been educated at the Santee School in Nebraska. In 1895, Thunder was appointed the missionary on the Oak Lake Reserve, the third in a succession of Dakota missionaries.

The Thunders threw themselves into the work at Oak Lake. Mrs. Thunder (there seems to be no record of her first name) taught sewing and knitting classes, while John Thunder led worship, preached, did pastoral care, and sought to transform the reserve into a Christian community. Thunder was able to report in 1901, after six years work on this small reserve, that 12 people had joined the church, 13 children and three adults had been baptized, and that six Christian marriages had been performed. As well, seven children from the reserve had gone to residential school; sadly, three of those, including the Thunders' daughter, had died while at school.[29]

In late 1901, things started to go wrong on the Oak Lake Reserve. John Thunder was one of the few people on the Reserve who could speak, read, and write English, and so when people went to the Hudson Bay Post to trade, they would ask Thunder to go with them. A number of people from the reserve began to accuse Thunder of skimming a portion of the transactions for himself. These accusations coincided with Thunder's public support for the banning of the "giveaway;" a practice outlawed by the Indian Act. Thunder was firmly opposed to much of Dakota social and religious practice, calling it "pagan." As early as 1887, before going to the Santee School, Thunder had expressed this view, signing a petition calling for "grass dancing and other heathen amusements" to be stopped.

"Giveaways" occurred at traditional native dances, when individual Dakota would share their resources with the others in their community, often giving away almost everything they had, including their means of making a living. This practice, therefore, violated the capitalist vision of a single farmer farming his own land and controlling his own means of production. It is impossible to determine if Thunder actually was skimming off the transactions he brokered or if the accusations were a response to his public support of the unpopular Indian Act. In any case, Thunder ceased to be the missionary at Oak Lake in late 1901. The Foreign Mission Committee reported to Assembly that Thunder had retired. Thunder believed he had been fired. Thunder returned home to Birdtail.[30]

In April 1902, Chaske Hanska, ruling elder in the Birdtail church, wrote to the Foreign Mission Committee asking that John Thunder be named the missionary to the Birdtail Reserve. The key reason for Thunder's appointment, was that he was a native speaker of the Dakota language. Worship had not been led at Birdtail by a native Dakota speaker in 14 years, since the departure of Tuankasuiciye. Hanska argued, "When the Holy Spirit was given as Jesus our Saviour promised, the disciples have been spoken [to] with lots of different languages. Therefore we knew it from the beginning that [having the gospel] spoken with native tongues was the work of the Holy Spirit." Despite this compelling argument for a native Dakota speaker, the Committee was not prepared to name Thunder as the missionary; instead he was named the translator to the minister who came to the reserve from Beulah.[31] Thunder, who had been a missionary in his own right at Oak Lake for six years, was clearly unhappy with this arrangement.

It was at this point in his career that Thunder began to emphasize how important it was for the missionaries on reserves to speak the language of the native people to whom they were ministering. It would be easy to see this campaign as Thunder's response to his being fired, or at least demoted from missionary to translator; however even after being re-appointed a missionary in 1907, Thunder remained adamant that missionaries, to be effective, should learn the native tongue of those to whom they were ministering.[32] In 1907, Thunder was appointed again to Pipestone-Oak Lake Reserve, and in 1908 was appointed to help set language study courses and exams for new missionaries arriving on the mission field of the Canadian prairies. The last mention of Thunder appears in Hugh McKellar's 1924 work, *Presbyterian Pioneer Missionaries*, which notes that Thunder is "still in the work" and at Pipestone in 1924.[33]

Despite the problems with the Dakota missionaries employed by the Presbyterian Church in Canada, the ministry of these individuals was significant. By 1912, the Foreign Missions Committee claimed that there were only seven individuals over the age of 15 on the Birdtail reserve who had not become communicant members of the Presbyterian Church. This, then, was for all intents and purposes a Christian reserve, standing in marked contrast to many of the other Dakota reserves on the Canadian prairies. By seeking out a Dakota missionary to carry the gospel to the Dakota people, the Presbyterian Church had come to understand the impact that indigenous missionaries can have in the spread of the gospel message. As well, Solomon Tunkasuiciye's ministry on the Birdtail Reserve as a Dakota missionary clearly served as a model and example to the three: Hunter, Ben, and Thunder. In addition, the Presbyterian Church's commitment to the Dakota peoples was shown in 1925, when most Native ministry went to the United Church of Canada and the Presbyterian Church in Canada retained its work at Birdtail and Oak Lake-Pipestone. It was only in the 1990's that there began to be serious discussion regarding the closure of the ministry on these two reserves. The creative risks taken more than 100 years earlier bore fruit in the Presbyterian Church's long standing commitment to the ministries on these two reserves.

EVANGELISTIC WORK AMONG THE NATIVE PEOPLE
While the ministry among Native people was being done under the direction of the Foreign Missions Committee, educational work was a recognized means of doing evangelism. The principals of the schools were also missionaries. Kate Gillespie, who was one of the most successful of the missionary-principals, each Sunday would leave the File Hills school, near Balcarres, Saskatchewan, to drive out in her horse-drawn buggy onto the reserves in the immediate neighbourhood to "preach to a congregation where one can be gathered, or failing that, speak to the ones and twos she may find at the houses at which she calls." Gillespie and her sister Janet, from Teeswater, Ontario, served the File Hills school for a number of years. Janet was the Matron of the school. Kate Gillespie married the well-known Saskatchewan farm activist, W.R. Motherwell, in 1908, and she and Janet both left the school. W.W. MacLaren, principal of the Birtle school, was also responsible for preaching in the church at the Birdtail Reserve just south of Birtle. It was not only the principals of residential schools who had this responsibility; the Rev. C.W. Bryden had to divide his time between being the teacher in the day school at the Mistawasis Reserve and leading the church on the reserve. Jonathan Beverly, who was Lucy Baker's replacement at Prince Albert, had not only to teach in the day school and preach, he was also the farm instructor. Certainly Beverly and Bryden would have found the day-to-day contact with the families on the reserve helpful in their work of building up the church. There would have been a completeness to their witness; they were seen living during the week the faith in Jesus Christ that they talked about on Sundays.[34]

Hugh McKay really wanted to do evangelistic work, and in 1911 he resigned from being the principal of the Round Lake school to devote himself full time to the proclamation of the gospel. By that time there were four congregations on the reserves near Whitewood, Saskatchewan. Many of the members of these congregations were former students of the Round Lake school who had long-standing relationships with McKay. But each time McKay tried to leave the responsibility for the school in someone else's hands so that he could devote himself full-time to "preach the gospel to his beloved Indians," events transpired against him and he was forced to come back to run the school.[35]

It was not just appointed and paid missionaries who were involved in the evangelistic effort. When, in 1907, the missionary at Lizard Point, Manitoba, left, the committee had been unable to find a missionary as quickly as they had hoped. An unnamed Presbyterian nurse at the government-run field hospital in the area showed herself "to be a true missionary," visiting in homes to offer along with healing for the body, healing for the soul. Each Sunday she gathered together as many people as she could and ran a Sunday School for all ages together.[36]

By the early 1900's the "Presbyterian Indian Workers" were getting together each summer to talk through issues of mutual concern and to act as a cohesive group in bending the ear and heart of the denominational leadership and the church at large. Growing out of the 1908 summer gathering came a commitment to carry out an evangelistic campaign through the schools and across the reserves where Presbyterian missionaries were working. At the Regina Industrial School, the principal, the Rev. R.B. Heron, invited long-time missionary Hugh McKay to be the guest preacher at a one week preaching mission. Heron reported that there was "no attempt to work on the emotions; no over urging;" it was clearly stated that anyone who "wished to make a start in the Christian life" could speak to either Heron or McKay privately after the meeting was over. Thirty-one young people took advantage of the invitation stating that "they wished to follow the Christ." At the closing meeting six of these stood voluntarily "to give testimony," and two girls lead the service in prayer. Heron was amazed that the shy young people he knew from the classroom would be willing not only to tell the story of their faith but to pray in a public context.[37]

The Rev. F.A. Clare invited Jacob Bear, a Cree who was assistant missionary at Round Lake to be part of the evangelistic effort at File Hills in January 1909. Clare reported, "It was a great joy to see the eager faces and the interested looks as Jacob delivered the message." In March of that year Bear was part of the team that was invited to the Mistawasis Reserve. Here the team went from house to house, visiting most of the families on the Reserve and having a short service of scripture reading, hymn singing and prayer wherever they went. Clare, who was part of the team, reported this approach as "being one of the most fruitful." Again Bear was the preacher,

"His messages came with great power showing what a great blessing he is for such services. The interest in his words was always so great and the faces were lighted up with attentive interest as he spoke such direct messages." Jacob Bear was clearly the star of these evangelistic events.[38]

In March of 1909, the Rev. W. W. McLaren, principal at Birtle Residential School and the missionary at Birdtail Reserve, together with John Thunder, a Dakota who was ministering at the Oak Lake and Pipestone Reserves, led a week-long mission at Birdtail. In the mornings they visited in homes holding times of prayer, and in the afternoons they had a series of Bible studies on the book of Amos, chosen for "its searching convicting power." The evenings were given over to regular evangelistic worship service. McLaren indicated that the plan was to repeat this evangelistic mission pattern at both the Okanase and Pipestone Reserves.[39]

The Cecilia Jeffrey School was located on Lake of the Woods and the motor launch, "The Wanderer," was used to pick up supplies from Kenora and students from the reserves around the lake. "The Wanderer" was also an evangelistic tool as the Rev. F. T. Dodds, the principal at the school in the 1910's, used the boat to visit the Native communities around the lake to hold worship services and to build relationships with the individuals.[40]

The Presbyterian mission to Native people involved as many or more staff than any other Foreign mission of the church, but it never received the profile within the denomination that the other foreign mission work of the church received. Some of the mission staff were highly committed to the work and seem to have been particularly well suited to it. Despite the deep commitment of these individuals, the Presbyterian mission among the Native people suffered from a rapid turnover of personnel. This greatly hampered the mission. It was hard for Native people to build relationships with the missionaries when the missionaries were constantly changing, and at its heart effective evangelistic work is built upon the relationship between two individuals.

EDUCATIONAL MINISTRY

One of the results of the 1885 Rebellion was an increased willingness on the part of the federal government to assist in funding "Indian schools." The Canadian establishment had been deeply frightened by the experience of 1885, and were prepared to put more resources into the education, which meant the "Canadianization" of the Native peoples on the prairies. Assisting in this process fit the Christendom vision of the Presbyterian Church, which saw "Canadianization" and "Christianization" as flip sides of the same coin. By the 1920's the vision for the church's educational ministry was that clearly set out by the Rev. F. E. Pitts, principal at Birtle and later at Cecilia Jeffrey,

...the Boarding School not only teaches them to read, write, etc., but tries to teach them new conditions of living. Teaches them to eat different food, to sleep in beds, to dress, wash, bath, to bake their bread, cook their food, keep their houses and make a living on farms, etc.—not like their parents have done but in a manner that shall enable them to live in civilized conditions in which they find themselves—tries to instill into them energy, perseverance, self-control, morals, and religion, and make these so much a part of their life, that they shall practice them as long as they live.[41]

The purpose behind teaching Native children was not so that they could read and write, it was to turn them into "civilized" people who would eat and sleep like "civilized" people did. It was to transform them from lazy people into people possessing "energy, perseverance, self-control." The agenda was nothing less than the social and moral reconstruction of the Native people. In the process they would become self-supporting, contributing members of Canadian society; all of which for many Canadians in the 1920's, was simply another way of saying that the goal was to make the Native people "good Christians."

The Presbyterian Church in Canada became involved in the education of Native peoples as soon as Nisbit reached Prince Albert. Education has always been one of the mission foci of Presbyterians. Teaching those who can not read to become literate was an important ministry because it allowed the new reader to read the Bible for themselves. For a denomination that values both the priesthood of all believers and learning in general, teaching people to read was an important mission activity. The first schools were day schools, with students walking to the school each day for their classes as they did in British-Canadian culture. The legendary Lucy Baker taught in a day school at Makoce Waste an unrecognized Dakota reserve from 1894 to 1904 when she retired from the mission field. She saw no conversions, and there have been questions about how educationally rigorous were the classes she taught. By the end of her time at Makoce Waste, she was deeply loved by the Dakota people among whom she worked. "The Misses Bruces" also ministered among the Dakota people at Swan Lake, southwest of Portage la Prairie, for eight years from 1911 to 1919. One of the sisters taught in the day school and the other was a missionary visiting in homes and leading Sunday worship. Both Baker and the Bruces had no desire to be involved with the residential school system, preferring instead to make their educational contribution through the one-room school.[42]

There were two problems with day schools from the missionaries' point of view. First, there was no truancy act governing the Native peoples as there was enforcing school attendance in the rest of Canadian society. Even if there had been such a law, it was uncertain who would have enforced it. The churches were no fans of the Indian agents, the people on the reserves who had the power to enforce laws. As well, Indian agents had made it clear to the Indian Affairs Department that had no desire to be turned into truancy officers. Thus attendance at most day schools hovered below 50 percent, and in some cases only a quarter of the school-aged children attended. It was not that parents were opposed to their children being educated; it was rather that part of a Native child's education was being with their parents on the trapline and hunting and working in the fields at seeding and harvest time. Going to school was not the highest priority. Kate Gillespie, in recalling what it was like to be a teacher in a day school on the reserve, wrote,

> …the attendance was irregular and not punctual and on bad days in order to secure anything like progress I had to walk up the road…in the forenoon (all the children happened to be living along the same road) go into [each] house, and hear and set lessons. In the afternoon return, correct exercises of the work, hear and set fresh lessons. The children could not come to school on bad days I had to go to them.[43]

Gillespie was clearly frustrated by this experience and hoped that the government would mandate boarding schools as the pattern for Native education. What Gillespie failed to recognize was that her modified teaching pattern, taking the lessons to the children if they would not come to her, was an effective means of addressing the educational needs of Native children in a culturally appropriate way. However, neither the churches nor the government were prepared to spend the money needed to do education in this teacher intensive way. Taking education to the students in their communities and homes was too expensive and inefficient. In fact, the churches were finding that some reserves were too small to justify a teacher, and so were adding boarding facilities to their day schools. As well, there were some remote reserves that were extremely difficult to staff and it was thought to be easier to have the children leave their home communities to board in a community that was larger and had the kind of schooling they required. The one great fear of residential schools, acknowledged by principals and denominational officials, was the illness and death of students. Disease could pass like wildfire through a school, and it was common for one or two students to die each year in the Presbyterian-operated schools. In 1907, two students at Cecilia Jeffrey School died of spinal meningitis.[44]

As Indian Affairs became interested in giving trade skills to the Native people, which they hoped would allow the Native people to become self-supporting, contributing members of Canadian society, the department started to fund the development of Industrial schools. These were boarding schools for older children, where the focus was on young men learning farming and carpentry skills and the like, and young women learning cooking, housekeeping, and sewing skills. The young women, it was hoped, would not only take back to their reserves a different lifestyle, but that some would become domestic servants in the homes of the settlers. The young men, it was anticipated, in taking their farm skills back to the reserves, would be examples and mentors to their neighbours of a new, better, and self-reliant lifestyle. The Presbyterian church operated one industrial school through an agreement with Indian Affairs, the Regina Industrial School. Opened in 1890, it was hailed as one of the finest schools of its kind in Canada, and a number of the students who attended the school were to speak of it in very positive terms in later life. The Regina Industrial School acquired a threshing machine, and at harvest time the students threshed grain for a number of the farmers neighbouring the school. In the print shop other students acquired enough skills to become press operators for some of the community papers in Saskatchewan. By 1910, Indians Affairs in Ottawa was disenchanted with the industrial schools; they were too costly with their large overhead equipment costs and the schools were not teaching enough students to have the impact that the government desired. Therefore the industrial schools were phased out in favour of residential schools; in 1912, the Regina Industrial school was the first industrial school to be closed by Indian Affairs.

Not only did Indian Affairs favour residential schools, so did those Presbyterians who were working among the Native peoples. In 1909 "The Indian Workers' Association of the Presbyterian Church for Saskatchewan and Manitoba" produced a document detailing how Native education should take place. Smaller residential schools were better than larger ones it was argued; there should be about 25 pupils in each school, as this would allow for a more family-like feeling within the school, rather than the institutional feel of the larger schools. Small schools also gave teachers and other staff the opportunity for "more efficient work especially in moral training." The Association wanted school attendance made compulsory for all Native children ages six to 15. It was argued that children should attend day schools on their home reserves until they were 12 years of age, and only then be transferred to the residential school. While the Association was concerned about the quality of education that their young charges received, it was "the moral training of Indian children" that was the predominant concern. "Rigid regulations" should be introduced to ensure that the moral training that was provided in the school was not undermined, "Nothing that encourages the survival of previous Indian customs, the excessive desire of sports, or associations with the evilly disposed white population should be permitted." Fear that the hard work of training students to "become good citizens of Canada" might be wiped out when graduates returned to their home reserves, the Indian Workers' Association advocated the establishment of a Colony system. Graduates would be clustered together as settlers on their own land, "at the same time they are under the guiding restraint of a Government official and are protected from the parasitic habits of their worthless friends." For the Indian Workers' Association, it was not enough to educate the students in the schools, nor was it enough to proclaim the gospel message to the students; it was also necessary to remove from the students their social and cultural makeup. The only way for the Native people to become successful members of Canadian society was for them to stop being "Indian."[45] Therefore by the early 1910's there was no room for middle ground; either one was part of Indian culture or one was part of the dominant British-Canadian culture. It was impossible to have a foot in both.

The story of the McLarens of Birtle illustrates this loss of middle ground most poignantly. The Rev. W.W. McLaren, a graduate of Knox College, became the principal of the Birtle School in 1905, to his own great surprise. It was not his choice to "go into the Indian work." In fact, he had never thought of being involved in this mission of the church, partly because, he, like many of his classmates, was hardly aware that the Presbyterian Church had a ministry among the Native peoples of Canada. McLaren suffered from health problems that his doctors told him would keep him doing traditional parish ministry. Even though he had been trained for full-time ministry, McLaren was anticipating going "into mercantile life." A letter from The Rev. R.P. McKay, convenor of the Foreign Mission Committee, raised the possibility of McLaren being able to do native ministry. As McLaren would say eight years later, "the call seemed to me providential." McLaren intended to only stay at Birtle a year; instead he stayed eight.[46]

In 1909, in one of his many letters reporting on various aspects of Native ministry in the Birtle area, McLaren wrote,

> We have a very clever girl in Birtle, Susette Blackbird, she is in full charge of Miss McLeod's department while the latter is in the east for a month. Although only 18 years of age she is doing admirably. To provide meals for 53 people is a pretty big undertaking for an Indian girl—yet she is doing it—keeping all the girls in good control.[47]

Blackbird was "an Indian girl" and a gifted person who was doing the important job of keeping the kitchen going, which she was doing surprisingly well. McLaren had a foot firmly planted in the dominant culture's understanding of what native people were capable of accomplishing. McLaren did recognize in Blackbird ministry potential, and he was able to arrange through funds provided by benefactors in Scotland for Blackbird to spend the school year 1910-1911 taking "special subjects" at the Presbyterian Missionary and Deaconess Training Home in Toronto. Upon finishing her courses at the Training Home, She returned to the Birtle School where she became Assistant Nurse and Matron.[48]

In late 1911, McLaren and Blackbird were married. There was in the Birtle School an unused classroom. The McLarens asked permission to turn that classroom into their living quarters. The reaction from the church and government was "No." McKay, in writing to Frank Pedley of Indian Affairs, indicated that there were two problems with the McLarens' proposal. First, there was great unrest within the school because "the bride does not appreciate the delicacy of her position." A number of teachers had complained that Susette McLaren spoke to the students in their native tongue and therefore had an advantage over the white teachers. The teachers were deeply concerned that McLaren would use this advantage for some unidentified, yet nefarious, purpose. Second, the Women's Missionary Society, who played a substantial role in the management of the residential schools, believed that W. W. McLaren's actually living in the building would limit his ability to function as the principal of the school. Again there were no specifics provided as to how that might happen, except a sense that the McLaren's did not have enough distance from the students to be able to effectively model the lifestyle that the dominant society wanted native peoples to live. The bottom line for the group leading the mission was, "Mr. McLaren's marriage has rather impaired conditions at Birtle," and he would be moved from the school at Birtle to the one at Round Lake, Saskatchewan.[49]

In response to all the furor his marriage had caused and his transfer to Round Lake, W. W. McLaren wrote a seven page letter to R. P. McKay. McLaren's vision and passion is clear as he wrote,

> The Future of Canada is as much bound up with its 110,000 Indians as with an equal number of Galicians—Jews or any other race and I felt that if we were to weld out of many people one truly Christian nation—the moral welfare of the Indian deserved the best I could give as much as any other race. I took a step further than many of my fellow Canadians and married a member of the Indian race. Some whose Christian profession should have taught them the essential equality of all peoples as followers of Christ have said and done things regarding this matter that have hurt more than anything that has been done to me. It is a poor lookout for the future of our church and of our Dominion when the union of Christian peoples of different races is made a ground of offense.[50]

McLaren had moved from having a foot firmly in the dominant culture to trying to create a new culture, in which the middle ground of "the union of Christian peoples of different races" would be as accepted as any other marriage would. For McLaren, his marriage was a litmus test of how far the church had moved toward his new found vision of "one truly Christian nation." W.W. McLaren died in 1915, and his widow vanished from the records of the church.

In 1923, the Rev. R.B. Heron, former principal at the Regina Industrial School, read a paper before the Regina Presbytery in which he attacked the residential school system. His critique, built on the contention that many of the students were "kept out at work that produces revenue for the School," was that the students were cheap labour for the "farms and gardens and laundries and bake-shops and kitchens in connection with Indian Schools." The per capita grants provided by Indian Affairs were predicated on the assumption that students would only spend half days in the classroom. Thus even the most motivated Native pupil was unlikely to achieve a grade 6 educational standing by the time they turned 18 and were no longer eligible to be a student. It took two years in the classroom in a residential school to cover the same material that was covered in one year in the classrooms of white day schools. Heron recounted the following story to show how poor the education being received in the residential schools was:

> The ex-pupils of our Indian Schools have such faulty education that very few of them are capable of interpreting Cree into English, or vice versa. A story is told of a clergyman who attempted to preach to an Indian congregation through an Interpreter, from the text: (Matt. 14:27) "It is I, be not afraid," when this came to the ears of the congregation in their own language, it was: "Hit him in the eye, don't be afraid!"

Heron placed the blame for this failure squarely at the feet of the educational system. He believed that Native children were as capable of learning, even of excelling in the classroom setting, as were their non-Native contemporaries. Heron believed that parents of children in the residential schools expected their children to be in the classroom for the full day, and that the churches and the government were failing to fulfill the promises they had made to these parents about the education these young people would receive. Historian J.R. Miller has said of the half-day of academic learning that was part of the residential school system, "there was always a 'buckskin ceiling' over the heads of the Native students." Heron's most telling criticism grew out of conversations he had had with missionaries who had worked among the Native people for many years. He reported that they "agree that the younger men have not as high sense of honour as, and are less self-reliant than, the old Indians who have never been in School." The residential school was not only failing educationally, it was also failing to create self-supporting, contributing Native people. But above all, in view of the churches' goals, the residential schools were turning out students with a lower sense of honour and, by extension, morality, than their un-schooled parents and grandparents.[51]

Heron's critique produced a host of angry responses within Presbyte-rian circles. The Indian Secretary for the Women's Missionary Society, Ad-elaide Clark, after casting aspersions as to why Heron was no longer the principal at the Regina Industrial School, argued that the cause of the failure of the residential school system was not the schools but the reserves and in particular the homes from which the pupils came. Native children were just not strong enough physically "for many years [of] close applica-tion to study." The goal of the residential school system should be to get children to a grade 7 or 8 level and with only a few exceptions should Native youth "be advanced further." The Rev. F.E. Pitts, Principal at Birtle at the time, said of Heron's critique that students were spending too little time in the classroom, "This is the Indian complaint. Nothing would please the Indian better than to sit down and have the White man feed, clothe, and wait on him. If we did this for the children in the school we would be making them worse Indians and unfitting them still more for the condi-tions of civilized life." The level of anger produced by Heron's comments make clear there were rumblings of dissatisfaction with the residential school system being expressed in other quarters as well. Heron's paper produced no change in the system, and the general view of the leadership overseeing the work of the residential schools was that this is a "good work although it sometimes seems slow."[52]

With the views just outlined being the way that denominational lead-ers saw the Residential schools and their pupils, it was easy for racism to be part of the culture of the school. Certainly the treatment received by Susette (Blackbird) McLaren was racial and cultural abuse, as was the aim of the school system to cut Native pupils off from their cultural roots. The two oldest daughters of Thomas and Mary Aspdin from near Moose Jaw at-tended the Regina Industrial School in the 1890's. Although Thomas was a white, the language of the home was Sioux because Mary was one of the Sioux who had come north with Sitting Bull. Thomas wanted his children to know English fluently and so he sent his daughters to the Regina school. The two sisters were punished by teachers at the school for speaking Sioux to one another in private. This was part of the process of the Aspdin sisters being "civilized."[53] As "Canadianization" became the goal of the schools, the church's missionaries began to proclaim a gospel of conformity with the dominant society's social values. In the process the Christian gospel became lost in the proclamation of "Canadian social religion."

There was also physical abuse in the schools. Physical discipline was, at times, more severe in the residential schools than what occurred in the white schools of the day. Parents lodged complaints against a teacher at the Cecilia Jeffrey School for the excessive use of the strap. The complaints were severe enough that the principal, Mr. Dodds, was forced to meet with the parents. They asked for a guarantee "that their children should never be whipped (by anyone)." Dodds would not agree to this, but did agree that the teacher in question would not be permitted to "whip" anyone. In a letter to the Foreign Mission Committee, which was doing a further investigation of the complaint, the teacher reported, "From that day on I have never touched the strap, though on a few occasions I have used a ruler." A more severe approach was taken by the principal of the Crowstand School in Saskatchewan. There was an outbreak of male students running away from the school in 1907. The principal, upon catching the runaways, "tied ropes about their arms and made them run behind the buggy from their houses to the school." Not surprisingly the boys' parents, who witnessed this treatment, complained, saying "that their children are not dogs." When the complaints were reported to James Farquharson, the convenor of the Foreign Mission Committee for the Synod of Manitoba and the North West, he responded, "Surely, there is some mistake about this charge." Nonetheless a committee was appointed to "inquire" into the complaint. Hugh McKay, longtime missionary to the Native people, a former residential school principal, and a trusted confidante of the Native people, wrote to R.P. Mckay, convenor of the Assembly's Foreign Mission Committee, about a story told to him by a young girl at the Round Lake School. The school matron, in this case the wife of the principal, had struck the girl on the ear so hard that she had knocked the child down. Hugh Mackay went on to write, "The ingovernable [sic] temper of both Principal and Matron is the cause of the trouble."[54]

As well, sexual improprieties occurred in some of the Presbyterian schools. There were problems at both Birtle and Crowstand in the 1890s when older male and female students were involved in sexual activity with one another. This was the result of improper supervision. A similar problem arose at the Round Lake school in 1919. Two males, former students at Round Lake and two friends, former pupils from the Qu'Appelle Industrial School, broke into the school one night and spent time in the senior girls' room. At first, none of the female students would say anything, but eventually it came out that the boys had been in search of a sexual encounter, which may or may not have happened. The principal was mortified, and ended his response to the police investigation report, by saying, "During the 35 years we have been here in charge of the school there has not been a single case of a girl going astray and leaving the school in disgrace."

The principal was about to retire for a second time when the break-in took place. The school was in a chaotic state, discipline was lax, staff morale was low, and the teaching was of a poor quality. This lack of positive leadership opened the door to the events described in the police report.[55]

A small number of cases of sexual abuse were reported as occurring in the schools. From the Round Lake school in 1912, the following incident was reported. A group of boys were bathing in a small room that had four windows. The principal saw one of them standing near a window, naked. In order to punish the boy, the principal took hold of the boy and dragged him naked out of the bathroom and into a room where his wife was sitting and then into a room where one of the teachers and some of the female students were. "In this room they struggled, the boy objecting to be taken where the ladies were naked. He caught on a bed, both pupil and principal fell to the floor." It was the teacher who was witnessing this scene who suggested to the principal that he should get the boy something with which he could cover himself. At Cecilia Jeffrey School in 1910-1911, a number of girls told the assistant matron that the principal had had them "put their hands under his clothing and [play] with his breasts," and that the principal "was in the habit of kissing the old girls." The former staff member who brought the charges was interviewed by R.P. Mackay, convenor of the Assembly's Foreign Missions Committee and reported "some things even more unpleasant."[56]

The most difficult part of the residential school experience, according to former students, was the loneliness. J. R. Miller, in his interviews with former students of the residential school system, notes that over and over again people told of being "lonely all the time." The schools were not intensely nurturing environments to begin with, and as the government's funding formula encouraged ever greater economies of scale, the schools became more and more institutional in order to function financially. Miller, in summing up the students' experience of residential schools, writes,

> For a sizable group of former students, the legacy of residential school was not bitter at all. It would be misleading to leave the impression that all or even most staff of residential schools were oppressive or slipshod in their care of schoolchildren, just as it would be erroneous to suggest that all former residential school-children carried bad memories away with them when they left school....A number of ex-students have testified publicly that their experience was a positive one.[57]

Throughout the history of the residential schools the churches and the government debated who was responsible for the schools, and what was the exact nature of that responsibility. There were regular complaints from school principals that they did not have enough money to purchase food or to provide the other necessities of life for the students under their care. School principals, who were also the financial officers for their schools, had three options about how to respond to the funding crises they faced. Some, like Jennie Cunningham, wrote fiery letters to both sides demanding action. Fed up with the stonewalling she was getting from both the Foreign Mission Committee in Toronto and Indian Affairs in Ottawa about who was responsible for expanding the school at File Hills, she highlighted the depth of the problem she and her students faced. "For two years now the oldest boys have been sleeping in a tent. All our house room is full to its capacity." Students were living in a tent through the cold of the prairie winter. Cunningham was able to get action; the File Hills school was enlarged. Other school administrators were not as lucky as Cunningham in getting either the church or the government to help with the issues of feeding, clothing, and housing the students of the school.

If embarrassing the powers that were into action did not work, a second option was to follow what Kate and Janet Gillespie did; between 1901 and 1904 they put almost $550 of their own money into the File Hills school. That was a third of their combined income for those years. If no one else would help finance the schools, the staff kicked in themselves. A third option was to find ways for the school to generate its own financial resources, or at least ways to stretch the available dollars to the maximum, which is exactly what Heron had accused the residential system of doing—turning students into cheap labour, whose work kept the schools open.[58]

In 1907, of the total amount of money spent by the Presbyterian Church on Native ministry, three-quarters of it went into educational ministry, both residential and day schools. The other quarter of the funding went to evangelistic and church work on the reserves, which was funded by the Foreign Mission Committee. The expense of the schools was almost equally divided between the Department of Indian Affairs, which picked up 47 percent of the cost, and the Women's Foreign Missionary Society, which carried 53 percent of the cost of the schools. The numbers would shift somewhat, with the schools themselves raising more and more money to cover their costs. The government was a major financial player at the table as were the women of the church. In fact, after 1910, the government carried a larger portion of the costs. The government was able to increase its support of residential schools, in part because funds had been freed up in the phasing out of the industrial schools. There was little additional money available for residential schools; the government was only willing to commit so much money to the Native people of Canada. By 1923, the federal government was paying for about two-thirds of the costs of Native education in both residential and day schools, and the Women's Missionary Society was paying the rest.[59]

The frustration church officials experienced in their dealings with Indian Affairs is caught in the correspondence between W.W. McLaren and R.P. Mackay. In analyzing the thinking of the Minister of the Interior, Frank Oliver, who was also responsible for Indian Affairs, McLaren said, "his whole attitude is not one of interest in the Indian so much as one of interest in the administration of Indian Affairs at a minimum of worry and expense." McLaren, from his position as principal of Birtle School, had come to recognize that the goal of Indian Affairs was not to find ways to best serve the Native people; instead it was to spend as little as possible on serving the Native people. Mackay, who dealt with the government on a regular basis regarding funding for the schools, agreed with McLaren's assessment; the government does "not propose to increase the expenditure on Indian work—they rather think that too much is expended for the work done." The work of the schools would be under increasing financial pressure; the government was about to further cut their funding and the church maintained it could not find any additional money for the schools. The only remaining option was to make the schools self-sufficient by turning them into money-making operations, which meant using the students as unpaid servants. Which was exactly the criticism that R.B. Heron would direct at the schools in 1923, 14 years after McLaren and Mackay had so clearly recognized the government's desire to pay as little as possible for the education of Native people.[60]

The flurry of letters that passed between the leadership of the Home Mission Board of the Presbyterian Church and various government officials between July 1914 and July 1915, shows how neither side was willing to accept responsibility for the schools. The presenting problem was that the land being used to teach the boys at the Birtle School how to farm did not belong to the school; it was being rented from a third party who no longer wished to rent the land to the school, but instead wanted to sell it. Learning of this opportunity to bring the land under the direct control of the school, the Rev. Andrew Grant, superintendent of Home Missions for the Presbyterian Church, wrote to D.C. Scott, deputy superintendent general, Department of Indian Affairs, in Ottawa asking that the government buy the quarter section of land immediately adjacent to the school, to be used in the school's educational mission. It was up to the government to purchase the land, because the church had "decided not to put any more money in land or equipment for this educational work among the Indians."[61] The church was prepared to put funding into classroom costs and into clothing and feeding the students, but capital costs were the government's responsibility. G.J.J. Keon, inspector of Indian Affairs responsible for the Birtle area, was asked by his superiors in Ottawa for his opinion of the request. Keon agreed that the land should be purchased for the school to use to teach farming methods, especially if the goal was "to farm on a large scale and make the institution profitable."[62] But Keon's views did not change the mind of the Indian Affairs officials in Ottawa, who rejected buying the land. The Rev. Grant wrote a stinging response upon hearing the department's rejection. He wrote,

> Of course it must be distinctly understood that these Indians are wards of the Government, and, if, you insist on large buildings, institutional work and farming as conditions connected with these schools, the Government will have to furnish the equipment that is necessary, as we are not going to do this any longer. So that, if we cannot get the land, it simply means that we cannot do the work, and this department will have to be neglected.[63]

If the government wanted the students of the residential schools to acquire a certain set of skills, then the government was responsible for providing the schools with the resources so that those skills could be taught. If the government failed to provide those resources, then it was the government who was responsible for the outcome, not the church or the schools themselves. The owner of the land did not take "No" so easily, and he wrote directly to the Indian Affairs department asking them to buy the land. D.C. Scott of Indian Affairs responded with the government's position; "this school is owned by the Presbyterian Church and the Department merely pays for the management at a per capita grant for the Indian pupils in attendance."[64] Department officials were at pains to indicate that they "merely" provided funding to the school and nothing more.

Neither the church nor the government was prepared to take complete responsibility for the residential schools. The government sought to remain at arms length from the schools, not funding them directly, but rather sending grant monies to the denominational offices for the number of children in the schools of that denomination. Yet at the same time the department sought to use that funding to control the nature of the education that was being delivered. The churches on the other hand, sought to ensure that religious and spiritual values were instilled in the students, but they were not willing to accept the financial burden that reaching that goal would have required. The churches were prepared to lay much of the blame for the problems in the schools at the door of the Indian Affairs department instead of owning their role in the educational process. Both sides were able to turn the other into the scapegoat for the problems in the schools.

The Challenges of Native Ministry

Many of the missionaries found working with the Native people frustrating and disappointing. A missionary might see development and growth take place, and be hopeful that a break through had been made, only to see what had looked like development evaporate overnight. The missionaries laid the blame for their lack of success in two places.

First, they held white traders responsible for plying Native people with alcohol. Missionaries regularly reported the impact of alcohol had on people they knew on the reserves. Miss McIlwaine, missionary at Swan Lake in 1908, noted that drunkenness often led to fights, fires and other accidents; she also recounted seeing one person who had died and of trying to help another who was dying from drinking wood alcohol. The missionaries were clear that it was a society which allowed the sale of alcohol that was the problem, and that the introduction of prohibition would end the problem.[65]

The second place the missionaries laid blame for the slow growth of the church among the Native people was with the still deeply held "heathen" and "pagan" worldview of many living on the reserves. The missionaries saw Native marriage, divorce, and common-law practices as hampering the proper moral development of the reserves. In 1922, a situation on the Birdtail Reserve so concerned the Home Mission Board that General Secretary Edmison wrote to Indian Affairs in Ottawa to see if the department would use its legal powers to rectify the living arrangements of two couples on the reserve. In both cases, the partners were married and living with people to whom they were not married. The government's response was since it was not a case of bigamy, the newly-formed couples were not married, and the government had no role.[66]

Not only did the missionaries find traditional Native social customs hard to end, there were reserves where traditional Native spirituality was still followed. One such reserve was where Lucy Baker had taught. The band was "a strong-hold of paganism, under the influence of medicine men." In the summer of 1909, right on the heels of the sustained evangelistic effort, a group of Native people, including a number from this same reserve who had shown interest in Christianity, "went away to a lonely spot and there celebrated heathen rites." What made this especially disconcerting, was that one of the participants in these activities was a recent graduate from the Birtle school who had "professed faith in Christ." This wholesale "return to heathenism" had left the missionary at Prince Albert, Jonathan Bailey, without a translator, severely limiting his ability to carry on his ministry. The advice and support he got from the Mission Committee was that he was "dealing with aborigines who are primitive in their morals as in all else." He would "require a little patience."[67]

In the first decade of the 20th century the Soul Society burst onto the scene, first noted by Presbyterians when Kate Gillespie reported a spiritual movement that anticipated the coming of the imminent return of the Messiah. Upon the Messiah's return, all those who were not found wearing traditional Native clothing would be expelled from the land. The Messiah's return would also mean the return of the buffalo and other wild animals of the plains in sufficient numbers for the Native people to be self-sufficient. Gillespie said of this movement, "so the true Gospel of Jesus was blotted out and heathen worship of the same Jesus substituted." John Thunder reported the opposition that he experienced from members of the Soul Society in his work at Pipestone, writing that although the society had picked up certain Christian terms, he viewed it as a return to Native religion.[68]

With these "temptations" lurking on the reserves ready to ensnare the graduates of the residential school system, it was clear to many missionaries that it was necessary to see dramatic improvement in the conditions on the reserves before "it may be safe to send our graduates back to their homes." The reserve could so easily undo all of the good that the schools had accomplished. In response to this problem, W.H. Graham, the Indian Agent for the reserves clustered around the File Hills School, developed the File Hills School Colony. Open only to the graduates of the residential school system, it regimented the colonists' lives in its elimination of all Native social and cultural life, replacing it with baseball, brass bands and the like. The ultimate purpose of the Colony was to make self-sufficient farmers. And that it accomplished very well. The star of the colony was Fred Dieter, a graduate of the File Hills School. Dieter did so well that he was able to employ a farm hand who was white. It was in Dieter's home that the Presbyterian congregation met before erecting its own church building. Traveling ministers were not an unfamiliar sight at the Dieter kitchen table.[69]

Kate Gillespie, after her resignation from the File Hills School, stayed involved with the Colony, assisting at the weddings of former students, using her position as the wife of the provincial and then federal cabinet minister to get the Colony the support it needed. A Presbyterian church was built on the colony and by 1921, there was a deaconess appointed fulltime to work among the families. She lived in the manse, which was right next to the church.[70]

The delicate balance between Christianity and Native tradition that Keeseekoowenin and George Flett had worked out had been rejected in the drive to turn Native people into productive members of society. The Presbyterian Church's discouragement at their inability to reach the Native people with their double message of educational and spiritual salvation is evidenced by the fact that no new work among the Native people was started after 1905. The enthusiasm that led to expansion of the church's mission in other areas was clearly lacking from the church's mission among the Native people of the prairies.

CONCLUSION

Reading through the reports of the Presbyterian church's work among the Native people in Manitoba and Saskatchewan reveals a gradual eroding of the middle ground between the 1880s and 1911. There was increasingly less willingness on the part of the missionaries to try to bridge their way into the Native culture, language, or way of life. But the value of finding that middle ground was still recognized until 1909. That year, with the report from the Presbyterian Indian Workers Conference, the educational goals of transforming Native children into functional and contributing members of the dominant society began to take precedence in the actions and decision making of the missionaries and the mission leaders in Toronto. The events of 1912 and 1914 guaranteed that educational and social values would become the first priority in the future mission. The Foreign Mission Committee, which had been responsible for the work in the residential schools and on the reserves, gave that work to the Home Mission Board, so that the Foreign Mission Committee could spend all of its time working on mission outside of Canada. With this change in responsibility came a new emphasis in the ministry. Up until 1912, the reports to the General Assembly about Native work almost equally balanced descriptions of evangelistic work with accounts of the work of the schools. The principals of the schools were seen as missionary-principals. After 1912, that changed. Descriptions of the educational work took up 80 percent or more of the reports, and the principals were solely principals who on rare occasions did mission work outside of the schools. A further organizational change took place in 1914. That year, the Women's Foreign Missionary Society and the Women's Home Missionary Society merged to create the Women's Missionary Society (Western Division); with that shift the church's entire mission among Native peoples became de facto, the work of the WMS. Only once in the 10 years from 1915 leading up to church union did the Home Mission Board itself report to the Assembly anything about the work among Native peoples, and then only to report on negotiations being held with the government about who was financially responsible for the schools. Thus emphasis of the mission was on the schools and education of young Native people; it was no longer about proclaiming good news about Jesus and raising up a Native Presbyterian church.

As this shift took place, salvation became measured in very material terms. It was the mission work of the church to teach the Native people self-reliance so they would "overcome as far as possible the old habit of looking to Church and State to feed and clothe them." The success of the mission work was to be seen in the improved standard of living of Native people, who now had "linoleum, iron beds, spring mattresses, sideboards, etc., that will compare favourable with the average white settler's home." When the Chief of the Rolling River Reserve in Manitoba became a

Christian in 1913, the proof that he had truly turned his life around, was his comment, "Now that I have God in my heart I want to see all the children of the reserve educated." As the evangelistic task shifted from the salvation of people souls to the social, material, and educational "uplift" of the Native people, the church moved from proclaiming the gospel of Jesus Christ to proclaiming a form of Canadian social religion. And with that change the church lost the spiritual reason for being involved in this mission venture among the Native people. Therefore as early as 1917, long-time missionaries among the Native people were voicing aloud the question, "Do you think the Church wishes to keep up the work?"[71]

In 1909, Jonathan Beverly, missionary at the Round Plain Indian Reserve near Prince Albert, wrote, "Sometimes we are disappointed, by not having any real decision for Christ, but we believe, that if we sow the seed in the Spirit of Christ we shall assuredly see in future the results."[72] The future results were certainly not what Beverly would have hoped for. In 1920, the Board of Home Mission and Social Service of the Presbyterian Church put together a briefing document to support their claim for additional funding. The authors estimated that there were 106,000 "Indians" in Canada. Of this number, 3,000 were connected with Presbyterian mission work. There were approximately 500 communicant members of the Presbyterian Church among 18 mission fields operated by the church on the prairies. At the time the church was operating five day schools with a total of 130 students; in total, there were approximately 7,750 Native students in day schools in Canada. The Women's Missionary Society was managing seven residential schools, five on the Prairies and two in British Columbia, with a total of 400 students; there were 2,500 students in church-managed residential schools across Canada.[73] These figures indicate just how small a role the Presbyterian Church has played in the Christian mission to the Native people.

One lasting heritage is the presence, in the year 2000, the Presbyterian Church still has on the Mistawasis Reserve in Saskatchewan and the Birdtail Reserve in Manitoba. These ministries date back to the work of John McKay and Solomon Tunkasuiciye, Native people who did ministry among their own people in the name of Jesus Christ. The longevity of these ministries indicates that commissioning indigenous missionaries to carry the gospel to their own people is a highly effective missionary strategy, one that was recognized and valued over a hundred years ago.

File Hills Native Residential School, circa 1907.
(Presbyterian Church Archives)

Birtle Native Residential School, circa 1910.
It was against government policy for parents to visit their children
at the school, but the school principal was allowing this visit to take place.
(Presbyterian Church Archives)

Miss Baker and visitors at Makoce Waste School House,
near Prince Albert, SK, late 1890's.
(United Church of Canada/Victoria University Archives, 93.049P/1681)

Indian women and Mrs. McEwen of the Women's Foreign Missionary Society,
Pipestone, MB, 1909.
(United Church of Canada/Victoria University Archives, 93.049P/1952S)

Staff and students at the Regina Industrial School
which operated from 1890 to 1911, photo from 1909.
(United Church of Canada/Victoria University Archives, 93.049P/1684N)

"...no mission to these people?": The Presbyterian Mission to Non-Anglo-Saxon Immigrants

The charts at the 1913 Pre-Assembly Congress clearly raised the question. One entitled "Canada: The Melting Pot of the Nations" outlined that the immigrants arriving in Canada in 1912 came from 59 different cultural groups. In 1912, 395,804 people came to Canada seeking a new home. In 1911, 350,000 had arrived. The banner asked the question, "Will they make Christian Canadians?" Answering its own question, the banner issued a challenge, "It is the Church's Problem." The flood of immigrants had begun in earnest in 1903, when over 120,000 new arrivals came seeking a place to live, increasing the population of Canada by 2.3 percent in one year. In 1912, immigration increased Canada's population by 5 percent in a single year. The impact of immigration was even more evident on the prairies, where three years in a row (1911-1913) immigration increased the population by 10 percent each year. In 1912 alone, 140,000 new people arrived to set up their homes in the three prairie provinces. What this meant to the longer term residents of the prairies, people who had been homesteading or living in a town for a decade or more, is that every third person greeted on the street, met at the grain elevator, or whose children went to school, had not been there three years earlier. Many a prairie town felt off kilter, swept along in a tide of humanity that was shaking the very fabric of the prairie community, and the church on the prairies was also shaken.[1]

Even more unsettling, this tide of humanity was made up of people from dozens of cultural groups that the average Anglo-Saxon Canadian may never of heard of before, let alone met in person. The *Record*, in 1919, published some facts about the west: more than 40 percent of the population was not of British origin; 58 different dialects were spoken in Manitoba; one third of the population was non-Anglo-Saxon, and over 100 different religious denominations, sects, or groups were represented. The linguistic and cultural challenges faced by township governments and school districts were enormous, as they sought to respond to the needs of the residents of their township who might speak as many as eighteen different languages. Just as prairie communities were struggling to find ways of responding to this influx, so was the Presbyterian Church. This chapter outlines how the church responded to the new Canadians of non-Anglo-Saxon background, describing the ministries undertaken, and marking the changes that took place in the mission philosophy.[2]

"Work Among Foreigners," 1885-1896

The first group of non-English speaking immigrants the Presbyterian Church sought intentionally to reach was the Icelandic community. Robertson reported to the Assembly in 1888, that no missionary society was reaching out to this community, "and it is feared that they must suffer spiritually if not looked after." Although they were "Lutheran in religion," Robertson believed that the Presbyterian Church had a responsibility to minister to the "Icelanders," as he called them. To that end Robertson had found Jonas Johnson, "[o]ne of themselves, a young man of good ability, of great zeal and Christian earnestness…a man of the right spirit, and he is to be our first missionary in this work."[3]

A year later, Robertson could report that a church had been built for the Icelandic mission, with a seating capacity of 200. There was a membership roll of 58, with an average attendance of 120 at Sunday worship. In 1891, Johnson was ordained and was therefore "capable of discharging all ministerial functions" at Martin Luther Church, the name chosen for the Icelandic-speaking congregation. The congregational name makes it easy to wonder how firm were the Presbyterian roots. It was a clear indication of how little denominationalism mattered to Robertson and the other Presbyterian clergy in the West during this time. The bottom line was, immigrants were arriving in the west "for whose religious well-being no adequate provision was made." The Presbyterian leadership in the west believed that their church had a responsibility to make such a provision.[4]

In 1892, tragedy struck the Icelandic mission. Jonas Johnson died. And the church lost a pastor "of deep convictions, of good preaching power, evangelical in his views and tireless in advancing the welfare of his countrymen." Johnson had left a legacy; his brother took over the leadership of Martin Luther Church and two young men from that congregation were studying theology at Manitoba College. These two had summer charges in Icelandic communities on the shores of Lake Manitoba and Lake Winnipeg.[5]

The success of the Icelandic Mission gave Presbyterians a model to copy when seeking to minister to other non-English speaking groups. Instead of seeking to assimilate the ethno-cultural grouping into an existing English speaking congregation, they sought to find a spiritually gifted individual who spoke the language of the people group they were seeking to reach. Through mentoring and some formal course work, this individual was trained on the job to be the minister of the new ethnic congregation. Over time it was hoped that the congregation would be drawn ever more closely into the Presbyterian Church. This is the model that is presently used in starting up churches among ethnic groups around the world, which is often referred to as the "homogeneous unit principle." It is remarkable that the Presbyterian Church and other Canadian Churches were using this model in the late 1800's, a full 70 years before those who study and plan mission methods defined it as the way to plant churches in ethnic communities.[6]

This model became a central part of the Presbyterian Church's response to the growing "foreign" population on the prairies. By the summer of 1894 there were: a German speaking minister working among German immigrants near Edmonton; a Hungarian speaking minister, recruited from Hungary, ministering among Hungarians at Bekevar near Whitewood, Saskatchewan; and a Scandinavian missionary ministering to three Scandinavian communities also near Whitewood, Saskatchewan. The recruitment happened in one of two ways. One way was to seek out among the newly arrived immigrants people with spiritual enthusiasm and leadership skills, who could be trained either on the job, or more formally at Manitoba College. Robertson was always on the look out for such gifted young people among recently arrived immigrants. He was prepared to offer them free tuition at Manitoba College and guaranteed summer employment during their schooling. The other model was direct recruitment from the home country. As the first wave of Hungarians began to arrive on the prairies in the early 1890's, Robertson wrote to Dr. Andras Moody, a minister of Hungarian Reformed Church in Budapest. Moody was able to recommend a gifted clergy person, who Robertson then recruited and enabled to emigrate to Canada. A variation on this approach occurred in 1895, when a group of Germans of the Reformed faith near Edmonton asked for a minister. Robertson was able to find and recruit a highly recommended person from the Reformed Church in the United States.[7]

In early 1901, James Robertson toured Europe visiting Budapest, Debreczen, Kinusenburg, Vienna, Prague, and Berlin looking for Hungarian, Ukrainian, Austrian, Czech, and German speaking clergy to minister on the prairies. He reported that only four suitable clergy had been found, although many more than that offered themselves, "The same dearth of suitable men for Christian work is found on the continent that prevails in Britain; and the moral conditions existing on the Continent demand that the utmost care be exercised in the selection of men." Robertson was particularly concerned about finding Ukrainians to work among that group which was starting to flow on to the prairies. But his trip to Europe had convinced him, "[i]t seems almost impossible to get suitable men for the

Galicians from Europe." Robertson had come to the conclusion that if a Ukrainian and German-speaking professor could be found who would teach at Manitoba College, "He would solve this problem for us, for Canadian-trained missionaries would best meet the needs of western Canada." Robertson was more and more convinced that western Canada was a unique situation and that only a Canadian trained—or more specifically western Canadian-trained—clergy could truly meet the needs of the western church.[8]

ROBERTSON'S VISION
James Robertson's vision for this "work among foreigners" was seemingly very simple. He argued:

> Our duty to provide for the children of the Church is evident, but what about the foreigners that come to sojourn among us? The German and Hungarian, the Icelander and Scandinavian, are sturdy Protestants. The boast of catholicity on our part...should be exemplified in caring for those who are not otherwise provided for, whatever their nationality or faith. To be a Presbyterian a man [sic] must not of necessity talk Gaelic, or broad Scotch, or hail from Ulster. The lack of an adequate revenue prevented us from undertaking this work in the past; the time, however, has come for broadening the scope of our work, and so showing that Presbyterianism is not a creed of race or locality, but adapted for all nationalities and races. It stands high in the estimation of Western people for its energy and adaptability; let us shew them its catholicity![9]

Presbyterianism was not Scottish or Irish; in fact the church should not limit itself to ministering to only people who claimed a Reformed heritage. Anyone on the prairies whose spiritual needs were uncared for was the responsibility of the Presbyterian Church. The catholicity of the Presbyterian church would be shown as it moved outside of its traditional constituency to ministry to all peoples regardless of "nationality or faith." This catholicity had a goal, as Robertson articulated in his 1889 Report to the General Assembly. After outlining the various ethnic groups that were arriving in the west, Robertson wrote:

> But the question arises whether the great work of State and Church is not to grind up, assimilate, and Christianize this heterogeneous mass. Schools and colleges powerfully help this process; but no power is superior to the Gospel of Christ in this great work, to give the Gospel to these people is, it must be repeated, the first duty of the Canadian Church today.[10]

The church and the state were to work together in the assimilation of the new immigrants, creating one nation with one vision out of the "heterogeneous mass." While working hand in hand, the church and the state had distinct roles to play in the process. The church was to proclaim the gospel, so that people were brought into a unity by the most powerful unifying force in the world, Jesus Christ. It was only in a common commitment to Jesus Christ that unity could be found. Robertson, and the many others impacted by his views, believed that a common faith was the building block that would lead to a common nationhood. Therefore he could write,

> If the West is dotted over with colonies, whose religious welfare is neglected, the whole religious tone must be lowered. Can we afford this? Have we as Presbyterians and as patriots no mission to these people? If the object of missions is to save souls, where could mission money be better invested than in giving the gospel to these strangers?[11]

The religious welfare of the west was an issue of patriotism. One needed only to look south to the United States to see what resulted from not taking seriously the religious welfare of the immigrants. "Christianity has suffered irreparable losses in the United States by early neglect; and Western Canada has not entirely escaped.[12] The American west and the impact of American immigration to the Canadian west became common concerns in the reports written by Presbyterian missionaries describing what might happen in the Canadian west if the church did not take its responsibility to proclaim the gospel seriously.

Thus in the period from 1885 through 1907 the Presbyterian Church saw itself as reaching out with the gospel to the non-English speaking immigrants regardless of their religious background. In so doing, not only were they saving souls, they were also creating a common nationhood built on a common commitment to Jesus Christ. It was a work that the church alone could do; it was a work that needed to precede the building of a nation.

Even though the church was called to minister to all immigrants regardless of their mother tongue or cultural background, Robertson had strong opinions about who was arriving in the Canadian west. Robertson knew that the west needed more people if it were to play the significant role in Canada that he envisioned for it. This made him, and all who listened to him, open to the immigration of non-English speaking peoples to western Canada. In 1900, Robertson wrote in his 1900 report to the Assembly about the Ukrainian and Doukhobour immigrants who were just beginning to arrive in the west:

As far as one can judge, these people are blessed with average
health, and are men and women of good physique. They do not
flock to cities and towns, but stay on the land, and they gladly
accept land that Canadians and others rejected years ago. Men and
women are not afraid of hard work; they are helping to solve the
"servant girl" problem, and the problem of cheap labour. They
have much to learn yet, but they are apt pupils, and because of
their industry and thrift, and their inexpensive mode of living,
they are sure to prosper in worldly matters.[13]

This is a very positive assessment of a group of immigrants whose arrival
was causing controversy in many circles. Robertson believed it was important that "care should be exercised in getting the right kind of people to
become settlers." He knew who should not get in: "None over thirty-five
years of age should be encouraged to come, nor should the diseased be
allowed to join any party upon the plea that Canada possesses a healthy
climate." Given the harshness of the winters in western Canada, Robertson
believed that people from northern Europe and northern Britain should
be courted as possible immigrants to Canada. He cared little about their
ethnic background; he was more concerned about their ability to adapt to
the Canadian west.[14]

How the immigrants were settled concerned Robertson. In discussing
the Scottish crofters, Robertson expressed the view that:

Instead of locating them as a colony it would be better to give
them locations among other settlers. They then would be able to
learn farming in a much shorter time, they could get work more
readily, be able to maintain their families, and parents and children
would be far more apt to acquire the English language and so be
more readily absorbed among the rest of the population.[15]

A Presbyterian clergyperson, born in Scotland and who spoke Gaelic, was
advocating that Gaelic-speaking immigrants should be assimilated into the
English-speaking culture. Robertson believed that this absorption into
mainstream Canadian culture not only helped the immigrants, it assisted
the church in reaching the immigrants with the good news of the gospel.
For this was his ultimate goal; to have people live Christian lives.

Robertson held in tension his commitment to the rapid assimilation
of immigrant groups into mainstream Canadian culture and his missionary
passion to respond to the spiritual needs of the immigrants. While he believed that immigrants should learn English as fast as possible, he was committed to finding and recruiting ethnic language speakers to be the clergy
in ethnic speaking congregations. Robertson did not see any contradiction

here. It was more important that the immigrants hear the Gospel proclaimed in a language that they could understand than it was for them to
be culturally assimilated. If the new arrivals were assimilated into the culture without making a commitment to the gospel of Jesus Christ, the church
would have failed in its primary task.

Local Congregations Respond

Ultimately the church's response to non-English speaking immigrants took
place at the level of the local congregation or presbytery. It was in the
prairie communities that people made face-to-face contact with immigrants who came from another part of the world, speaking another language. The immigrants came from parts of the world that many Canadians
of British origin knew little or nothing about—Russia, parts of the Austro-
Hungarian Empire, and China. Many of these immigrants brought with
them religious commitments and socio-economic lifestyles which Cana-
dian-born Presbyterians found strange. It was these strangers that Presbyterian congregations across the prairies were called to welcome. There was a
concerted effort to encourage the Presbyterians who sat in the pews Sunday by Sunday to actively work at befriending the "New Canadians." New
Canadians was the most appropriate name, it was argued, for "They do not
come as travellers through our domains, as do foreigners. They come as
home seekers, to live here, and their children after them." New Canadians
were to be met in the presence of the boy delivering milk, the seamstress
hired to make a dress, the customer at the counter. These people were to be
befriended, for they were people just like the older Canadians: "with the
same heart hunger for the old home," and "the same human ambitions for
themselves and their children." The challenge went out, "Let us show our-
selves friendly to these lonely ones and interpret our Christian convictions
to them in the terms of friendship and service." In 1913, the Board of
Social Service and Evangelism endorsed the widespread use of the YMCA's
"system of teaching English to non-Anglo-Saxons." The course was designed to be used by lay people in their contacts with neighbours and
domestic help who came from non-English speaking countries. By proclaiming the gospel through friendship and caring service, a door of opportunity to speak the Christian message would be opened.[16]

Certainly friendship and service were important parts reaching out to
new Canadians on a one-on-one basis, but the fact remained, the local
congregation had to find a way to draw people from the wide diversity
existing on an increasingly multi-cultural prairie. In 1903 in Yorkton, Saskatchewan, there were 18 different languages spoken by people in town
and its neighbourhood. This multilingual population would have created a
substantial challenge for any local Presbyterian congregation or minister
seeking to carry out their ministry. In the first quarter of the 20th century,

most Presbyterian clergy in rural or small town areas of the prairies had three- to six-point charges. One point on a pastoral charge might be in a town that was entirely English-speaking, while a rural point might have a strong non-English speaking presence but not be large enough to justify the hiring of a ethnic-speaking clergy person. So the local minister would be expected to meet the needs of both congregations. As well, during the rapid population growth on the prairies, a small community's ethnic mix could change quite dramatically. In southern Manitoba, near Winkler, the pastoral charge of Mountain City in 1905 was "a rapidly diminishing…mission to English speaking people" because Mennonite households were buying additional land from "the Canadian farmers." The Mennonite community was not fertile ground for Presbyterians. Attempting to put the best possible face on the situation, it was reported, "Out of this work no permanent Presbyterian congregation can spring, but if spiritual life is deepened among these people and some are led to Christ, the labour of our missionary will not have been in vain." It was in situations of often unpredictable change, that clergy and congregations were called to minister.[17]

In most cases, as non-English speaking immigrants moved into areas that already had Presbyterian congregations, the local minister committed himself to reaching out to these new Canadians. It was reported from Mountain City, in the Rock Lake Presbytery, "As these newer regions are settled by Icelanders and people from northern Europe, and the missionary spends a large proportion of his time amongst them, this might take rank among our other missions to settlers of foreign origin." Ministers were expected to adapt their focus to meet the needs of the community in which they were located, even if that meant doing cross-cultural ministry. Generally, clergy within the Presbyterian Church believed that whoever was resident in the community, regardless of ethnic background, was part of the parish and deserved ministry. In 1909, the minister at Buchanan, Saskatchewan, noted that he was trying to reach, "considerable Doukhobours who have broken away from the thraldom of the community and are known as Free Doukhobours." It was commonplace to read in the Annual Reports of the Home Mission Committee (hereafter HMC) of Presbyterian congregations where a variety of ethnic groups worshipped together in a single service. One unnamed congregation in rural Alberta in 1910 had an average worship attendance of 50 people, representing 10 to 12 different countries of origin.[18]

At times, the movement of a large number of non-English speaking immigrants into an area meant that the style of ministry had to change. The Mountain City pastoral charge in southern Manitoba reported in 1906, "It is for the most part work among foreigners whose knowledge of the English language is limited. The best work is done by house to house visitation and distribution of literature."[19] The church was coming to understand that if they were going to minister effectively to these new Canadians the process would be a long and slow one, a process of house to house visiting, rather than calling people to attend church in a language they did not fully understand. This ability to respond in a flexible manner to the changing situation required a great deal of wisdom and patience on the part of both clergy and congregational leaders.

It was at the community and congregational level that church leaders saw the conflicts between various ethnic groups. The Hilton pastoral charge in southern Manitoba was a notoriously difficult charge. It was "made up of English-speaking people and Crofters, and these two elements do not work very harmoniously together." These tensions were also present when what had been an ethnic enclave was inundated by English-speaking settlers. The minister at Esterhazy, Saskatchewan, raised concerns about what would happen as English and Irish immigrants moved into what had been an almost exclusively Hungarian community.[20]

It was also at the congregational level that church leaders experienced conflict between the new Canadians and the Presbyterian system. The new immigrants often did not understand how the Presbyterian church functioned. The 1910 report from Otthon in the Yorkton Presbytery typifies this difficulty,: "Many of these foreign colonies are kept back by not getting sooner into line with the mode of work of the Church with which they become associated in this country." The structures of elders and sessions, presbyteries and home mission committees, were all a strange world to these newly-minted Presbyterians. Many of the new Canadians came from countries where there was a state church, and the free church approach of the Canadian religious scene was a new experience. In Esterhazy, Saskatchewan it was reported, "There are many Hungarian and Bohemian families who adhere to our church. These while adding to the work of the field, have not so far added very much to its revenue." The HMC's policy of moving congregations from being mission charges to augmented charges to self-supporting charges meant little to those new Presbyterians who came from state-supported churches. The free church tradition was outside their experiential frame, creating tensions between the budget watchers on the HMC and congregations of new Canadians.[21]

Despite these difficulties and tensions, virtually none of the reports from congregations, presbyteries, synods, or Assembly make derogatory comments about the non-Anglo-Saxon immigrants. In fact, the 1908 comment that in the High River Presbytery, "There are practically none of the inferior grades of European immigrants—i.e. Galicians, etc." is noteworthy because it is largely the exception to what was a generally an open response to non-English speaking immigrants prior to World War I. That is not to say that the church encouraged the new Canadians to maintain their culture and language. Most presbyteries in the west would have agreed with the view that "we have a tremendous problem to face both in evangelization and in citizenship." The church was an instrument in the process of the Canadianization of the immigrants, to Christianize—more precisely to Protestantize—was to Canadianize. By the same token, however, the church used the broader society's desire for the Canadianization of these immigrant groups as a means to their evangelization. This double focus that we already noted in Robertson's vision could still be found expressed into the 1910's by people like W.D. Reid, superintendent of missions for Alberta, who wrote in 1912, "Among all these peoples our church is at work, endeavouring to give them the Gospel. This is the material out of which we are endeavouring to build a nation, which shall be established in righteousness, whose God is the Lord." To teach English to Ukrainian or Chinese immigrants was part of an assimilation process, to use the gospel of Mark as the text to teach English reading was to evangelize. For most Presbyterians this was a natural connection to make.[22]

THE 1914 SURVEY

At the height of the immigrant flood, in order to gain an understanding of the breadth of the challenge that faced the church, A. S. Grant, general secretary of the Board of Home Missions in November 1913 requested all Presbyteries to survey the "Non-Anglo-Saxon Races" settled in their district. The Presbyteries' responses to this request provide a snapshot of how Presbyteries and local congregations were responding to the influx and the attitudes held towards the newly arrived immigrants.

In Manitoba, the primary concern was the Ukrainian community (who were called Ruthenians in the 1913 survey). The Dauphin Presbytery knew of over 13,000 Ukrainians who had settled in their area; there were three Presbyterian Missions to the Ukrainian community that were within Dauphin Presbytery: Ethelbert, Sifton, and Venlaw. The challenge presented by the Ukrainian community was so large that the Icelandic community in the Swan River region was largely ignored. The Presbytery of Brandon reported that they had no great challenges, having a minister in Brandon ministering to the Ukrainian community.[23]

In Saskatchewan, the Doukhobour community remained an engima. From Yorkton Presbytery it was reported, "No church has done anything amongst the Doukhobors (sic)." There was not even a recognition that they might have their own faith community. The Saskatoon Presbytery did recognize that the Doukhobour community had worship as they noted a small Doukhobour village "with their own church east of Warman." The call of the gospel to spread the good news about Jesus to all people needed to be balanced with the ability to recognize the new-to-Canada religious commitments of some of the immigrant groups as Christian. For example, the Regina Presbytery saw the Ruthenian community as a legitimate mission field because, they "have no church of their own." But the "Roumanian" (sic) community had a church in the city of Regina and therefore was to be responded to differently. The new-to-Canada faith communities were checked out by Presbyterians in the west, as the Regina Presbytery reported in its study, "Nazarene appears to be a Protestant organization." A similar need to recognize the work of other Christian churches existed with the Scandinavian (more precisely Swedish) communities dotted through the Yorkton, Prince Albert, and Qu'Appelle regions. These communities were having their spiritual needs adequately cared for by the Lutheran Church. The German communities in Regina and the Qu'Appelle also had sufficient care provided by either Lutheran or Roman Catholic clergy. Both Moose Jaw and Saskatoon Presbyteries were seeking ways to minister to the Chinese community in these cities. In Saskatoon it was reported that "many churches" were working with the Chinese, while in Moose Jaw the Methodists and Presbyterians were working together, seeing "the Meth[odists] take the lead." It was not enough to simply recognize the work of others; at times it was necessary to assist and support other denominations in their ministry.[24]

The dominant concern in Saskatchewan, as it had been in Manitoba, was the Ukrainian community from Northern Saskatchewan, the Prince Albert Presbytery noted that the "colony" at Petrofka "is growing rapidly and demands immediate attention." Presbyterian hospitals had been set up at Wakaw and Canora, to provide the community with basic health care and as a means to reaching into the community through a ministry of care and presence. An additional group to create interest was the Hungarian communities at Kipling and Esterhazy, where ethnic Hungarian Presbyterian clergy were working.[25]

The need to balance the mission of the Presbyterian church with recognizing the work of other Christian denominations, was also clear in Alberta. From Medicine Hat it was reported that of the 500 foreigners in the city, "German speaking people predominate; being cared for by two Lutheran Churches and a well organized German Evangelical Church. Not necessary for our Church to attempt any work here." That did not mean, however, that Presbyterians had no responsibility to provide for the spiritual needs of people whose most natural connection was not to the Presbyterian Church. From Edmonton, it was noted that the Scandinavian and German communities "adhere chiefly to the Lutheran, the German Reformed, and Baptist churches...These churches seem to be making an honest but inadequate effort to meet the spiritual needs of their people." That meant that there was room for the Presbyterian Church to send clergy to minister among this traditionally Lutheran community. A Scandinavian minister from the United States had offered to work with "his people" at the Castor and

Coronation areas, but his offer was rejected because "all the people speak English and read it too." Once the new Canadians had learned English and could therefore understand sermons preached in English, there was no need to provide them ethnic clergy. The Finnish community, as distinct from the Scandinavian community, provided a number of Alberta Presbyteries with challenges as did the Russian and Slavic communities. Painting with a broad brush, the Medicine Hat Presbytery described their challenges, "What is wanted is someone to look after the spiritual interests of the Russians, whose children have no chance of being educated. The Norwegians are of a religious nature, but the Russians and Finns and Polish Germans are not." The Ukrainian community was the concern of the Edmonton Presbytery, within whose bounds the Vegreville Hospital was located.[26]

In the area covered by the Edmonton Presbytery there were two small black communities numbering about eighty families and 400 to 500 people in total. A Presbyterian missionary had been invited by some white settlers to hold worship services in the area in one of the settler's homes, "on condition that no negros [sic] attended the services." There were similar problems in the public school as the whites in the community would not allow their children to attend school with black children. The leadership of the Edmonton Presbytery was at a loss as to how the church should respond to this situation which they clearly saw as a problem.[27]

MINISTRY WITH SPECIFIC ETHNIC GROUPS AFTER 1896
In attempting to respond to the multilingual, multi-ethnic world of the Prairie provinces, the Presbyterian church continued their earlier practice of recruiting, training, and ordaining speakers of various languages where the numbers warranted such a response.

THE HUNGARIANS
Some work had been done among the Hungarians at Bekevar prior to 1896, but the missionary had returned to Hungary and no ministry was attempted again until 1903. That year, Louis Kovacsi reopened the ministry at Bekevar, which quickly became a congregation of approximately 40 families. In the summer of 1904, he was invited to the Crooked Lakes area south of Prince Albert to minister among 200 newly arrived Hungarian families, half of whom were Roman Catholic. These Hungarian-speaking immigrants moving into the Wakaw (a Native word meaning "bent lake") area, arrived the same year that the Women's Home Missionary Society (hereafter WHMS) opened the Anna Turnbull Hospital. The hospital had been intended to minister almost entirely to the Ukrainian community already present, but as the region was further settled by people from various cultural groups, it was clear that the hospital would have a broader mandate.[28]

By 1906, there were four Hungarian-speaking congregations: at Otthon (near Yorkton), Bekevar (south of Whitewood), Wakaw (south of Prince Albert), and in Winnipeg (the congregation worshipped in Point Douglas Presbyterian Church.) Kovacsi, who was a student at Manitoba College, had in the summer of 1905 worked to resolve some significant internal congregation struggles at Otthon, and upon returning to school that fall had begun the congregation in Winnipeg. Early in the Presbyterian Church's ministry among the Hungarians, a problem arose that would be a continual area of conflict. In 1907, the Hungarian congregations provided no financial support to their clergy, leaving the HMC to carry the financial responsibility. At Otthon, the congregation contributed generously to the building of church, but they would not pay their minister. Carmichael, superintendent of missions, stated, "From this time on generous support of their missionaries should be required and expected." By 1916, the problem was so severe, that Colin Young, district superintendent for Northern Saskatchewan, wrote, "if the present policy of supporting almost entirely the ministers of non-English speaking peoples is continued, the people will look upon this support as their right and will fail to learn that one of the largest gifts in Christian experience is the gift of benevolent service." The clash of cultural expectations was now clear; the voluntary Presbyterian tradition in which the congregation supported the minister financially was the exact opposite of the state-church experience of the Reformed Church of Hungary, where the state provided the resources needed to pay the clergy. Despite this ongoing conflict, mission among the Hungarian-speaking community continued.[29]

In 1910, the Rev. John Kovach was appointed a special assistant to the superintendent of mission to take two months off from his ministry at Otthon to visit the other Hungarian-speaking congregations in the west. This was an attempt to do two things: first, to solidify the Presbyterian church's ministry among the Hungarian-speaking community; and secondly, to respond to the seemingly never-ending struggles that affected these congregations. It was hoped that Kovach, "a well educated gentleman" who spoke English fluently, would be able to solve the problems of his countrymen in a way that would please both them and the English Canadian leadership of the Home Mission Board. Kovach was to stand in the gap, bridging both cultures. The problem that led to this appointment was a series of accusations from members of Bekevar congregation that their minister was a "Spiritualist" and not a Christian. Kovach's solution to the problem was to switch the minister at Bekevar with the minister of the Hungarian-speaking congregation in Winnipeg, the Rev. Louis Kovachy. This only made matters worse, as the elders of the congregation in Winnipeg rose up en masse to reject the idea, preferring to leave the denomination than to lose their minister. Kovachy was a remarkable person; the president of the Hungarian Brotherhood of Canada and editor of the *Canadian Hungarian Farmer,* while being the minister of the Winnipeg Hungarian Reformed Church. Kovach's next plan was that he would go to Bekevar and the Rev. J. Kovacs would move from Bekevar to Otthon. By this time, the HMC was convinced that Kovacs was more trouble than he was worth and did not want him in their employ. They listened, however, to Kovach's pleas to give Kovacs one more chance. Late in 1911, Kovach himself had had enough and agreed that Kovacs needed to go. The denominational leadership essentially let the Hungarian congregations deal with this problem on their own, within the parameters of Presbyterianism. Various parties did appeal at times to English-Canadian leaders in the church, whose response was to soothe the ruffled feathers and tell the Hungarians to solve the problem with the help of the local Presbytery.[30]

By 1914, there were three Hungarian-speaking clergy on the prairies. Kovach dreamed of broader ministry. Since 1886 there had been a cluster of Hungarians working the coal mines at Lethbridge, but a specifically ethnic ministry to this group never materialized. As the war started, Louis E. Kovachy was in Winnipeg, ministering to a congregation of 113 members; Louis Kovacy, at Otthon, ministered in a four-point charge that was a mixture of Hungarian and British cultural groups; and John Kovach was at Bekevar, where 157 people were members. By 1924, the Bekevar congregation had grown to 200 members and Kovach was still the minister. The ethnically mixed congregation at Wakaw had an Anglo-Saxon minister.[31]

World War I was a significant moment in the life of the Hungarian community on the prairies. Canada was at war with Germany and the Austro-Hungarian empire, and the Hungarians were viewed in some quarters as potential enemies within the nation. The Hungarian-speaking congregation in Winnipeg had shrunk significantly by the middle of 1915, and the decision was made to close this ministry, believing that the members of the former congregation "would do well to affiliate with existing Protestant congregations" in the city. The clear implication was the Hungarians should join English-speaking congregations. In his 1916 report to the General Assembly, Colin Young, district superintendent for Northern Saskatchewan, laid out his plan for the Hungarian speaking congregation at Otthon: "a Canadian trained minister of British birth should be sent, and his services ought to be in the English language." It was time for the Hungarians and any other immigrants from the enemy nations to be brought into line and their loyalty ensured. Peter Strang, District Superintendent for Southern Saskatchewan, expressed a very different view. He visited the Bekevar church in 1917, describing it as "one of the most beautiful church buildings to be found anywhere in the province." Strang showed great pastoral courage visiting a Hungarian-speaking congregation during the war and speaking of it in such positive terms.[32]

Following the war, the HMC was able to recruit Dr. Frank Hoffmann, a former university professor from Hungary to be the missionary at Otthon. This scope of ministry was too limiting, so Hoffmann launched "The Otthon" a monthly Hungarian-language newspaper, in 1922. Hoffmann was also appointed "missionary at large" to the Hungarian people, keeping in touch with 12 widely scattered groups of Hungarian-speaking Protestants. The Presbyterian Church in Canada recognized among the Hungarians arriving in this country people who were theologically their brothers and sisters, members of the Reformed tradition of Christianity. Sharing common religious roots allowed Canadian Presbyterians to overlook the fact that "[t]heir traditions, customs and manners differ from ours in many ways." And to set as a goal, "Let us give them a chance to develop in their new homes in this free country, and help them all we can. Surely a people with such a history is worthy our best efforts."[33]

The Doukhobours
Four Doukhobour delegates visited Saskatchewan in September 1898 to determine if the land was suitable for their mixed farming methods and cattle raising. And between January and July 1899, 7,500 Doukhobours arrived from Russia. They were pacifist and lived a radical separation of church and state, believing the state should have no role in their faith, which encompassed every aspect of their lives. They were fleeing persecution in Russia where they were regarded as traitors to the state. The Doukhobours were helped by the Society of Friends (Quakers) in England in their move to the Canadian prairies. They were settled in the areas of eastern Saskatchewan: near Yorkton, in the Rosthern area (where they would soon be joined by Ukrainians and Hungarians), and in the Thunder Hill district.[34]

In 1902, J.A. Carmichael, superintendent of missions, heard about the work of Michael Sherbinin, a Russian, who was a gifted linguist, speaking Russian, Ukrainian, German and English fluently. Sherbinin had been converted through the work of the Quakers in England, and it was under their auspices that he was working among the Doukhobours at Rosthern. The HMC decided to support his work, financing the building of a school house at Rosthern to enhance his ministry. After some negotiations with the various parties, Sherbinin became a missionary with the HMC among the Doukhobours east of Rosthern. By 1903, however, Sherbinin's involvement had changed, as the number of Ukrainians arriving in the west continued increasing and the plans were put in place to educate young Ukrainians at Manitoba College to be teachers and ministers. The church settled on Sherbinin as the one who was best qualified to be the professor to the Ukrainians. With Sherbinin's removal to Winnipeg, the ministry among the Doukhobours collapsed. Even if Sherbinin had stayed it is not likely that much impact would have been made on the community. A series of conflicts between Peter Verigin, a charismatic Doukhobour leader, and the government around issues related to communal farming, registration of marriages, divorces and other vital statistics, and the meaning of the "full liberty" they had been promised even as they emigrated to the new land, reached a climax in 1905. That year, approximately three-quarters of the Doukhobours in Saskatchewan followed Verigin to British Columbia.[35]

There was little attempt to do any work among the remaining Doukhobours in Saskatchewan until 1914, when the Rev. George Eccleston, the newly appointed minister at Buchanan, Saskatchewan, near Yorkton, began to visit those Doukhobours who were no longer living communally. Eccleston had learned to speak Russian, which would have immediately broken down some of the barriers. He was particularly interested in having children attend the Sunday School programme of the church, and he began a night school programme to teach English to people from the wide variety of nationalities in the Yorkton area. For three years Eccleston did this ministry among the Doukhobours, while at the same time working with a three-point English speaking charge. In 1917, the work among the Doukhobours was considered important enough to release Eccleston to the work on a fulltime basis. He covered four preaching points, where he led worship in Russian, and he continued to teach English in the night school. Eccleston also made use of the government-mandated half-hour a week of religious instruction, teaching in five different schools. So effective was this model that, in 1923, Lydia Gruchy, a highly gifted graduate of the theological college in Saskatoon, was named the missionary in charge of duplicating in Veregin, Saskatchewan, what Eccleston had done north of Yorkton. It was reported that she had "laid good foundations for successful work in that strong Doukhobour centre."[36]

The Doukhobours were a puzzle to Presbyterians; deeply religious, peaceful, industrious, clean, and "thoroughly honourable in their business dealing," they should have been the perfect neighbours, the perfect new Canadians. But there was the communal land holding, the closely knit community, the foreign language, and the fact that they seemed "easily swayed by forceful, fanatical leaders." In 1903, Carmichael was predicting, "they will speedily become loyal and valuable citizens." By 1924, however the assessment was very different. One Presbyterian summed up the views of many; "their Canadianism is of somewhat doubtful quality."[37]

THE SCANDINAVIANS

Earlier we saw that work was done among the Icelandic people in Manitoba, and work was begun among the Scandinavians in Saskatchewan. Local ministries of this kind continued after 1896. The church in 1908 was seeking a missionary who could preach in both Norwegian and English to minister at Helma outside Vermilion, Alberta, but no one was available who met this description. The church was more successful in finding Mr. Hegh to minister to Swedish speaking people in Calgary. The church was aware that many of the Swedes were Lutheran, but in the time before the Lutheran church had clergy present the Presbyterian Church saw itself as responsible for providing worship services to those who had no opportunity to worship God in their mother tongue.[38]

The work among the Finns was much more widespread. The Rev. A.A. Harju (or Hargu) was working among a group of Finns in 1913 that were located between Sylvan Lake and Rocky Mountain House in Alberta. He had five preaching points, made up of 60 families and 78 single people. By 1919, the ministry had grown to the point where there were two Finnish speaking ministers working fulltime and in the summer of 1918, Miss Luoma assisted them in their work. She visited the sick and helped with the worship services "playing the organ or guitar, singing, teaching, reading the scripture, offering prayer, speaking a few words." Hargu was forced to leave the work in the foothills in 1919, because his children could not get an adequate education in the still pioneer land. In 1922, there was a Finnish-speaking congregation at Manyberries on the western edge of the Cypress Hills, south of Medicine Hat. The non-ordained minister was Miss V.S. Heinonen "who has met a trying situation with singular ability and good judgement." Through the 1920's as the Finnish community in Port Arthur grew, so did the Presbyterian Church's desire to do ministry in their midst.[39]

The Finns were highly politicized. In describing them to Canadians of British origin, Edmison, said, "Perhaps no class of settlers have held more radical views on social problems and labour questions." He went on to say that although most Finns had been Lutheran, many had cut their denominational ties in favour of their "socialistic societies." Despite this challenge the church would continue to reach out to the Finnish community with the gospel, and found "a devoted company of people who have responded readily to evangelistic effort."[40]

OUTREACH TO FRANCOPHONES
The district superintendent for Northern Alberta, William Simons, was always on the lookout for new ministry opportunities among new Canadians or other recent arrivals in the West. He encouraged the clergy in his district to do the same. In 1914, the Rev. J.E. Duclos, the bilingual minister at Erskine Presbyterian Church in Edmonton started a service for French-speaking Protestants. The congregation was made up of settlers from France, Belgium, and Switzerland and young French-Canadians who rejected "the ministrations of the Roman Catholic Church." This ministry was going so well that the Presbytery of Edmonton was seeking ways to free Duclos

from many of his day-to-day responsibilities with the English-speaking congregation so he would have more time for the Francophone congregation.[41]

Word of this ministry reached the ears of "a colony of thirty French-Canadian families" at Bonnyville, in north-eastern Alberta. They wrote to Duclos, asking him to find them a French-speaking Protestant minister. In the spring of 1916, Simons surveyed the situation and determined that such a ministry was indeed worth pursuing. In the fall of that year, Duclos became the missionary among the French-speakers of Bonnyville. During the winter, the Duclos' as a couple taught adults in night school and children in day school to read English, using the Bible as their primary textbook. In a year and a half, 46 people had professed their faith in Jesus Christ, joining the Presbyterian Church. One of the questions that Duclos asked the new members was, "Do you promise to seek forgiveness and reconciliation with those with whom you have quarrelled?" The next morning a number of those who had made this promise "went to be reconciled to neighbours with whom they had been at variance." The work grew rapidly. First, the Swedes, Norwegians, Anglophone Canadians, and Americans joined with the existing Francophone congregation in petitioning for a bilingual church, which became the new model for the charge's ministry. Second, in March, 1917, Simons asked the WMS(WD) to consider opening a hospital at Bonnyville, which was 45 minutes from the closest doctor. A six-bed hospital was opened that October under the direction of Miss Jean Stewart, with Mrs. Duclos as a volunteer. The hospital staff was almost immediately run off their feet as the influenza epidemic hit less than a year after the hospital opened its doors. It was "a haven of refuge to many stricken people who would probably have perished, but for the treatment given by the nurses." Third, the ministry expanded geographically. Duclos, with the help of a couple of lay missionaries, added the Cold Lake area to the charge. And then in 1919, with the Rev. A.C. Rochedieu covering the work at Bonnyville and Cold Lake, Duclos opened a new ministry at St. Paul de Métis, just southwest of Bonnyville. As the town's name indicates it was a firmly Roman Catholic community, and there was strong, even violent, opposition to Duclos' ministry. Duclos persisted, finally being able to acquire land for a church and hospital. The hospital was never built. However, in 1919 the Cold Lake nursing station was added to the work of the Bonnyville Hospital, with a focus on home visiting and public health. In 1921, the Bonnyville Hospital was rebuilt. By 1923, there were 20 preaching points in the pastoral charge built around Cold Lake, Bonnyville, and St. Paul; bearing witness to what could happen when the right combination of missionary, superintendent, and a ready field came together.[42]

Duclos' departure from Edmonton in 1916, had meant the end of the

Francophone worship services. In the fall of 1919, French Protestants were again being gathered for worship under the leadership of a bilingual theology student from Robertson College.

MINISTRY WITH OTHER ETHNO-CULTURAL GROUPS
There were a number of other ethno-cultural groups among whom the Presbyterian Church sought to minister. In 1905, a group of 15 to 20 Armenian families north of Battleford, Saskatchewan, asked the church to provide them with a minister. It has not been possible to determine how the HMC responded to this request. The Presbyterian church's connection with the Armenian community can be seen in the ministry of the Rev. M.G. Garabedian, almost certainly of Armenian descent given his last name, who in 1924 was the minister at Orion south of Medicine Hat. In 1911, a small group of Persians in Fort William (Thunder Bay) asked the District Superintendent to provide them with ministry in their own language. Somehow, the Rev. S.C. Murray was able to find someone to lead this congregation for two or three years.[43]

With great expectations, a group of new Canadians from the province of Bohemia (part of the present-day Czech Republic) built a church building at Broderick, Saskatchewan, in 1910 in anticipation of a minister coming who could preach to them in their mother tongue. Many Bohemians are Reformed Protestants, and it was natural for the group at Broderick to turn to the Presbyterian Church in their search for a minister. *The Home Mission Pioneer* took up the cause of the Bohemians in 1911, outlining the religious history of their homeland, the land of John Hus, a Protestant martyr. "They are," the Pioneer argued, "worth all the attention that the Church can afford to give them." But it was not until 1917 and the arrival of the Rev. John Linka that all these hopes were realized. Linka had been doing post-graduate work in Edinburgh, and was not able to return to his homeland because of the war. The congregation grew rapidly under Linka's ministry, and there were hopes it would soon become self-supporting. Early in 1919, Linka left Canada, and the Home Mission Board "persuaded" the Rev. Oscar Odstricil, who also had been doing post-graduate work at Edinburgh, to come and minister at Broderick. Odstricil was mandated to visit "other colonies" of Bohemians to determine where else clergy should be placed. Given the enormous difficulty in finding clergy to meet the needs of this group of new Canadians, it seemed more likely that those who wanted to continue their connection with the Reformed branch of the Christian faith would need to follow the example of their compatriots in Esterhazy, who simply joined the English-speaking Presbyterian congregation.[44]

THE UKRAINIANS

Of all the groups of New Canadians, the Ukrainian community faced the Presbyterian Church with the greatest challenges, and it was in reaching out to the Ukrainian community that the denomination expended the greatest number of resources. As large numbers of Ukrainian immigrants poured onto the prairies after 1896, the Presbyterian Church realized that the old models for responding to new Canadians would not work, and a new way of responding to this group of immigrants had to be developed. As people without a country (there was no Ukraine until 1905) these people were often called Galicians, after the province in the Austro-Hungarian Empire in which they had resided, or Ruthenians, from the older ethnic name they used for themselves, Rusyn. The Ukrainian community in Canada grew from almost nothing in 1891 to 32,600 in 1901 to 225,600 20 years later. Eighty percent of this population lived on the prairies, settling in large blocks, notably around Teulon, north of Dauphin, and between Shoal Lake and Sandy Lake, all in Manitoba; around Wakaw and Rosthern in Saskatchewan; and around Vegreville, Alberta.[45]

In 1900, James Robertson and Dr. J.T. Reid, a medical missionary, travelled to the Sifton area north of Dauphin to start a mission to the Ukrainians. During this trip, they contacted two leaders in the Ukrainian community whom they knew of through Manitoba College. John Bodrug and John Negrich were part of a small group of Ukrainian intellegensia who were among the new arrivals. These intellectuals dreamed of establishing a distinct Ukrainian identity in the new land. They were told by fellow countryman, Cyril Genik, that the Christian denominations in Canada were offering free theological training to anyone who had completed high school. Genik, Bodrug, and Negrich set out to find which Canadian denomination was compatible with their hopes and theological understanding. The historical tensions between the Uniate Ukrainian Church and the Roman Catholic Church meant attending a Roman Catholic school was immediately rejected. Bodrug, in later life, gave two reasons why they chose the Presbyterian Church. First, they liked Presbyterian worship: the Anglicanism they experienced felt too much like the Catholic Church; Methodists were too pious and said "Amen" during the sermon; while Presbyterians acted with dignity and preached understandable and intelligent sermons. Secondly, the Presbyterian Church was offering assistance to "diverse religious groups of various denominations" on the prairies. The Presbyterian Church had a reputation for trying to reach immigrants who were not part of their traditional ethnic base. Having made their choice, Bodrug, Negrich, and Genik met with the principal of Manitoba College, John Mark King, and Bodrug and Negrich became fulltime students at the college in 1898. Bodrug was quickly recognized as a valuable translator for his Ukrainian compatriots, the church, and the government. In this role, he was able to interpret the two sides to one another. Bodrug's connections in the Presbyterian Church enabled him to get grants from both lay people in Winnipeg and the Church and Manse Fund for the building of two school houses in the Sifton area.[46]

Reid established a medical clinic and dispensary at Sifton, and in exceptional cases had patients stay overnight. He also visited in the surrounding communities and held Bible classes. In early 1902, the dispensary burned down, and Reid moved his base of operation to Ethelbert, northwest of Sifton. The Presbyterian Church's missionary approach to the Ukrainians was different than the approach the church took in reaching any other non-English speaking immigrant group in Canada. The primary focus was not to quickly establish a church, but rather through medical care, meeting the physical needs of the people by supplying them with clothes, mittens, and blankets, and providing educational opportunities for their children. It was hoped that the barriers would be "broken down and prejudices removed." It was the style of ministry that Presbyterians used in reaching people on a foreign missionary field. One of the missionaries wrote, "The people have never shown themselves otherwise than friendly....They are very religious in their own way, and yet in many ways ignorant. They have not much knowledge of the Bible." It was with trepidation that missionaries entered into this endeavour; their fears were allayed as they discovered the Ukrainians to be friendly and even religious. But the missionaries had much work to do because the Ukrainians were unfamiliar with "Canadian" ways; many were illiterate and tremendously impoverished. The evangelization of the Ukrainians would be a slow process,

> It will be the aim of the missionaries to help these people to a knowledge of the needs and the spirit of the gospel. Such a work will not be spectacular; it will need to be carried on with quietness and discretion, with the object of fulfilling and not destroying their religious conceptions, with the supreme aim of bringing them to the knowledge and love of a personal Saviour.[47]

Those working with the Ukrainian community had a strong sense that these were a deeply religious people who simply needed to be shown the full truth of the gospel. It was not necessary to undo their religious beliefs; rather all they needed was to see in Jesus the fulfilment of their religious convictions that would lead them to love Jesus as their personal Saviour.[48]

The medical work among the Ukrainians was turned over to the Women's Home Missionary Society in 1903, when the mandate and membership of the Atlin Nurses Committee was expanded. In 1903, land was purchased at Sifton for a small hospital, which was completed shortly after. The WHMS sent its first nurse to Sifton in 1906. She was also responsible for continuing the work at Ethelbert, which remained a nursing station. In 1904, the Teulon hospital, 40 miles north of Winnipeg, opened with the medically-trained minister, Alexander J. Hunter as medical missionary and his mother as matron. A.J. Hunter continued serving at Teulon until his death in 1940. The Rolland M. Boswell Hospital at Vegreville was opened in 1906, and in 1908 the Rev. George Arthur, M.D., arrived. Arthur was to add the School Home to the mission of the Society in 1910. Also in 1906, the children of the Sunday School at West Church, Toronto, contributed enough funds to build the Anna Turnbull Hospital at Wakaw, Saskatchewan. The pictures of the hospitals at Teulon, Vegreville, and Wakaw show large two-storey houses, with dormer windows on the third floor. The hospitals had three or four wards, with a total of 12 to 15 beds. They were in a word, small country hospitals. Much more ambitious was the Hugh Waddell Memorial Hospital in Canora, Saskatchewan. Not built until 1913, it was an impressive five-floor building with 60 beds. These hospitals were busy places; in 1922, the hospital in Vegreville reported that it had seen more than 3,300 patient days in the previous year. The hospital in Ethelbert and its nursing station in Pine River had handled almost 2,000 cases that year. While each of these facilities provided medical care to all who came through the doors, the focus of the ministry was on reaching the Ukrainian community and other non-Anglo-Saxon groups in the hospital's catchment area. The facilities were funded through fees charged to patients and their families, grants from various levels of government, and funds raised by the WHMS.[49]

The hospitals were run by the female leadership of the WHMS who hired and fired staff, made decisions regarding renovations and additions to the buildings, the purchase of equipment and the expansion of medical services to be offered, and were responsible for the quality of care delivered. Through the years of rapid expansion, 1903-1913, Jean Kipp exercised effective leadership as the WHMS's secretary for Home Mission Hospitals, allowing hospital staff room to make decisions as best fit the needs of the moment and the location, but being in enough contact both by mail and through her frequent visits to the hospitals to sense when staff needed to be held back or re-directed. The WHMS was able to attract well-qualified nurses to their hospital venture. A large number of the nurses were graduates of the Nursing-at-Home programme offered in Toronto; some had gone on to do post-graduate work at other institutions, including Emily Sprague who had gone to New York for further study before being appointed to Wakaw. A number of the nurses had lengthy careers in the hospitals, not always staying in the same facility for their entire medical ministry. Further historical work needs to be done on these nurses so that they move beyond simply being names on a sheet of paper to become more well-rounded individuals.[50]

The medical work was an important part of the church's outreach to Ukrainian community. George Arthur, medical missionary at the Vegreville Hospital, argued such work "should prepare the hearts of these people to receive the gospel, but we must see that we have educated men to live and preach the gospel." It was not enough that the good news was lived out by the medical staff; it had to be spoken. So deeply held was this conviction that for the vast majority of the doctors employed by the WHMS to work in the hospitals were also ordained ministers.[51]

Various women's groups across the Presbyterian Church sought to respond to the needs of the Ukrainian community by collecting clothing to be distributed to those in need. John Bodrug reported that these clothes were well received: "Our children, who had not been able to go outdoors throughout entire winters, now became clothed. Women, who froze in tattered clothing brought from the Old Country, now had a chance, even in winter, to 'appear among the people.'"[52]

The Ukrainian community in western Canada felt abandoned by their spiritual guides in the Ukraine. The mother church, which was Greek Orthodox rite, showed little interest in sending clergy to Canada to meet the spiritual needs of the immigrants. The Roman Catholic Church tried to fill the gap, but many Ukrainians were uninterested in becoming involved with the Roman Catholics given the historical tensions between Roman Catholics and Ukrainian Greek Orthodox. To meet their spiritual needs, a small number of well educated Ukrainians, led by John Bodrug, approached the Presbyterian Church in 1902 with a proposal which they had been working on for some time. The Presbyterian Church was asked to fund the development of an entirely Ukrainian-led denomination. The clergy of the denomination would be trained at Manitoba College. What the Presbyterian Church got out of this was the hope that this denomination would act as a bridge along which the Ukrainian community would move to become Presbyterians. And so, in 1903, the Independent Greek Church of Canada was born. The principle of faith was "The Word of God according to the Old and the New Testaments." The doctrinal basis was the Apostles' Creed, the Nicene Creed, and the Athanasian Creed. The catechism was the Shorter Catechism of the Christian Faith, which had been translated into Ukrainian. The order of service was to be a blended service using the Greek rite but with a longer sermon and greater focus on the Scripture, and the total service length was to be less than 90 minutes. These latter two elements were changes asked for by the Presbyterian leadership. There would be only two sacraments, but the five mysteries would still be part of the church's life. The denomination was to have a synod made up of the clergyperson and one elder from each congregation in the denomination. The elders were to be democratically elected to their position. It was this body which had the power to ordain new ministers. The new denomination would call its clergy priests. This truly remarkable agreement was brokered, on the Presbyterian side, by William Patrick, principal of Manitoba College. Yet nowhere in the constitution of the newly born denomination was there any reference to the Presbyterian Church; this was to be an independent denomination with its own governance structure.[53]

A description of the worship in a Independent Greek Church provides an interesting insight into the blending of the Orthodox and Reformed traditions:

> An onlooker finds difficulty in seeing a Presbyterian element in their service, for with their crosses, pictures, candles, incense, etc., one would think them of the Roman Catholic faith. They have no seats in their church, and remain standing throughout their long service, which lasts from 8 a.m. to 1 or 2 p.m. They prostrate themselves and the minister intones much of the service, as the Independent Greek Church has not discarded the Ritual of John Crysostom [sic] of the Orthodox Greek Church. They get their ritual from John Crysostom, but their theology from Manitoba College.[54]

The liturgy provided the familiar link for the Ukrainians, while the Presbyterian emphasis on the preached word and theological truth was recognized in the preaching and theological formulations of the church.

Some historians writing about the Independent Greek Church have implied that the Presbyterian Church in Canada had a hidden agenda and used the Independent Greek Church as a front. While it is true that the Presbyterians provided extensive funding to the new denomination, and that the hope was that it would lead to Ukrainians joining the Presbyterian Church, there is no evidence that Presbyterians were surreptitious or hidden about their connection with the Independent Greek Church. The Independent Greek Church reported its activities to the General Assembly each year, and that report was published in the widely available, annually produced *Acts and Proceedings* of the General Assembly. In May of 1912, as the plans were being laid to merge the Independent Greek Church into the Presbyterian Church in Canada, the Rev. Dr. Charles Gordon was at pains to point out that, "all assistance in the formation of their Church and the direction of their work was at each stage given at the request of the Ruthenian religious leaders themselves." In the minds of the Presbyterian leadership, they had been approached by recognized religious leaders from within the Ukrainian community, and all the developments that had taken place within the Independent Greek Church, had been with the full knowledge and input, and at the initiative of those recognized Ukrainian leaders.[55]

The Independent Greek Church produced a weekly paper called *Ranok*, initially funded by the Presbyterian Church. By the 1920's it was jointly funded by the Presbyterian and Methodist Churches. A series of articles printed in *Ranok* during 1911-1912 drew the ire of the Roman Catholic Church and that denomination pressured the Canadian Post Office to put pressure on those responsible for *Ranok* to change their ways. The Post Office officials knew who was the funding body for *Ranok* and came knocking on the door of the Presbyterian Church. The article in question was entitled "Celibacy" and was a direct attack on the Roman Catholic Church's practice of having celibate priests. The following quote gives the flavour of the article series, originally written in Ukrainian and translated into English by A.J. Hunter, the long-time medical missionary at the Presbyterian hospital at Teulon,

> This celibacy destroys among the clergy all natural feelings of family life and hands them over entirely to the control of the popes. In order to extend his despotism over the people the pope furnishes his priesthood with a sort of net which is the mystery of auriculur confession. By this instrument Rome enslaves both the labourer and his field.[56]

The Presbyterian leadership was unanimous in saying that parts of the series were clearly unacceptable, and were committed to ensuring that "no articles in any such form will appear again in Ranok." But the leadership did feel that there was "a good deal to be said in excuse for the article." Not the least being that, "[t]hese people just now are face to face with having a Celibate Priesthood thrust upon them." Having come from a Uniate Church, many Ukrainians in Canada wanted to maintain their married priests, but the ethnic Ukrainian Catholic clergy were not being allowed to marry. Finally, the Presbyterian leadership believed that the Ukrainians "have not reached our stage of culture and what we would look upon as being obscene they take to be quite right. For the same reason they are accustomed to have things spoken out pretty bluntly to them and would probably miss the point if the terms were less blunt than they are accustomed to." Some within the Presbyterian leadership did not think of the Ukrainians as their equals in terms of culture; this blatantly racist view can be seen in the ways in which the Ukrainian community was spoken of in various reports about Presbyterian work going on within that community. The Ukrainian community not surprisingly resented "the superior airs of the Anglo-Saxons" and the all-out push to convert them "to the Anglo-Saxon view point."[57]

Clearly then the Independent Greek Church was never intended to be for the long term; it was always to be a bridge for Ukrainians to travel along to becoming "Canadian." For a decade this unique bridge worked.

In 1903, Manitoba College hired Michael Sherbinin to teach a basic college course in Ukrainian to prospective ministers. Principal Patrick taught a one-month course each summer to clergy in the Independent Greek Church with the goal of improving their quality of preaching and helping them understand Presbyterian theology. The number of clergy in the denomination grew as did the number of congregations. In 1905, there were 20 clergy in the denomination, 13 of whom were employed by the Presbyterian Church as colporteurs, and about 25,000 Ukrainians claimed allegiance to the Independent Church. By 1907 there were 23 clergy ministering to 2,300 identified families. Bodrug could write happily, "For the first time in its history, our nation had lived to see a church of its very own, founded on the Word of God, a church that could be administered according to its own wishes, without feeling over it the patronage of Rome or of the Patriarchs."[58]

By 1911 changes were taking place that would spell the end to this remarkable bridging denomination. First, there was a conflict among the leadership of the Independent Church as to what the long term goal of the denomination was. Bodrug, as we have seen, was a nationalist who believed that finally the Ukrainian community had a church that was free from any outside influence. This church of their "very own" should continue forever. On the other hand, Maxim Zalizniak, minister in Edmonton, believed, "the Independent Greek Church is just a bridge to the Presbyterian and of course it is no use to continue any longer to be *Independent,* but we must be *real Presbyterians* (emphasis in original)." Second, the church was under attack from within the Ukrainian community. The Ukrainian Greek Orthodox Church had begun to send clergy over to minister to the new Canadians on the prairies. These priests charged that the Independent Church clergy were traitors to the Ukrainian cause. These charges were creating dissension among the lay members of the Independent Church. Recognizing the new situation, the clergy of the Independent Greek Church wrote to the Presbyterian Church in Canada, "we believe that the Independent Greek Church as an organization has done its work as far as it could do." The time had come for the merger of the two churches. The clergy of the Independent Greek Church stated they "would gladly join [the] Presbyterian Church as ministers in full standing or as ministers with temporary ordination, and that as such we are prepared to bring to our people the message of the Gospel and the idea of Great Presbyterianism."[59]

From the Presbyterian Church's side of the equation there were additional concerns. The Independent Church was becoming increasingly expensive for the Presbyterian Church. With more clergy being ordained and the Independent Greek clergy asking to be paid at the same level as the clergy in the Presbyterian Church, the financial burden seemed to be spinning out of control. As well, the Independent Church wanted financial help in building church buildings and manses, which would be owned by the Independent Greek Church but paid for by the Presbyterians. The Presbyterian leadership felt they were being asked to foot the bill, but had no control over what the Independent Greek Church did. As the Rev. Dr. Andrew Grant wrote, "It seems to me that the more we render them assistance of this kind the more likely they are to look to us for it." Therefore when faced with a huge financial shortfall in 1912, the HMC of the Presbyterian Church decided that it would cut its support to the Independent Greek Church. A.J. Hunter, from his position as a medical missionary among the Ukrainians, believed that the Independent Greek Church was bound to fail. It was impossible for the Presbyterian Church to not seek eventually to absorb the Independent Church; assimilation was inevitable. Hunter also believed that the priests of the Independent Church were far more Protestant than the congregations they served, and eventually clergy and congregation would have gone their own way.[60]

In preparation for the amalgamation of the two denominations, a three member committee of Presbyterian clergy interviewed 22 clergy from the Independent Greek Church in October 1912 to determine if they could become Presbyterian clergy. During these interviews the Independent church priests were asked about their life, their decision to become Protestants, and what they would say to a person who was seeking God. A number of those interviewed identified that while still in the Ukraine they had been dissatisfied with Catholicism. N. Sekora stated, "[h]e entered the Independent Greek Church because he had been favourably impressed with Protestantism before leaving his Native Land, and he was anxious that his fellow countrymen should know the truth." P. Uhrynuik reported, "[i]n early life while a Catholic outwardly, he was not so in heart—that he had been led by a teacher who was a Christian to think of Christ and of Protestantism." J. Danylchuk said, "a rich lady wished to make him a priest but that he declined because of difficulties regarding the doctrines of the Roman Catholic Church." Many of those interviewed had been involved with other Protestant churches before arriving in the Independent Greek Church. M.P. Berezniski had been Baptist, G. Tymnchuk became a Protestant by reading "Lutheran books," and J. Gregorach had taken the Methodist Evangelist Course. All those interviewed expressed thoroughly evangelical views of salvation and conversion. M. Hutney stated that if a person came to him asking the way to God, he would tell them they had "to become a Christian and believe in the Lord Jesus, that he must repent of sin and ask Jesus what [Jesus] would have him do." J. Zazulak said, "a man is a Christian who reads his Bible, prays and lives a good life. If a man is not a Christian, to enter the new life he must be born again."[61] At the General Assembly of 1913, 21 clergy from the Independent Greek Church became Presbyterian clergy, to the loud applause of those who had gathered, and the Independent

Greek Church was no more. John Bodrug was not among those who joined the Presbyterian Church. In his memoirs he wrote,

> The Presbyterian Church, a creation arising out of the spirit and culture of the Scottish people, however genuinely Christian and highly cultured it might be, was NOT UKRAINIAN. Every people has its own peculiar psychology and culture and every church must fit the psychology and culture of a given people. And when reform does come to a given church, such reform must take place step-by-step, according to the spiritual growth and traditions of that nation. It must emanate from the standard of thinking and level of culture within the given nation.[62]

The end of the Independent Greek Church did not mean that the Presbyterian Church had no interest in ministering to Ukrainians. With 21 Ukrainian-speaking clergy on the roll, there was still a great deal of interest in the Ukrainian community. But there was a new focus for that attention: the education of children. Both the government and the church recognized the educational needs of the Ukrainian community, but it was next to impossible to run effective school programmes at the local level in the Ukrainian communities that dotted the prairie landscape. Few Ukrainian families, as well, had the financial resources or the connections to send their children to a school in a neighbouring community. This problem faced not just the Ukrainian community, but all those families who due to their isolation were unable to send their children to a day school. In 1910, George Arthur, of Vegreville, tried to respond to this problem by taking boys into his home as boarders as they attended the nearby high school. The school was responsible for the secular education, the home for the religious education. The idea took off and by 1923 the WMS had 12 school homes in nine different prairie towns. These homes, usually located in or near a Ukrainian community—like Vegreville, Teulon and Battleford, Saskatchewan, were open to all students and families needed to make use of them, although the majority of students had a Ukrainian background. Usually the homes were segregated boys and girls, with an average of 20 young people resident in a school-home. The school home in Battleford broke both of those generalizations, being co-educational and in 1922 being home to 62 young people.[63]

The historian Michael Owen has argued that the children in these schools "were subjected to an intense effort to replace their cultural and, in most instances, their religious heritage with carefully delineated British Canadian sentiments as well as an evangelical Protestant (Presbyterian) religion."[64] Clearly one of the purposes of the school homes was to confront children with the claims of the gospel. These homes were being run by a

Christian mission agency; it would have been strange if the school home parents did not talk to their charges about their Christian beliefs. However, it is less clear that the purpose of the homes was to replace the student's cultural heritage. A.J. Hunter, the long time missionary among the Ukrainians at Teulon, wrote of the purpose of the school homes regarding the Ukrainian culture,

> …we shall be making a great mistake if we meet it with antagonism. We are all proud of our ancestry; it is little to our credit if we are not. We do find some who are trying to forget that they are Ruthenians, changing their names, and seeking, in other ways, to separate themselves from their people, but it is quite certain that these are not the ones whom the missionary finds most helpful. We do not want our boys to forget they were Ruthenians, but we do want them to learn from us, that which is best, and to take it back to their people.[65]

The point of school-homes was not to make the Ukrainians forget their heritage; rather it was to add to their heritage that which was "good" from the English-speaking culture. Hunter and many of the other missionaries among the Ukrainians were fully prepared to admit that there were things in the dominant culture that were not "good."

The Presbyterian Church had made an enormous investment in the evangelization and Canadianization of the Ukrainian community. Through the hospitals, school-homes, and in practical aid, the church had used the mission methods of the foreign mission field to gain a hearing among the Ukrainian community. With the Independent Greek Church, the Presbyterians had sought to meet the spiritual needs of the Ukrainian community in developing a church model that was far outside the traditional pattern of Presbyterianism. Although the Independent Greek Church had failed to achieve its goal, the fact that it had existed indicates how committed the Presbyterian church was to proclaim the gospel among the non-Anglo-Saxons who were making Canada their home. They were, as the saying goes, "Willing to try anything once." This openness to risk and try new ministry models was part of the mission ethos of the Presbyterian Church on the prairies.

THE URBAN CHALLENGE

During the period of most rapid population growth, 1901 to 1911, the urban population of the prairies more than quadrupled from 109,000 to 474,000, meaning that by 1911, one-third of the population of the prairie provinces lived in a city or town setting. These urbanizing centres drew new groups of immigrants to the prairies, people groups that were used to urban life and those who had shopkeeping skills saw in the cities and towns of the prairie provinces a place for themselves.[66]

As the railroad was completed, many Chinese stayed in Canada, opening laundries and restaurants across the west. The mission to the Chinese was operated under the direction of the Foreign Missions Committee of Presbyterian Church until 1912. The Presbyterian work among the Chinese in Winnipeg was the passion of James Thomson, a lay person who in 1890, at the age of 60 began to work quietly among the Chinese community. For 20 years he visited the laundries and restaurants, visiting each one every three months, "being an amount of pastoral work that might be considered arduous for a younger man." The churches in Winnipeg had caught a vision for the mission to the Chinese; 38 lay people were involved in teaching English as a second language. In 1910, C. A. Colman, a Presbyterian appointee who was financially supported by both the Presbyterians and the Methodists, started a mission to the Chinese in Winnipeg. A mission hall was purchased to serve as a base for the outreach, and a small congregation was started made up of Chinese who had converted to Christianity "as a result of work in places from which they come." By 1914, Colman reported that there were about 1,300 adult Chinese living in Winnipeg, 800 of them employed in the 160 laundries in the city. There were Sunday evening services held in one of the Methodist churches in Winnipeg, which drew an average of 40 ethnic Chinese each week. By 1916, there were 13 classes in Winnipeg alone attended by 300 Chinese who were learning English. Colman toured through the prairie provinces in 1912 and 1913, finding Chinese in between 30 and 40 towns across the west. In each of these communities he encouraged and supported the development of a mission to reach this immigrant community.[67]

There was a ministry among the Italian community in Winnipeg. There had been a briefly lived ministry in 1908-9, but the missionary had moved on to Toronto. Then in 1913, the Presbytery of Winnipeg's missions convenor discovered Mr. and Mrs. D'Augustino leading a small group who had attended the Italian mission before it was closed. The D'Augustinos were calling it a Presbyterian mission. The missions convenor saw this as an opportunity, and took the D'Augustinos and the mission under his wing. Working closely with the congregation, he nurtured the D'Augustinos understanding of the Christian faith to the point that by 1915, Mr. D'Augustino was named a missionary of the Presbyterian Church, being a catechist. In 1914, 20 people were converted through this ministry.[68]

In 1911, William Shearer, another creative, mission-focused district superintendent, was told by a black "gentleman" of the burial of a black man in Calgary at which no minister was present, not because the family wanted it that way, but because no one was doing ministry in the black community. Following a series of conversations with key players in the black community, Shearer arranged for the rental of the Moravian Church in Calgary so that afternoon services could be held. The services were well attended at first, but given the lack of consistent leadership the services ran out of steam and the project "fell through." Mr. F. W. Bell, a black theological student from Presbyterian College, Montreal, came to take up this work for six months in the summer of 1913. This time a storefront was rented in the south part of Calgary, chairs were borrowed from Knox Church and an organ was rented. In addition to the Sunday services, there was a mid-week prayer meeting. Again the congregation tried to keep the services going following Bell's return to classes in Montreal, but again the services collapsed. In the summer of 1914, Bell again ministered in Calgary. By early 1915, the black community in Calgary had shrunk dramatically and the decision was that the size of the remaining community did not warrant continuing the ministry.[69]

A SHIFT IN PHILOSOPHY

Through their daily contact with newly arrived Canadians, the Immigration Chaplains had a wide-ranging experience with immigrants upon which to draw when they commented on the changes large scale immigration was bringing to Canada. Dr. A Paterson, a medical doctor and also Immigration Chaplain, wrote in 1913 outlining some of the "evils" that had to be "overthrown if we are to have a united country and "Canada for Christ.""

Among the concerns were, "The foreigners, with their multiplicity of languages, their illiteracy, their low moral standards, and their ignorance of personal responsibility, many of them coming from countries where there is maladministration." This point of view being expressed by an Immigration Chaplain in their annual report to the General Assembly carried a great deal of weight. There is here a strong nativist sentiment; the foreign element was not to be trusted, particularly in areas of morals and public life. J.A. Bowman, the Immigration Chaplain in Winnipeg, contended that the problem was not so much the morals of the immigrants on their arrival, but "allowing them to live under evil conditions" once they got to Canada. The newly arrived did not know better, had no understanding of a higher set of values or ideals. "The Christian Church must deal in some way with these—not to proselytize—but to inspire to new ideals of life and conduct." This was a major shift in thinking for the Presbyterian Church, moving away from the double focus of Gospel proclamation and cultural assimilation, to the single focus of cultural assimilation and the outright rejection of proselytizing.[70]

This same shift in thinking can be seen in Ralph Connor's (Charles Gordon's) *The Foreigner: A Tale of Saskatchewan,* first published in 1909. Kalman Kalmar, the foreigner, as he is growing up in the north end of Winnipeg ends up in conflict with Rosenblatt, another immigrant with nefarious intentions of all kinds. Kalman is sent for his safety and moral salvation to work on the ranch of Jack French, an Anglo-Saxon alcoholic bachelor. Near French's Night Hawk Ranch there is a colony of Ukrainian immigrants. Working among these people is Brown (we are never told his first name). Brown is a renaissance man, minister, doctor, teacher, and entrepreneur. When French pushes Brown and asks him if he is a preacher, Brown replies,

> Well, I may be, though I can't preach much. But my main line is the kiddies. I can teach them English, and then I am going to doctor them, and, if they'll let me, teach them some of the elements of domestic science; in short, do anything to make them good Christians and good Canadians, which is the same thing.[71]

But the process of turning the Ukrainians, who Brown calls Galicians, into good Christians and good Canadians has little to do with the proclamation of the gospel or conversion. We are never given the content of one of Brown's sermons, and all we know about the worship at the mission is that they sang hymns. In another conversation with French, Brown asserts,

> I am not sent here to proselytize. My church is not in that business. We are doing business, but we are in the business of making good citizens. We tried to get the Government to establish schools among the Galicans. The Government declined. We took it up, and hence this school. We tried to get Greek Catholic priests from Europe to look after the religion and morals of these people. We absolutely failed to get a decent man to offer. Remember, I say decent man. We had offers, plenty of them, but we could not lay our hands on a single, clean, honest-minded man with the fear of God in his heart, and the desire to help these people.[72]

Brown's church is the Presbyterian Church, and in his speech here we have Charles Gordon's view of the mission of the church. This is a far cry from the vision that was articulated by James Robertson less than a decade earlier and by W.D. Reid and others who were contemporaries of Gordon's. The church was to make good citizens, it was a tool of socialization and assimilation. The success of the church in fulfilling its "business" was to be measured not in terms of conversions or church attendance, but in terms of how well those touched by the church adopted the values and ideals of the dominant culture. This transformation was to be seen not only among the non-English speaking immigrants but also among the recalcitrant Anglo-Saxon pioneers who had first come to the prairie pulled by the wide open spaces and the freedom from the social mores of the civilization.

> The call of the New Time, and the appeal of the New Ideal, that
> came through the railroad, the mine, but more than both, through
> the Mission and its founder, found response in the heart of Jack
> French. The old laissez faire of the pioneer days gave place to a
> sense of responsibility for opportunity, and to habits of decisive
> and prompt attention to the business of the hour. Five years of
> intelligent study of conditions, of steady application to duty, had
> brought success not in wealth alone, but in character and influ-
> ence.[73]

This was how the church should measure its success: in the wealth, character, and influence of its parishioners. There is nothing here about souls
saved, or even of the kingdom of God being expanded. *The Foreigner* ends
with Marjorie Menzies, the daughter of the Scottish capitalist, Sir Robert
Menzies, who earlier had vowed that she could "never, never" love "one of
those foreigners," asserting her love for her "Canadian foreigner," Kalman
Kalmar. The foreigner is no longer a foreigner because he has fully adopted
the Canadian social religion of hard-work, success, and moral responsibility, and therefore can be accepted into Canadian society.

Gordon was not the only Presbyterian to argue that the social and
educational needs of the non-English speaking communities must be placed
ahead of their religious and spiritual needs. A.J. Hunter put it very suc-
cinctly: "These people must be brought from one mental attitude to another, before they can be changed form one spiritual attitude to another."[74]
The education of the mind to Canadian social values had to precede the
transformation of souls. Colin Young, superintendent of missions for Northern Saskatchewan in 1916, made a similar point,

> At this stage in the history of non-English speaking communities
> it is quite probable that the preparatory work will be done by the
> school rather than the Church. If the educational work is well
> done there will be a demand for the higher life to which only the
> Church can minister. Our present obligation seems to be to nour-
> ish the institution which creates the environment in which the
> Church is to do its work.[75]

The church was out of the loop—the focus had to be the school; no longer
was the church to be an equal partner with the state in the building of a
unified nation. That could only happen after the non-English speaking
immigrants had been Canadianized. It was the church leadership who were
pulling back, leaving the arena open to the government and the school.
Arriving at this point was the result of a massive shift in thinking in the
space of just over a decade.

A second major shift in mission philosophy was articulated by Principal Edmund Oliver of Saskatoon College. In a letter outlining his plan for
solving the "problem" of the Ukrainians, he contended it was better to
have Anglophone clergy who had learned Ukrainian than Ukrainian clergy
who had learned English. This was because it was "absolutely necessary
that we should know what we are doing, and my observation is that this is
not possible through the Ruthenians themselves." The Ukrainian clergy
were not to be trusted was the implied condemnation. And with that the
whole philosophy upon which the ministry to non-Anglo-Saxons had
been predicated was wiped out. Oliver was disparaging of the Ukrainians,
saying that the Home Mission Board should be on the look out for some
young Anglo-Saxon clergy "devoted enough to endure bad ventilation
and evil smells, and perhaps even Bukowinian fleas for the sake of the
Gospel." The goal of the mission to the Ukrainians was not to make them
Presbyterians or even to tell them the gospel story, rather it was to make
them "Canadian." Everything else needed to be forgotten; instead "we must
remember Canadianism." Oliver, as the principal of one of the theological
colleges, was a leading figure in the denomination and a strong advocate of
union. His views carried weight and there would have been many on the
prairies who would have followed his lead. He urged the church to set up
bursaries to help Anglo-Saxon students get the appropriate training to enter this new form of "non-Anglo-Saxon mission," a mission whose goal
was "the task of Canadianization." Many of the mission leaders in the Presbyterian Church by 1918 would have agreed with Oliver that the church
needed to stop using non-Anglo-Saxons in its mission endeavour, for the
non-Anglo-Saxons did not advance the new mission of the church:
"Canadianism."[76]

The complete triumph of this new vision is seen in the fact that J.H.
Edmison, general secretary of Board of Home Mission and Social Services
had to remind the church in his 1923 Report to Assembly that the church
still needed to be in the business of proselytizing or it would die. He quoted
an unnamed American authority as stating, that the church must become
involved in the evangelization of the immigrants, "even if it bring her
under suspicion of proselytizing. Indeed one of the growing weaknesses is
the loss of those deep convictions which make proselytizing easy." The loss
of confidence and conviction in what the church was supposed to be about
lay at the root of the problem. Having given up its partnership with the
state in the welcoming of the stranger; the church now had no role to play
in reaching out to the non-English speaking New Canadians. Not everyone
had bought into the new policy. William Simons wrote of the city mission
work that took place in Edmonton in 1923, "In all these varied activities of
the church our aim is not simply to educate nor to Canadianize, but to
Christianize the people, to enlighten them in the precepts of the Gospel,

and in the practice of the teachings of Jesus Christ." The call to Canadianize was so dominant that Simons had to remind his readers that there was a secondary purpose behind all this effort—the proclamation of the gospel of Jesus Christ.[77]

Conclusion

Historian John Webster Grant has argued that there was a general opening of the churches toward the New Canadians in the first couple of decades of the 20th century.[78] This chapter has argued the opposite: that while there was a shift in language, moving from talk of the foreigner to talk of the new Canadian, certainly the attitudes toward the New Canadians became harder and the goal more fixed.

Robertson's vision had been to use anyone and everyone possible in the cause of carrying the message of the gospel to the non-English speaking immigrants. He recognized the need to have people of the same ethnic and cultural group to proclaim the gospel in these new communities, and scoured the European continent looking for appropriate clergy. He also offered free education and guaranteed employment to gifted young men in the newly arrived groups who wished to become ministers in the Presbyterian Church. He opened a very big umbrella, inviting former Lutherans, Roman Catholics, Greek Orthodox, anyone who was not being ministered to, to come and be part of the worship and congregational life of the Presbyterian Church. That openness continued after his death, as Michael Sherbinin was co-opted and the Independent Greek Church was given birth and nurtured by the Presbyterian Church. This intentional use of clergy whose mother tongue was not English and whose cultural background was often very different than the leadership of the church, meant that these New Canadians were trusted. This openness and trust combined with a breadth of vision that allowed Presbyterians to take risks as they sought to reach New Canadians with the good news about Jesus. Lay people took risks in beginning new ministries and responding to opportunities around them, women took risks in playing ever larger leadership roles in churches, including becoming ministers in some congregations.

It is hard to imagine how this trust of the New Canadian exhibited in an earlier day could survive in the face of the new mission philosophy articulated by Charles Gordon and Edmund Oliver. The landscape had changed; no longer was the primary goal giving people the gospel with the anticipation that that would be a step on the road to their becoming Canadians. The new goal was to make the new arrivals Canadians—in fact it was a new religion, "Canadianism."

In the face of massive immigration from non-English speaking countries, the Presbyterian Church in Canada responded to what they saw to be the spiritual needs of the immigrants. The church sent missionaries, established churches, found clergy who could speak to the immigrants in their own language, and provided some of the new Canadians with schools, hospitals, and clothing—all as a way of reaching these foreigners and aliens with the good news about Jesus Christ. At times the church's response seemed to be seeking a cultural conversion rather than a conversion of the heart. But for many Presbyterians who believed that to be Canadian was to be Christian, it was an easy equation to make. Through a tremendous, and at times sacrificial commitment, the Presbyterian Church became the largest denomination on the prairies, keeping pace with the population explosion that took place in the first 15 years of this century. The church heard the call to evangelize the west, reaching out not just to those with a Presbyterian pedigree, but to all who were willing to respond to the gospel, regardless of their ethnic or linguistic background.

Miss M. McArthur going on home visiting rounds
at the Pine River Nursing Unit in Manitoba.
(United Church of Canada/Victoria University Archives, 93.049P/2046)

The Hugh Waddell Memorial Hospital, Canora, SK, built in 1913.
(Presbyterian Church Archives)

Four unnamed priests from the Independent Greek Church, 1903-1912.
(United Church of Canada/Victoria University Archives, 93.049P/3257N)

"God has given us an opportunity. . ."[1]: The Presbyterian Church in the Yukon and the Prairie Near North

The opening up of the North presented the Presbyterian Church in the west with a new challenge: How to do ministry among the settlers, gold-seekers, and others who were moving into this new land? The harsh climate, the great distances and the overwhelming remoteness which those distances created, and the here-today-gone-tomorrow nature of community life meant that new ways of doing ministry had to be found. As John Pringle wrote from Glenora, British Columbia, on the edge of the Klondike, in late 1898, "No one not on the ground has any conception of the conditions which as your missionary I have had to face here."[2] In the face of these great challenges the Presbyterian Church sought to minister.

THE KLONDIKE

In 1887, George Dawson, son of famous geologist William Dawson, led a Geological Survey of Canada team up the Stikine River and into the Yukon. Among the things that Dawson's expedition did was describe the gold-bearing gravel in the area and used glacial patterns to predict that there were workable gold deposits in the Yukon. Two editions of Dawson's report, including geological maps and a description of the access routes into the Yukon, sold out. In recognition of his role in the opening up of the Klondike, Dawson City was named for George Dawson, a Presbyterian.[3]

Robert Henderson, a Presbyterian from Big Island, Nova Scotia, arrived in the Yukon in 1894. Henderson had been prospecting in Colorado since 1880, and now was going to try his luck in the North. In July, 1896, he and his partner were working on Gold Bottom Creek, a tributary of Hunker Creek, and they were finding some promising showings in their pans. In August, they were visited by George Washington Carmack, an American who had lived in the Yukon for a decade, living with and working with the Stick Native People. Carmack and his partners, Skookum Jim and Tagish Charlie, stayed with the Henderson group only briefly before heading back toward Dawson. To do that they crossed the ridge to Bonanza Creek and slowly made their way down. They headed towards Klondike River, panning for gold as they went. About the point where Eldorado Creek flows into Bonanza, they made a big find. They staked their claim, and headed to Forty Mile to have their claims recorded. So excited were they by their discovery, they forgot all about Henderson, never telling him about what they had found. By the time Henderson heard about what had been discovered on Bonanza and its tributaries, the claims had all been staked, and even the best spots on Gold Bottom Creek had been staked by other parties.[4]

By January 1897, most of the North knew what had been found, and many people were on their way to the Klondike. But it was not until July that the rest of the world knew, as the first Klondikers arrived in Seattle and San Francisco. There was a small rush of people into the Klondike in the autumn of 1897, especially from those who were experienced with Canadian winters. But the big rush did not start until the spring of 1898. James Robertson stood on the docks of Vancouver in the summer of 1897, watching the first eager outsiders push their way on to the steamers headed for Skagway, Alaska. Little did some of these people know the arduous journey that lay ahead of them once they had reached Skagway. Robertson saw in this mass of humanity a mission field, and he began to plan for a way to reach out to these people who were headed north. Robertson and Charles Gordon (Ralph Connor) had in mind the individual they wanted to send to the Yukon; Robert M. Dickey, who had just completed his second year of theological study at Manitoba College. Gordon spoke to Dickey about what Robertson and he had in mind, but asked Dickey not to make any decision until Robertson was back in Winnipeg for the opening Convocation of the fall term at Manitoba College. Robertson addressed the Convocation with a call to the mission of the church in the Yukon. He said,

> These men have souls. Some of them will make fortunes and be tempted to destruction; some will be disappointed in their search; all will endure hardships, and many of them will die; many will be broken down. We must send with them some one to tell them of the treasure more precious than gold, some one to warn them in their day of prosperity, or remind them in their day of calamity, that God reigneth, some one to stand by the dying bed and point men to Christ. These men who are facing a thousand peril have grit, courage, endurance: we must send a man to turn the faces of these strong men heavenward.... God has given us an opportunity which we dare not neglect.[5]

Dickey was in the audience that heard this challenge, and on October 2,

1897, he boarded the S.S. Quadro in Vancouver headed to Skagway and the Klondike.

Robertson had seen a need and had acted with his characteristic decisiveness and speed. But there was discontent about the fact that Robertson had acted outside of the rules. There had been no time to call together the HMC to get their blessing for a mission to the Yukon. It was necessary to get someone at least as far as Skagway before winter. Robertson had committed the HMC to a very expensive venture, without any consultation. On top of that Robertson had taken a student who had only completed two years of theological study at Manitoba College, and had ordained him using an obscure regulation which allowed the superintendent to ordain people to a specific task under special circumstances. The faculty at Manitoba College was resentful of what they perceived to be Robertson's cavalier action in stealing one of their students. The growing centralization and bureaucratization of the mission of the church were getting in the way of responding to what Robertson saw as a clear need. He believed that there was "no recklessness in the methods employed" and that the HMC was "too timid about a deficit." When the souls of human beings were in the balance what was a deficit and what was the bending of a few rules, if that is what it took to get the mission off the ground.[6]

The Klondike, and the Yukon as a whole, had fired the imagination of the Presbyterian Church at large. At the worship service designating A.S. Grant for ministry in the Yukon, held on Dec. 30, 1897 at St. James' Square Presbyterian Church in Toronto, "a good audience" heard from leading Presbyterians, including: Sir Oliver Mowat, Premier of Ontario, and Principal George Grant of Queen's University. It would be hard to name two Presbyterians with higher profiles either in the church or in society at large. Presbyterians were eager to donate to the cause, and a number of clergy volunteered to become part of the team going to the Yukon. The mind of the church was kept focused on the Yukon; in the 23 issues of the *Presbyterian Record* between December 1897 and October 1899, 19 articles about the Klondike and the church's ministry there were published. One of the articles closed with the question: "Who will take shares in this Klondike expedition, with guaranteed permanent dividends in saved men?"[7]

The *Westminster* chastised the Home Missions Committee for their caution in committing the money and personnel to the Klondike that Robertson and others thought was needed. "Gentlemen of the Home Mission Committee," the editor wrote, "the Presbyterian Church in Canada is able and willing and ready, waiting only for the policy you did not adopt, the call you did not issue, the leadership you have not shown." In the end it was Robertson's approach, somewhat tempered by the concerns raised by the HMC, that won the day. By June 1898, the official report to the General Assembly on the work of Home Missions in the Yukon stated, "the

Committee should be ready to act promptly as soon as the way is clear, else much of the advantage already gained may be lost." The Committee itself was prepared to acknowledge the need to move with dispatch as ministry opportunities presented themselves in the North. For as they noted in their 1899 report to Assembly, "Wherever gold is found men are sure to flock, and the Church must follow the people and be prepared to make the sacrifices needed to meet their religious wants. The salvation of men's souls is first, the building up of congregations subordinate." The goal of the mission to the Yukon was now agreed; the salvation of souls was the clarion call to the church. Robertson's hand-picked missionaries held this same vision of their ministry. Whatever it took to get the ministry done was what they would do, regardless of whether the Home Missions Committee had given its official approval. The missionaries were chosen not only for their ministry gifts, but also for their ability to see ministry opportunities and to seize them even when those ministry opportunities required doing ministry in non-traditional and unconventional ways.[8]

There were three routes into the Klondike. The fastest, but most physically demanding was to go by steamer to the Alaskan port of Skagway, and then pull or carry one's possessions over either Chilkoot Pass or White Pass to Tagish on Lake Lebarge, there build a boat to travel down the Yukon River to Dawson City. The problems with this route were the physical demands of getting people and materials over either pass and secondly that the route went through the United States. The discovery of gold in the Yukon coincided with the heating up of the Alaska Boundary dispute, and there was great fear among Canadians that the Americans might seize the Klondike if the opportunity presented itself. Certainly the discovery of gold presented them with a motive for such a seizure. Given these concerns and the physical demands of the route through Skagway, the Canadian government promoted a route through Telegraph Creek and Atlin, British Columbia. The rails went as far as Telegraph Creek, and then the Dominion Government cut a trail from there to Atlin. Atlin Lake fed into the Yukon River upon which Dawson was located, and there was only one set of rapids to be contended with along the route, the imposing White Horse Rapids. By 1899 there was regular paddle boat traffic on the Yukon River moving people and materials along the Atlin to the Dawson City lake and river system. Traveling through Atlin took more time, but it was an entirely Canadian route and was by far the safest. A third option was to pass through Edmonton and use the traditional fur trade route into the Yukon.

It was Robertson's plan to place Presbyterian clergy on the first two routes, which were by far the most heavily traveled. He wanted two clergy to work in Dawson City and the area of the Creeks; a third clergyperson was to work the Lake Bennett and Tagish route to cover those gold-seekers who were prepared to face the danger of coming over the passes, and a fourth minister would do ministry in the Telegraph Creek, Glenora and Atlin regions of northern British Columbia covering the second travel route into the North.

Dickey went to Skagway in October 1897, but it was too late in the season to push over the passes to Whitehorse and beyond, so he settled down in Skagway for the winter. He held a worship service on Oct. 10, 1897, in one of the few community halls in town. Seventy people attended and following the service a building committee was appointed. The new church building was to be a union church, not belonging to one denomination or religious group. Funds were raised not just from Anglicans, Methodists, Presbyterians and the like, but also from the Theosophists and the tiny Jewish community in Skagway. The church building was dedicated on Dec. 12, 1897, with a series of five services led by representatives of the faith communities who would be using the building. But the church building was not merely a church. Starting in January it was the schoolhouse, Monday to Friday during the day. Each evening it was opened as a reading room, where people could gather in a place that was not the saloon. It also became the home of the local literary and music societies. The multiple, shared uses of church buildings became a hallmark of the missionary effort in the Yukon area.[9]

In January 1898, The Rev. Andrew S. Grant joined Dickey in Skagway. Grant, who was described as "a tall, brawny, freckle-faced Scotchman...able, resourceful" had spent seven years ministering in Almonte, Ontario before being chosen by Robertson to be one of the Presbyterian missionaries in the Yukon. Grant had a wife and children whom he left behind in Ontario while he entered upon this northern adventure. Grant also had three years of medical school training, which would stand him in good stead in the Klondike.[10] Grant, who seems to have been as headstrong as Robertson, arrived in Skagway and decided that he would immediately go over the passes to Lake Bennett, where about a thousand people were waiting out the winter, before pushing on to the Klondike. In February, Grant went over White Pass to Bennett. He wrote to Robertson,

> The herculean task of my life was the encountering of the Skagway trail; all the way from Skagway over the White Pass, and on to Bennett, the way is difficult. We encountered storms and severe cold, all our party were sick, one had to return, and for two days I lay in a tent at the foot of the summit in rather a critical condition. Had I not known what to do I would have fared worse. There have been so many deaths, and so much sickness that I was often compelled after a hard day's work to minister to the sick, and perhaps overtaxed my energies.[11]

Grant, who was not in the habit exaggerating, described his physical situation as "critical," that only his medical knowledge prevented him from having "fared worse" than he did. But the physical demands of the trail and the struggle to stay alive did not mean that Grant had any thought of giving up on his goal of reaching Dawson City as shortly after spring break-up as possible. Grant kept to his schedule, arriving in Dawson in early May 1898, only to find that The Rev. Hall Young, an American Presbyterian, was already there. Young, commissioned by the Board of Home Missions of the Presbyterian Church in the United States of America (North), had arrived in Dawson in the fall of 1897, and had been ministering to a multi-denominational congregation. Grant was taken aback to find an American Presbyterian in what Grant considered a Canadian mission field and the first words out of Grant's mouth were, "What are you doing here?"

In one of those strange historical coincidences, the readers of *The Presbyterian Record* knew that Hall Young was in Dawson City before Grant did. One of Young's letters to the American Home Missions Board, dated Dec. 1, 1897, was printed in the April 1898 issue of the *Record*. Grant would not have received a copy of the April issue until well into the summer of 1898, if he ever received one, given the haphazard nature of the mail and his being constantly on the move. In the letter Young asked the American Home Mission Board to ensure that they sent someone to do ministry in Skagway, since it was expected to be "a booming town for years." And at the end of his lengthy correspondence he asked the Board to contact Robertson about Young's presence in Dawson City, "I am really in his jurisdiction, though the great majority of my adherents are Americans." So in an ironic twist, Robert Dickey, the Canadian, began the Presbyterian ministry in Skagway, Alaska; while Hall Young, the American began the Presbyterian ministry in Dawson City, Yukon Territory.[12]

The editor of the *Record* noted that Dickey and Grant were on their way to the Klondike, stating that they would "find in Mr. Hall [sic] a congenial spirit." Certainly Grant's first conversation with Young did not begin in a congenial way. Despite this brusque start to the relationship, Grant and Young were able to work out a mutually satisfactory solution. Grant became the minister of the congregation that Young had started on June 1, 1898, and Young stayed around the Klondike area ministering until 1900.

Dickey followed Grant to Lake Bennett, and from there he wrote about the medical needs he saw along the way, and about the desperate need for nurses in the Klondike. He stated, "If trained nurses with the Love of Christ in their hearts could be sent there would be a great work for them to do. The people are mostly too eager after gold to care for the sick."[13] Dickey's comments came both to the attention of Lady Aberdeen, the founder of the Victorian Order of Nurses in Canada, and a Presbyterian, and to the attention of a group of Presbyterian women in Toronto. Together Lady Aberdeen and these women arranged for four Victorian Order of Nurses to go to the Klondike. In the summer of 1898, Dickey followed Grant to Dawson. John A. Sinclair, who had been sent out early in 1898 to take up the work at Lake Bennett, was detained in Skagway because the American Presbyterians had not yet sent a minister to cover this congregation. Sinclair ended up splitting his time between Lake Bennett and Skagway, traveling over the passes on a regular basis, but by now, fortunately, there was a train between the two points. The fourth member of the Presbyterian pioneers was John Pringle, who was sent to secure the Telegraph Creek, Glenora, and Atlin route.

Grant quickly became involved in the life of Dawson. There were two hospitals in Dawson; a Roman Catholic-operated facility, and the Good Samaritan Hospital, which had a community board. Prior to Grant's arrival, the Good Samaritan Hospital had not had the leadership it needed. In December 1898, barely seven months after his arrival in Dawson, Grant wrote to Robertson,

> There is a great deal of sickness and a considerable number of deaths yet. Many are leaving for their homes discouraged and many are in destitute circumstances. The local council have already spent over fifty thousand dollars in caring for indigent sick. The general hospital of which I am Superintendent has now a capacity of over one hundred patients and its wards have proved a haven for many a homeless destitute sick miner. I have interviewed as many as forty persons in one day on hospital matters.[14]

Not only was Grant the minister of the Presbyterian Church, he was also superintending the Good Samaritan Hospital, a job he was qualified to undertake given his medical training and his obvious organizational skills. Grant was to become so deeply involved in the operation of the hospital that on his second stint in Dawson, from 1902 to 1908, he asked the Home Mission Committee to take over the hospital as a Presbyterian hospital. He had secured substantial financial commitments from the federal government, the local city council, and the Yukon Council, so that the Presbyterian Church's responsibility were primarily in the areas of management and personnel. The Home Mission Committee chose not to take on this mission opportunity.[15]

Grant in his letters to Robertson was brutally frank about the challenges of ministry. He had left his family behind in the south as he went on this adventure; to Robertson he wrote, "I cannot tell you how terrible it is for me to be separated from my family." The congregation in Dawson, aware of the loneliness Grant was feeling, suggested that he move his family to

Dawson and become their called minister. Grant wrote to Robertson, "They insist that I am their pastor but I am not; and could not be as I would never bring my family into this camp, and could not accept a position that would mean separation from them." The conditions in Dawson were not the kind Grant wanted to raise his family in; it was to his mind nothing more than a camp. It is easy to understand how Grant could write, "There is so much to discourage and depress and so little to encourage and elevate our spirits in the work here, yet the call to duty, for the Master's sake lights up the darkness." It was Grant's profound commitment to Jesus Christ and the mission of Jesus that allowed him to stay the course in his ministry in Dawson.[16]

In July 1898, Dickey arrived in Dawson City and was given the responsibility of doing ministry in the area of the Eldorado and Bonanza Creeks. Where the two creeks joined a community had sprung up, called interchangeably Grand Forks, The Forks or Eldorado. The ministry in the area came in two forms. Much of this work required visiting prospectors and miners in their cabins scattered along the creeks and streams that fed into the Klondike River. It was not a typical form of ministry, having less to do with formal Sunday worship and more to do with face-to-face contact and leading ad hoc worship services in cabins and in other unusual settings. The second way in which ministry took place was that Dickey was able to acquire land and build a church building. Every effort was made to establish the church building as the centre of the community rather than the saloon. The building functioned as a reading room, having the most up-to-date newspapers that were available; as well as a small library, there was a small gym and games room. The building was open daily, providing a gathering place for miners to socialize in a location free from alcohol. The church had light, provided by oil lamps, a major benefit in the winter in the land north of the 60th parallel. Dickey's two years of all out ministry had exhausted him and he resigned from the work in the Klondike in 1899.[17]

The work on the Creeks and in Eldorado continued after Dickey's departure. He was replaced by Daniel Cock, a 25-year old minister from Truro, N.S., who had worked for a year with Dr. Wilfred Grenfell in Labrador. In early 1900, Sinclair, who had overseen the building of the church at Lake Bennett and had collected enough materials to build a church in White Horse (throughout the period under discussion the name of the community is given as two words, not one), went to minister in the Creeks for the summer. Sinclair, like Grant was separated from his family, and was not willing to spend a third winter in the Yukon. None of the four pioneer Presbyterian clergy spent more than two and a half years in the Klondike before leaving for some kind of break. Dickey and Sinclair left never to return; Grant left for two years before returning, and Pringle took a leave of absence during what would have been his third winter in the north before returning to do ministry in the Creeks. Doing ministry in the early chaotic and turbulent days of the Klondike was physically demanding and spiritually draining.

Ministry in the Creeks was challenging, as John Pringle noted: "We are a kind of gypsy crowd here. Half of my congregation may, within a week, be stampeding or prospecting fifty miles off." As the areas in the immediate vicinity of the first find was staked, prospectors were moving farther and farther afield in their search for a new strike. And as they moved, so did the Presbyterian Church. The Pringle brothers, John and George, loved working with the miners in whatever place they found them. George was already doing some of this ministry as he moved among the people scattered along Hunker and Eureka Creeks. John also wanted to do this,

> There are scores of outlying points which we cannot touch, and no one else thinks about. I wish the Home Mission Committee would appoint a good man for Eldorado, who could preach and visit, and let me loose to have the untouched and outlying dis- tricts as my parish, districts inhabited mostly by prospectors. These far away boys appreciate a minister's visits as mothers do.[18]

The model for this ministry was quite simple, Pringle would travel by boat, on foot, or by dog team to visit with people right where they were, leading short worship services, out-of-doors if the weather permitted, or in the cramped shacks or tents of the prospectors. Many of these prospectors rarely saw another human being, and having someone to speak to who also brought news from the outside world, was a major blessing for "these far away boys." It was a sign that the church had not forgotten about them while almost everyone else had. In the fall of 1903, John Pringle was granted his wish as he was released to ministry "on the trail." While "on the trail" on Christmas Day 1903, Pringle and Richard Fullerton found gold on what came to be called Christmas Creek, which flows into Christmas Bay on Kulane Lake. Pringle and Fullerton staked claims on the creek.

Even though the Pringles wanted to spend their time doing ministry "on the trail," which had little structure and was all about face to face relationships, it became necessary at times to establish congregations and meeting times and even at times buildings needed to be erected. George Pringle by 1905 had what amounted to a six-point charge. He preached and led worship at Gold Run and Sulphur Creek every third Sunday, "the people carrying on a song service and sort of C[hristian] E[ndeavour] when I am not present." Christian Endeavour was a programme for youth and young adults, which produced devotional and study materials. Two Sun- days out of three he preached and led worship at Gold Bottom Village and

Gold Bottom Creek. He also led mid-week services at Granville and Last Chance. A model of ministry was developed that fit the realities of the Klondike, allowing people to worship God as a corporate group on a regular basis, even when that meant lay people led the worship service, or that the service was held on a Thursday evening. The openness of ministry "on the trail" allowed new ways of being the people of God to bubble up.

From the very start of the mission to the Klondike the clergy involved saw themselves playing a role in the moral development of the territory, as well as the spiritual development. The following clearly outlined their views:

> Many young men of good morals and habits are going. But all the more need for mission work to save these men from sin; for there will be multitudes versed in all evil, and making gain by men's ruin. The drink shop, the gambling saloon, and the brothel, foul trinity of ill-will abound, and if left uncared for, multitudes of young men from good homes, and of hitherto clean, pure, lives, "somebody's boys," will fall victims. Of the greatest importance, therefore, is that the church be on the spot from the first, that it may give visibility to good, remind our boys, "somebody's boys," of home and heaven, and help to keep them from the way that goeth down to death.[19]

The church saw itself entering into the lists in the struggle for the hearts and souls of the men and women, but primarily men, who were heading north to seek their fortunes. In this struggle, the church needed to provide these young men, who were all "somebody's boys," with a clear moral alternative to the "trinity of ill" that they would find both in Dawson City and on the journey to Dawson. Grant took the role of being the voice for morality seriously. He was completely frustrated by the Government of Canada's 1901 flip-flop on the open gambling and dance halls in Dawson and wrote an angry letter to Prime Minister Wilfred Laurier. The Dominion Government had ordered that the dance halls and gambling dens be closed at midnight on Saturday, March 16. But a petition that circulated through Dawson City, which had not been taken seriously by Grant and others opposed to the dance halls, had asked the government for two months grace until June 1. The government agreed to the change. So midst "a regular carnival among the sporting fraternity of this place," the dance halls re-opened at noon on Monday, March 18. In Grant's letter dated March 19, he wrote,

> It is not with me as much a matter of allowing open gambling and prostitution, with all their con-commitant evils, for ten weeks more, as it is that the majesty of our British Law should be trampled

under foot, and that our Canadian Government should for a moment sanction this evil. It is nothing more or less than a standing disgrace to our country and an insult to the people of Dawson.[20]

Grant's goal was finally achieved, as by the end of 1902, the sale of liquour was forbidden in the dance halls and the prostitutes were banned from Dawson itself. In response the prostitutes and dance halls simply moved to Klondike City on the other side of the Klondike River. Almost certainly Grant would not have been happy with this arrangement. But it was John Pringle, not Grant, who took up the cause in 1903, demanding that the political authorities exercise moral authority. Pringle had in late 1901 moved from his ministry in Atlin to the Eldorado district south of Dawson, and in 1903 he was elected to the Yukon Territorial Council representing the people of Bonanza. From that position he sought to lobby Laurier to do something about the drinking, gambling, and prostitution. When Laurier failed to respond to his letters, Pringle took his campaign public, involving the eastern Canadian press, the Presbyterian Church, and the Conservative party in his agenda. As Pringle said before the General Assembly in 1908, "I shall meddle in politics as long as the devil meddles in politics."[21]

By 1901 the halcyon days of the Klondike were past and gold mining was settling down to be "an ordinary industry." Large companies were bringing in equipment and buying out small claims from those prospectors who did not have the resources to get the gold from the lower grade gravel and sand that were said to cover as much as 1,000 square miles in the Klondike River system. While this meant that there were fewer people in the Klondike region, there was more stability in the community as the mining became more and more mechanized. This stability meant three things to the mission to the Yukon.

First, stability meant that the government and private industry were able to begin building the infrastructure that the newly minted communities in the Yukon would need. This meant that some communities were entirely bypassed, leaving them little more than ghost towns. This was the case at Lake Bennett, which had been an important junction point between the overland route from Skagway and the water route to Dawson City. But the building of the Skagway to White Horse rail line meant that Lake Bennett was irrelevant. Therefore in 1902 the Presbyterian Church in Canada abandoned its work at Lake Bennett, leaving behind a church building, which in 1967 was declared a National Historic Site.[22]

The second thing that happened was that Presbyterian clergy on the ground in the Yukon became more settled themselves, staying for longer terms. This length of stay and the time to think about what was taking place in the Yukon as a whole gave leaders the opportunity to step back and determine where the key places were to develop new communities of faith. This reflection led to the planting of a congregation in White Horse. It made good sense for two reasons. First, it was the new terminus of the railway from Skagway, where everything headed to and from Dawson City would be transferred from train to paddlewheeler or vice versa. Second, LeRoy Mining had found copper near White Horse and people would be moving in to work the new mines. John Sinclair had laid the ground work for a church plant back in 1900, and in 1901, J.J. Wright was building on that foundation. Following the now familiar pattern, a church building was constructed that would function as a community centre with a reading and recreation room. By 1903, the HMC was expressing concerns about the long term viability of the congregation: "the progress of this mission field has not been as rapid as it at first seemed likely to be." By 1909, the population of White Horse was about 1,000 and the reading room was a great boon to the work of the missionary, but there seemed to be little chance that the congregation would grow. In 1914, there were 20 families and eight single people connected to the congregation, and that was not enough to justify continued funding from the Board of Home Mission and Social Service who were to face severe financial pressure during the war years. In late 1915 the congregation in White Horse was closed.[23]

Third, stability in the mining industry meant there were fewer people working on the creeks around Dawson and Bonanza and that meant a winding down of the ministry. By 1905 the congregation at Bonanza was in decline as prospectors and small time operators pulled up stakes and headed to what they hoped would be the next big find. In 1908, both Grant and John Pringle left the Klondike, leaving George Pringle to work the creeks further east of Dawson. On a rather ominous note, that year the Home Mission and Social Service Board reported to the Assembly, "Mining conditions having changed, some re-arrangement of our work may be necessary in the future." A minister, Archie Sinclair, was appointed to St. Andrew's, Dawson, but he left in 1910 and was not replaced. For a couple of years the minister in White Horse did supply work in Dawson City, but by 1912 Dawson was no longer listed as a mission charge. In 1910, George Pringle left the Creeks, ending his eight years of ministry there. Thus by 1912 the Presbyterian Church in Canada's 15 year adventure in the Klondike was basically over. After the war, the Rev. G.H. Findlay was sent to Dawson City. He also spent the summer preaching and visiting along the creeks, travelling by steamboat, canoe and on foot. Through the 1920's, White Horse asked for a minister, but the financial realties would not allow one to be sent.[24]

TELEGRAPH CREEK, GLENORA AND ATLIN

In March 1898, John Pringle was sent to Telegraph Creek and Glenora, in northern British Columbia. John Pringle was 46 years old when he went to Glenora; he had 20 years experience in ministry, primarily in western Canada and in Minnesota. He hauled his kit over the ice of the still-frozen Stikine River to arrive at Glenora. Faith Fenton, reporter with the Toronto *Globe* who was covering the Klondike, wrote of Pringle's ministry in glowing terms. He lived in a six-foot by eight-foot tent in Glenora but his mission field covered everyone within a 30- to 40-mile radius of Glenora. Fenton wrote, "His tall, slender, muscular figure is greeted with a shout of welcome as comes swinging up the hills." One of Pringle's tasks was to carry out going mail for the miners, prospectors, NWMP, and others in the back country areas of his "parish."[25]

As the route north to the Klondike through Telegraph Creek was being secured, gold was discovered on the Stikine River, creating a small boom. Thus there were miners and fortune seekers in small groups throughout the district. John Pringle wrote to Dr. Warden of the Home Missions Committee on Nov. 17, 1898, describing the context of his ministry,

> A crowd of gold-seekers on the wing need the gospel more than any other mass of men I ever met. There are the reckless, the indifferent, the professing Christian without back-bone, the earnest Christians, the discouraged, the despairing, good and bad men who have spent all and are at their wits end. They all need Christ very much, and are glad to hear the Saviour's name most of them....
> I can see, if not feel, the shadow of an acute home sickness falling over us up here. But we have after all the heart of the Christmas time, Jesus, and our thoughts about Him and our blessing from Him.[26]

It was impossible to draw together these scattered groups of people into one central location, and so Pringle traveled from cabin to cabin having "family altar" worship with the occupants. Pringle found this ministry pattern more effective than the traditional Sunday worship services which were held in Glenora each week. As he wrote to Robertson, "There is no church organization but men have carried Christ with them who had never let him into their hearts before."[27] There might not be any identifiable congregation; in fact Pringle could not find a single Presbyterian among the prospectors around Glenora, but people were responding to the gospel message they saw and heard in Pringle's life and words by making decisions to follow Jesus.

There is one truth about the gold-prospecting business—things can change quickly. As quickly as the Stikine River area boomed, the rush had passed and the focus moved to Atlin, British Columbia. And with the new excitement, half of the Glenora community was on the move to Atlin. In the fall of 1898, Pringle visited Atlin and decided he needed to pack up his ministry and move there with the people too. While the work at Glenora was important, "for scores at Glenora there will be thousands at Atlin." Without any agreement from either Robertson or the Home Missions Committee, Pringle changed his mission nine months after having been sent to Glenora. He arrived in Atlin to set up his new base of operations on March 6, 1899.[28]

Pringle, on his 1898 tour of the Atlin area, had seen first-hand what the absence of trained medical personnel meant to the miners and their families. In Ocober of that year, he wrote to the Home Missions Committee asking that some Christian nurses be sent at once. The HMC turned to the small group of women who had come together to send the four VON personnel to Dawson; again the women responded, hearing it as "a Macedonian cry." The Atlin Nurse Committee was formed with representatives from the virtually every Presbyterian church in Toronto. On June 28, 1899, Helen Bone and Elizabeth H. Mitchell, sister of the Rev. Mitchell of Mitchell, Ontario, were designated as missionary nurses, and they arrived in Atlin on July 22. By that time there were 1,200 miners in the immediate area. A government official gave the nurses a cabin to use as a hospital. It had a mud roof, sawdust floor, and only one window made of two small panes of glass. There was only room for four cots, when the hospital was full, patients were cared for in a tent, even in the middle of winter. The living accomodations for the nurses were not much better, being a shack 12 feet by 18 feet in which they both lived.[29] In spite of these challenges Bone and Mitchell made an impact in the community. Pringle wrote on Aug. 25, 1899, to the *Record* in glowing terms,

> The work of the nurses for one month has done more to make people believe we have the spirit of Christ, than a year's preaching could. I have no words to tell the church how glad and thankful I am for this beginning in Atlin. It has strengthened my hands and made the old church dearer to her own people, and exalted her in the opinion of those of other churches and of no church. Best of all, the gentle ministering hands of our nurses will open many a heart to the Gospel and Spirit of Jesus.[30]

Hospital work was evangelism, the actions of the nurses spoke even more powerfully than the words of a sermon.

In the summer of 1900, the one-ward St. Andrew's Hospital was built with volunteer labour from the community. The following year a Presbyterian church building was erected. In 1902, a second ward, intended as a women's ward, was added to the hospital. And in 1903 a new nurses' residence was built. In 1902, the government of British Columbia became a partner with the women in Toronto in the operation of the hospital. The

Atlin Committee would be responsible for paying the nursing staff, while the provincial government covered the operating costs. This sounded like a good idea; however the government did not provide adequate funding, and so the nurses became fundraisers for the hospital. One of the more creative ideas was the sale of "hospital tickets," which were a form of medical insurance. Individuals could purchase a month's hospital insurance for $5.00.[31]

The gold rush at Atlin was never as chaotic as the rush at Dawson. First, Atlin was in British Columbia and provincial rules regarding claims applied. In British Columbia claim stakers had to be Canadian citizens. This immediately limited the size of the rush. Second, the gold extraction process quickly moved from panning to mining, which meant a smaller but more stable community. Third, the presence of the church and its hospital acted as a moral compass within the community. All of this impacted the types of medical care the nurses provided. Between 1899 and 1902, frostbite and scurvy were common presenting ailments. Following 1902, the nurses saw more industrial accidents from either mining or lumbering. As well, there were maternity cases; 10 children were born in the hospital in 1904 and six in 1905. For most of the time under discussion, the nurses at St. Andrew's Hospital were the only trained medical personnel for 250 kilometers. There were short stints of a year or so when a doctor was present in the community, but for the vast majority of the time the nurses made all the medical decisions involved in the care of their patients. In 1904, a total of 111 patients received care. By 1912 that had reached a high of 240 patients, with only one death. As the community of Atlin began to shrink in the early 1920's, the number of patients declined as well; in 1923, there were only 20 patients admitted to the hospital. That does not cover out-patient services rendered by the nurses. This decline in numbers further complicated the financial situation of the hospital, whose provincial funding was partially tied to the number of patients cared for annually.[32]

During the 26 years from 1899 to 1925, Mr. J. A. Fraser served as the secretary-treasurer of the hospital board in Atlin, providing stability and corporate memory. During those years, a total of 13 different nurses worked at St. Andrew's Hospital. Three had direct connections to Presbyterian clergy: Elizabeth Mitchell's brother, Jean Kellock's father, and Lucy Pringle's two brothers were all ministers. Some who served in Atlin could not get it out of their system: both Margaret Emes and Rachel Hanna stayed seven years, only to return after being away for four and two years respectively; each served an additional two years during their second stint at Atlin. Lucy Pringle summed up the feeling of most of the nurses when she wrote, "This is the ideal we profess, to follow in the footsteps of the Great Physician counting no sacrifice too great, no service too small, careless of any praise but that of God and conscience."[33]

The success of St. Andrew's Hospital in opening up alternative models of ministry led to the creation of the Women's Home Missionary Society in 1903. There had been a cry from across the church for other hospitals to be established, a cry that was too large for the Atlin Nurse Committee to respond to. The WHMS was the result, which in 20 years would have established 15 hospitals or out-patient clinics in northern Ontario and the west. To their medical ministry they would add the school homes discussed in Chapter 4, the funding of deaconesses working in the inner city, and the support of home missionaries working on the prairies. The Atlin adventure proved that the women of the church had a vision for home mission. Now they had a way to make that vision a reality.

PEACE RIVER COUNTRY

With much fanfare HMC announced to the General Assembly in 1903 that a missionary was being sent to the Peace River country of the unorganized provisional district of Athabaska (in 1905 to become part of Alberta.) Using the language of the settler, R.A. Simpson was being sent "to break ground and undertake foundation work in a field 500 miles beyond Edmonton." Simpson and his wife were going "beyond the railways and the towns, into the dim distances and the pioneering days of a vast and vague country." Instead of waiting for the settlers to move into the Peace before sending in the messengers of the gospel, this time the Presbytery was sending a missionary ahead. In 1904, it was reported that Simpson had started three congregations at Grande Prairie, Peace River, and Pouce Coupe.[34] In the late summer of 1904 a log manse was built at Spirit River, where worship services were held in the sitting-room. During their time in Spirit River, the Simpson's first-born child died and was buried close to the manse. Late in 1905, the Simpsons left the Peace.[35]

For four years no Presbyterian ministry took place in the Peace, and in fact, in 1908, the Presbytery of Edmonton was seriously considering selling the property provided, as good Scots, "they could get out of it what they put into it" because "it is a little early to go into the Peace River country yet."[36] But by the summer of 1909 that had changed. The Rev. Alexander Forbes and his wife were commissioned by the Presbytery of Edmonton to tour the Peace River area to evaluate the possibility of again doing home mission work in the region. One of the most important things that had changed was the development of Marquis wheat in 1904. Marquis wheat is an earlier maturing wheat that allowed more northern regions of the prairies with their shorter growing season and shorter frost-free period, in this case specifically the Peace River, to be farmed. Marquis wheat was being used widely on the prairies by 1911, which coincides with the period when the Peace River country was first being settled in an intentional way.[37]

Mrs. Forbes, an avid supporter of the Women's Home Missionary Society, kept the editor of the Society's publication, *The Home Mission Pioneer*, well informed about what was happening in the Peace River country. On their 1,300 mile trip, the Forbes discovered that the Methodists and Anglicans were already present in the southern portion of the Peace River country, but that no Protestant ministry was taking place in the area of the Grande Prairie Valley. And in fact, Forbes was the first minister to lead worship at Beaver Lodge, Alberta. Mrs. Forbes returned to her home in Fort Saskatchewan, Alberta, saying, "This new country needs missionaries, 'Who shall go, Salvation's story telling; Looking to Jesus Counting not the cost!'"[38] The Presbytery of Edmonton was so convinced by Forbes' report in October 1909 that they decided to immediately find someone to go and minister at Grande Prairie and "organize the Pioneer work in that settlement of The Last Great West." In using this phrase, the presbytery was playing on the very popular promotional publication from the Department of the Interior, which was seeking to encourage immigrants to come to Canada, entitled, *The Last Best West*. After looking unsuccessfully for someone to fulfill this important task, it became clear to the presbytery who it was that should do this work: Alexander Forbes. So the presbytery persuaded the congregation at Fort Saskatchewan to release Forbes, who had been their minister for 15 years, "to oversee the church's work in this newest front of the last West." And on Feb. 21, 1910, the Forbes household left Fort Saskatchewan for the Grande Prairie. They arrived on May 10. They built a manse at Flying Shot.[39]

One of Forbes' tasks was to plant churches, gathering together small groups of people in the living rooms of obliging settlers, in the back rooms of stores and the like. Through an agreement with the Rev. Charles Hopkins of the Methodist Church in Canada, who was appointed to the Grande Prairie about the same time as Forbes, the Methodists took the west side of Lake Saskatoon and the Presbyterians the east side. Here Forbes was a free agent, able to make decisions on the fly, choosing to start a congregation in this location and without reference to any overseeing group. It was the same kind of freedom that James Robertson had enjoyed and that missionaries in the Yukon exercised when deciding the scope and nature of their ministry. By late 1912, it was clear that more ordained missionaries were needed if the Presbyterian Church was going to respond to the demands being placed on it. Things were moving so fast that there were no fewer than six small churches under construction in the fall of 1913. A request for two new ministers had been submitted to the Home Missions Committee. In July 1913, R. F. Thompson moved to Spirit River. In February, R. W. McVey took his place at Spirit River, so that Thompson could move to the British Columbia frontier and the Pouce Coupe territory, which was just opening up. In addition to that a minister was needed at Peace

River Crossing, which was growing in anticipation of the railroad that was coming in from Edmonton. The plan of the Presbytery of Edmonton's Home Mission Committee was, "we must try to possess the strategic points so that our missionaries could keep in touch with the pioneer settlers who are passing into the country."[40]

In 1911, it became clear that it was Grande Prairie and not Flying Shot that was going to become the larger centre, so Forbes filed a homestead claim for a quarter section of land immediately east of the Grande Prairie townsite. On this property a log building was erected; it was to function both as the Forbes' house as well as having "a room or two for the sick." Shortly after arriving on the Grande Prairie, Forbes had asked the Edmonton Women's Home Missionary Presbyterial Society to send a nurse to work in the mission. Seeing a need, Forbes challenged the closest group of Presbyterians he knew to meet that need, and the group willingly took on the challenge as their mission. The presbyterial found a nurse, Agnes Baird, and she agreed to become their missionary in the Peace River Country. She arrived in Flying Shot in late 1910. In an article published in *The Home Mission Pioneer* about a year after her arrival in the Peace, she outlined some of her work at the Pioneer Hospital, the name given by the locals to the facility. She had dealt with complicated fractures and gunshots. One patient had come having been burned in the fire that destroyed his home; he had gone back to retrieve his money bag, and then after having been burned froze while seeking shelter. Baird had worked hard with the patient not just caring for his physical needs, but "[w]e had hopes that his affliction would be a means of grace to him but, of late, he will not look at the Bible." Baird was clear; the hospital had a mission to "minister to the soul as well as the body." In 1913, the time was right to plan for a more permanent hospital structure, not just a couple of rooms in the Forbes' house. And so the cornerstone was laid by three women: Agnes Baird, Mrs. Forbes, and Dr. Higbee, who was the first medical doctor in Grande Prairie. In June 1914, "The Katharine H. Prittie Hospital" was formally opened, named for the daughter of Mr. and Mrs. Prittie of Toronto, who provided a $5,000 grant towards the building of the hospital. In the 1920s the WMS(WD) opened the Fort Vermilion Hospital Unit; located on the Peace River, north of the 58th parallel (175 kilometers south of the Arctic Circle).[41]

The ministry in the Peace River area continued to grow through the 1910's. In the rest of the west, immigration slowed to almost nothing during World War I, but in the Peace River region it continued. A major blow to the ministry in the region was the sudden death of Mrs. Forbes on Aug. 27, 1917. Alexander Forbes stayed in Grande Prairie after his wife's death, and in 1918 was inducted into the charge. Because of the number of churches and their great distance from Edmonton, on Sept. 1, 1920, the Presbytery of Peace River was formed. At that time there were four pastoral charges each served by an ordained minister, and there were five student fields that had ministry only in the summer time when students could be found. By 1925 there were six Augmented charges and six Mission Fields in the Peace River Presbytery, encompassing 51 preaching points.[42]

The arrival of more immigrants, the coming of the railroad, and the development of town infrastructures did not mean that there was no longer a rugged edge to life in the Peace. The missionary located in what was known at the time as "the Peace River block of British Columbia" spent two months at Pouce Coupe ministering in the area. Then at the start of the third month, he packed "his blankets and an emergency supply of canned goods and provisions" and started out on a month long circuit. He travelled first to Fort St. John where he stayed for 10 days to two weeks doing ministry. Then he would head off again going west toward Hudson's Hope and then south to the Pine River settlements, before turning east and passing through the Cutback communities and returning home at the start of the fourth month. He would spend months four and five in Pouce Coupe, and then at the start of month six again saddle up and head on his month-long circuit. Understaffed, but recognizing the need for the church to be present with the ranchers and other settlers in the district, the clergy who supplied Pouce Coupe met that need through personal sacrifice and an openness to doing ministry in non-traditional ways.[43]

A second innovative model of ministry that made sense in the remoteness of the Peace River was the mission lived by T.F. MacGregor, the minister of the Fort Vermilion Pastoral Charge, which consisted of settlers, traders, and prospectors scattered along the northern parts of the Peace River. The following description was given in 1923 of his work:

> Owing to the absence of roads, and the impassable character of the trails, the missionary has learned to make the river the main thoroughfare of his mission field during the summer. He comes up to the town of Peace River by steamer. There he purchases lumber and builds a boat, and starts down stream in his itinerary. At every landing along the river he moors his boat and starts on foot for the settlements of the interior, sometimes 40 miles distant. At night, he sleeps on the side of the trail where night overtakes him, and by day he visits the settlers and conducts service where a few families or bachelors or children can be brought together. This is real mission work, and the most encouraging part of his report is that at almost every service, one hundred percent of the people within reach of the service are in attendance at it. When he reaches the north end of his mission field, which is 360 miles long, he sells his boat to a trapper, and returns by steamer to Peace River here he again starts on his itinerary. In the winter he travels by mail-team, dog sled or by snowshoes.[44]

The official statistics indicate that there were nine preaching points on MacGregor's circuit with 31 households consisting of 150 people under his pastoral care. There was certainly still room for the pioneering minister in the northern parts of Canada.

With the coming of Church Union in 1925 the entire Presbyterian work in the Peace River Country went into the United Church of Canada. Alexander Forbes was opposed to union; he did not see that there was any overlapping of ministry that needed to be eliminated. Back in 1910 when he had arrived on Grande Prairie, he had worked out an agreement with the Methodists, an informal type of federation, made on the ground by those most affected by the decisions. Like a number of the veteran Presbyterian missionary-mined clergy, Forbes favoured a locally initiated federation model of church union.

OTHER NORTHERN MINISTRY

The Province of Manitoba remained postage stamp–sized until 1881, but it was not until 1912 when the northern section was incorporated into the province, making it the size that we are used to seeing on our maps today. And it was not until 1912 that Manitoba Presbyterians seemed to recognize that there might be a call for ministry further north than the Swan River Valley. That year, S.C. Murray, in his report to the Home Mission Committee of the General Assembly, noted that the railway had just reached The Pas and that a town was springing up there. Although no missionary had been appointed to this northern region, "conditions here must be examined into and the territory pre-empted for the Master, or the Adversary will occupy it for the promotion of his own special business."[45] Things move rapidly in the north with the boom and bust cycle, and in the summer of 1914, Presbyterians in The Pas organized themselves into a regular self-supporting congregation named Westminster, and the congregation called the Rev. J.A. Cormie to be their minister.[46] The coming of the war led to the development of the Mandy Mine with its rich copper ore near present day Flin Flon, but the church was in no position during the war to respond to these ministry opportunities.

With the war's end, S.C. Murray, superintendent of Home Mission for Manitoba, could speak in optimistic tones about Manitoba entering "a second Home Mission career" as Manitoba's "New North" was opened up through the development of its mining, forestry, and hydro-electric resources. In the spring of 1919, the Rev, Hector Ferguson, the minister at The Pas, was asked to do a survey tour of the areas north of the town. His recommendation to the Board of Home Mission and Social Service was that they appoint a roaming missionary who would ride the rails of the Hudson Bay Railway and its branch lines taking the gospel message to all along the route. The Board appointed William Holmes in 1920, who was then just graduating from Manitoba College, to this task. Holmes traveled the 300 miles of track, doing lantern talks, distributing literature and holding services wherever and whenever the opportunity presented itself. He was the only clergyperson who had regular contact with the mining, prospecting, and lumbering camps along the railway. It was noted, "[m]any reports from the field have made it abundantly clear that his ministry was much appreciated." However, in 1922 it was necessary to end the experiment, because there was not enough money for the Board to fund all of the mission projects that it had underway.[47]

While the Board did not have enough money or vision to maintain the mission experiment, the congregation of Westminster in The Pas and its minister, H. Wallace, sought to create and sustain a number of Sunday Schools along the railway. One of the Sunday Schools, which they supported with literature and organizational help, was located 320 kilometers from The Pas and drew 18 children. They saw an opportunity for mission and seized it. The congregation at The Pas was one of the stronger congregations in the Presbytery of Dauphin; by 1924 there were 115 households with 350 people under the pastoral care of the congregation. The vision and drive of this missional church shamed the Board of Home Mission who stated, "An appointment to this special field must be made as soon as the funds will permit."[48]

While the Board was ending one experiment in ministry, it was supporting a similar kind of ministry at the other end of the Synod of Manitoba and Northwestern Ontario. In 1922, the Board agreed to appoint a missionary to travel the 1,200 miles of track radiating north from Port Arthur and Fort William; here, particularly at the divisional points, were small communities to whom no church was ministering on a regular basis. Robert Dewar was appointed "a missionary with a roving commission" to this special field.[49]

CONCLUSION

As the Presbyterian Church faced the new mission front of the North, it sought to find creative ways of responding to the challenge. Much of the innovation in ministry grew out of people on the ground deciding to do ministry in new ways, ways that made sense for the new context of ministry. Often the decisions about changing the direction and nature of the ministry were made with little or no consultation with the HMC, or its successor. The missionaries and the congregations they led were turned into missional agents free to bend the style and form of the ministry into one that fit the new northern land. This freer approach is particularly evident in the story of the Yukon mission and the work in the Peace River Country. The northern ministry in Manitoba and Northwestern Ontario was more circumscribed by the decisions of church leaders far from the actual ministry. The Synod of Manitoba and Northwestern Ontario had become much more organizational and bureaucratic in its response to the call to mission than was the younger Synod of Alberta.

Doctor entering Katherine H. Prittie Hospital, Grande Prairie, AB.
(United Church of Canada/Victoria University Archives, 93.049P/1102)

Good Samaritan Hospital, Dawson City, Yukon.
(United Church of Canada/Victoria University Archives, 93.049P/4534)

Atlin Hospital, Atlin, BC.
(Presbyterian Church Archives)

CHAPTER 6

"by His own methods":[1]
The Rise of Evangelism and Social Service

As Presbyterian Church leaders looked around, they saw a host of problems: declining church attendance, a lessening of family prayer and other devotional practices, prostitution, drunkenness, and political corruption. Then there were the bigger problems of the city, rural depopulation, and the rise in labour activism. The leadership was confronted with an uncomfortable piece of logic; if the Christian faith were the truth, then why was the world still a mess? With the vast majority of Canadians being Christian, surely the problems that society was confronting should be no more. But that was not the case. The problems still existed and the older church patterns seemed unable to address these problems. Simply having people join together to worship God on Sunday and to have ministers do pastoral visiting was not impacting the society, was not changing people's lives. The answer to this problem, it was suggested, was the twin focuses of evangelism and social service. Evangelism was defined as "the quickening of the life of the Church for the extension of the Kingdom" of God; and social service was "removing hindrances to the extension of the Kingdom." The two went hand in glove; it was only through the removal of various roadblocks in people's lives and in society that the Kingdom of God would be able to advance drawing more people to experience God's reign, and the energy and organization necessary to remove those roadblocks would only come as people were enlivened spiritually and deepened their commitment to Jesus Christ. The Presbyterian Church was proud of the fact that it had succeeded in putting these two factors together in the mind and heart of the church. They fed each other, needed each other, as the Assembly heard in 1916, "What God hath joined together let no one put asunder." Historian Brian Fraser in his study of Presbyterian progressives describes the balance in their "comprehensive vision of the transformation of individual characters into the likeness of Christ and the gradual permeation of society by the moral and social values perfectly manifested in his character." Through evangelism and social service the church would begin to see the transformation of individuals and society, becoming the first signs of the coming kingdom of God.[2]

EVANGELISM

The Committee on Evangelism bluntly put its case in 1909,

> The Church exists for the purpose of evangelizing the world. The Church that ceases to be evangelistic ceases to be Christian. The minister that is dead to the spirit of evangelism has lost touch with his Lord. The congregations from which the spirit of evangelism has died, thereby demonstrates its need to be evangelized.[3]

The purpose of the church was to confront people with the good news about Jesus Christ. It was in the first decade of the 20th century that the Presbyterian Church became very intentional about its evangelistic role. To raise evangelism's profile one step further, the 1908 Assembly was addressed by American Presbyterian evangelist, the Rev. J. Wilbur Chapman, whose name was well known in Canadian Presbyterian circles as well. This emphasis on evangelism was felt on the prairies.

In 1908, under the leadership of the Rev. H.G. Crozier, the Presbytery of Minnedosa, Manitoba (north of Brandon), used a method often employed by the Chapman team in their campaigns; holding a simultaneous presbytery-wide evangelistic campaign. The Presbytery invited a number of ministers from neighbouring presbyteries and from as far away as Toronto to be part of the campaign, so that in every congregation in the presbytery evangelistic preaching services could be held simultaneously over a two week period. Having every congregation in the area participating built excitement among all the Presbyterians in the area, and drew the attention of non-church-goers. It would have been the talk of Minnedosa and the surrounding area. So successful was this approach that it was recommended that other presbyteries imitate the model.[4]

In 1910, there was an evangelistic campaign just on the Saskatchewan side of the border in the Presbytery of Yorkton. Here a different model was used. The numerous small preaching points were visited by one of a couple of teams over the summer and early fall. The teams would stay in a community for two weeks, no matter how small or how poor the response to the campaign, before moving to the next mission charge. This approach of progressing from one charge to another meant that this model became called a "progressive" campaign. Then in November and December a simultaneous mission was held in "the larger towns and villages." The impact of the Yorkton campaign was reported to the church at large, but with any identifying information removed from the report, therefore it is impossible to determine about which community or congregation a given comment was written. Some congregations had grown enough that they were able to move from being mission charges to become augmented charges. In other places the impact was seen in the deeper spiritual life of parishioners.

One pastor wrote of 100 people joining the church in the space of three months, "whole families" were coming to church, including the husbands and fathers. But the campaign also had its doubters; one lay person wrote, "Our Church has been too slack along these lines in the past and I do hope that hereafter from year to year we can so educate our people that they will no longer take offense with such appeals as are now being made." Some people had taken offense at the evangelistic message and the preaching campaigns, but largely because the church had been falling down on the job, failing to take seriously its evangelistic role. Many congregations had come to think that Presbyterians did not do things like evangelism and hold preaching missions.[5]

In the early part of the 1910's, these evangelistic missions developed along lines something like this: the minister of the congregation or charge hoping to host a preaching mission would contact a nearby, preferably Presbyterian, minister who was known for their evangelistic preaching to find out whether they would come. The invited clergyperson, who was usually the full-time minister of a congregation, would need the permission of their congregation to take two or more weeks to go and lead the mission at the other charge. These preaching missions were led almost entirely by local parish clergy, who were involved in evangelism on a part-time basis. By the late 1910's that had changed, the older style was still in use in some localities, but most of the evangelistic missions were lead by one of the four to six evangelistic teams working under the direction of the Board of Home Mission and Social Service. The teams were made up of two or three people. There was the preacher whose role it was to preach the evangelistic sermon and encourage people to come forward as a sign of their new commitment to follow Jesus. There was the director of song, who both led the congregational singing and who sang a couple of solos themselves as part of the service. A third person was sometimes included as an accompanist. In the teams under the Board's direction, all the preachers and most of the directors of song were men. Congregations interested in having a team visit would contact the Board and make arrangements from there. By the early 1920's there was a waiting list of over two years to book an evangelistic mission.

In the fall and winter of 1920-21, no less than four evangelistic teams were working among the Presbyterian churches on the prairies. The Rev. E. W. MacKay and director of song T.H. Nichol spent September through December, 1920 leading evangelistic meetings in Alberta. The Rev. D.T. McClintock had spent the first part of 1921 in Saskatchewan, leading services with director of song Miss A.B. Niven. Dr. Unsworth with Mr. Dunnington as director of song was spending the first part of 1921 in Alberta. And Dr. D.J. Craig, who had once been an evangelist paid by the Synod of Alberta, was in Peace River with his co-workers, the Weavers.[6]

By the late 1910's there was a pattern to these preaching missions. The team would be in the town for two and a half weeks for two weeks of actual preaching services. Every morning throughout the district to be covered by the preaching campaign there would be prayer meetings in homes. The purpose was to pray for the mission and that God would bless the church. As the Board of Evangelism reported, people would "come together and avoiding unnecessary conversation, just kneel down and pray." In the early afternoon there would be teaching sessions at the church building, focusing on the doctrinal truths of Christianity in the first week, and the need for and patterns of personal evangelism in the second week. These meetings were aimed at Christians to give them both the knowledge and the skills to continue the work of evangelism after the team had left the area. Also in the afternoon, after school had ended, there would be meetings for boys, girls, and youth, in the church building. These meetings would be held four times over the course of the mission. The missioners were in some communities invited into the schools; in the high schools a favourite topic was "sexual purity." Then in the evenings there would be a "preaching and song service" at which people would be invited to make a commitment to Jesus, confessing their sin and turning to Him as their personal Saviour. In addition, there would be some special meetings: one for women only; another for men only, which was held not at the church but in the town hall or a local theatre, a neutral space that might be more attractive to men; and new believers meetings, which were to nurture the new converts in their faith. It was an intense two-and-a-half weeks of ministry and outreach, that often had an energy that carried the evangelistic passion beyond the departure of the missioner team. In the eight months from September 1922 to April 1923, 87 such preaching missions based in Presbyterian congregations were undertaken; half of them were held in one of the prairie provinces.[7]

In 1920, the Presbyterian Church arranged for well-known American evangelist Gipsy Smith to visit four cities in Canada, one being Winnipeg. In 1921, the Board of Home Mission and Social Service brought in the American evangelist, G. Campbell Morgan, to Canada for two months. Among the places he preached were Calgary, Moose Jaw, and Saskatoon. Both Smith and Morgan fit the more orderly and restrained style of Presbyterianism. There was a clear call to conversion delivered by a gifted orator, but neither of these men were as emotional as some of the evangelists of the 1920's.[8]

Clergy and other church leaders saw five distinct effects that the church's commitment to evangelism was having. People were more open to the idea of evangelism. The "prayerful caution" and "sane methods" used by the Presbyterian evangelists had overcome nearly "all prejudices" against evangelism. Congregation members now understood why the Committee on Evangelism had made such a strong statement about the need for evangelism in the church, and what role they might play in its being moved forward. Second, individuals were being converted and were becoming part of the life of the church. As souls were saved, the church grew. Which leads directly into the third impact; the spiritual temperature of the whole church was raised as the evangelistic crusade caused old members to deepen their commitment to Jesus, and the newly converted brought their excitement to the congregation. Fourth, there was a new awareness of the social needs of the community. Growing out of these evangelistic meetings groups rose to tackle the identified social issues of the day: prostitution, the alcohol trade, gambling, and similar concerns. Finally, these campaigns became opportunities for young people to step forward, committing themselves to serve God full time as minister, missionary, or deaconess.[9]

During the summer of 1914, four students from the theological department at Manitoba College formed a gospel team and toured through most of Manitoba, presenting the "gospel by address and song and life." The purpose was to reach young people, not only that they might hear the gospel message, but also to challenge youth to consider a lifetime of service to God. The team used many of the same methods of the full-time evangelists although they stayed in a given location only a week to 10 days. This team also did street preaching, using a dry-goods box as a stage and speaking and singing on street corners and at factory gates.[10]

By the 1920's there was a sense that all of these evangelistic methods were not reaching the working classes, and that new methods needed to be found. William and Virginia Asher led evangelistic crusades that focused on the working classes, entering the saloons and preaching at the factory gates, intentionally seeking to touch the working classes with the good news of Jesus. The Ashers had been part of the Chapman campaign team before going on their own; William Asher, born in Scotland, had grown up in Ontario. The Ashers' campaigns were supported by the Presbyterians in the communities they visited. In October 1907, almost 500 people "jammed into the bar" at the Queen's Hotel in Winnipeg to hear the Ashers speak. Although people were converted under the Ashers' ministry, few of the working class males, who were predominantly their audience, were able to overcome the social barriers that divided them from the increasingly middle class church in Canada. There was a need for "a new evangelism," one that would "deal adequately with Christian truth, making God real to men, and at the same time doing justice to the needs of the present hour."[11] Evangelism and social service belonged together. The Presbyterian church recognized that social service was an important part of the church's mission, but they were equally clear that evangelism was to have the priority. The words spoken by the Rev. John Shearer, a leader among those Presbyterians seeking to mobilize the church in the struggle for moral and social reform, at the Pre-Assembly Congress in 1913 still rang in their ears,

It is not enough to change the environment; it is not enough to transform social life. That is necessary, but it not sufficient. It is essential that the heart be regenerated, that the people should be saved, that character should be transformed; and that can be done to the full only by bringing the people in contact with the living, life-giving, risen, glorious and glorified Son of Man. There is no other way.[12]

MORAL AND SOCIAL REFORM

The moral redemption of the nation went hand in hand with the religious salvation of the nation; the two were inseparable. Faith was a public commitment and a lifestyle. When this was combined with the Presbyterian understanding that the church was to be the conscience of the state, the Presbyterian Church was prepared, in fact, felt compelled, to become involved in the great moral crusades of the first quarter of the 20th century. The three crusades this chapter will look at in some detail are: the crusade against the "social evil," or, prostitution; Sabbath observance; and the temperance campaign.

The Board of Moral and Social Reform brought to the Assembly in 1910 a two-pronged recommendation regarding "the social evil." The church was asked to find ways of giving "refuge and offering help to women of the underworld who may desire to reform," and secondly to educate "particularly the women of the church of the extent of the Social Evil, and the traffic in girls for immoral purposes." The goals were clear: redeem the prostitute and prevent the further spread of prostitution.[13]

The church established Redemption Homes, sometimes called Rescue Missions, across Canada. On the prairies there were homes located in Winnipeg, Calgary, and Medicine Hat. Six years after Assembly approved the development of these homes, the Board of Home Mission and Social Service felt compelled to defend the church's decision in making this part of its work. The need of these women was "exceptional." These women were social outcasts, hopeless and depressed, with nowhere to turn for help; it was the church's responsibility to care. Jesus' own example called the church to receive, forgive, and speak compassionately to those seeking help from the redemptive homes. These homes had three purposes. First, they provided a place for prostitutes who were wishing to get out of the business to go while they cut their ties to their former life and sought to begin a new life. They also became home to prostitutes and unmarried women who were pregnant and had nowhere else to turn. Of the 16 new residents admitted to the Winnipeg home in 1918, 15 were either "motherless" or their mothers lived in "the old country." Besides providing a home environment for these women, there was an educational programme that taught the women homemaking skills like cooking, washing, sewing, and the like. By giving the young women, and many of the residents were young, these life skills, it was hoped they were acquiring what they would need in the future once they had left the home. Thirdly, there was a religious component to the homes' work. There was daily prayer time, and on Sundays a worship service was held at the home for those residents who were unable to attend worship at one of the nearby churches. Residents were confronted with the claims of the gospel, the need for repentance, the promise of forgiveness in Jesus Christ, and the promise of the Holy Spirit to give them the strength to live a new, reformed life. These were redemptive homes, and for the church complete redemption could not be found apart from making a commitment to Jesus Christ. Those who ran these facilities estimated that 40 percent of those who spent some time in one of the Presbyterian redemptive homes made a public confession of their faith in Jesus Christ. In Calgary, there were two, three-storey houses used as the redemption home, which was under the direction of two trained deaconesses, Miss Sage and Miss Pettigrew. In 1915, 75 women made use of the Calgary facility, with an average of 20 women in residence at any given time. In 1923, the Winnipeg home moved from the downtown core to a ten-acre site in suburban Winnipeg.[14]

Fulfilling the second prong of the Board's recommendation was more complex. The Board of Moral and Social Reform quickly realized that educating women about the dangers of "white slavery" would not end prostitution. There had to be a change in how men acted. The Board published a pamphlet outlining a double standard, "Barbarous and civilized people alike, Buddhist, Christian, and Moslem peoples alike, have insisted strongly on chastity in women; but not one of them has ever seemed to expect a like chastity in ordinary men." The pamphlet went on to argue, "The same virtue is needed in both sexes for the happy development of that family life on which the security of the [human] race and the progress of civilization depend." The double standard had to go, chastity was to be as expected of men as of women. The Board was unable to see anyway of ensuring male chastity apart from using the law, the police, and the courts. Church officials put pressure on politicians in Ottawa seeking to have a number of laws amended or added to the books: the age of consent for women raised from 14 to 16 years, the criminalization of adultery, and the protection female employees from the sexual harassment of their male employers. On a local level, Presbyterian clergy encouraged city officials and police to use their powers to stamp out prostitution. By 1910, most municipal politicians had decided that they would do better to limit prostitution to a small area in their city rather than seek to stamp it out, which would simply drive it underground.[15]

SABBATH OBSERVANCE

The enforcement of Sunday as a day of rest grew out of three factors. First, to work on Sunday was a violation of one of the Ten Commandments, which most Presbyterians saw as the blueprint for living a moral life. Second, by enforcing that no work would be done on the Sunday, everyone was given the opportunity to attend worship, to reflect on the spiritual side of life. Third, by having one day in the week on which factories stopped their production, offices were closed, and business of buying and selling was shut down, working families had one day of rest together as a family each week. For the church the struggle was between those who saw "the chief end of life" being "to get rich quick" and those who saw the primary purpose of life being to "glorify God and enjoy God forever." The churches had been so convincing in their argument that the government in Ottawa had adopted the Lord's Day Act which was to be enforced across the country.[16]

By 1909, there were two glaring areas of Sabbath breaking on the prairies. At harvest time, farmers ran their binders and threshers right through Sunday, on the principle that they needed to get the harvest in before it got rained on or the like. Peter Strang, district superintendent in Southern Saskatchewan, during the 1915 harvest came across two binders out in the field working on a Sunday. Strang went to talk to people operating the binders, who after their conversation with Strang unhitched their teams and went home. On another occasion, Strang stopped to have "a quiet talk" with the leader of a threshing team that was working on Sunday. After the conversation the leader shut down the threshing operation and sent everyone home. Strang was pleased that there were whole townships in Saskatchewan where no work was done on the Sabbath, even at the height of the harvest season. The second concern related to what forms of entertainment were appropriate for a Sunday. Strang wanted the young men who were playing baseball on Sunday afternoons in June and July charged as Sabbath breakers. William Shearer, district superintendent of Central Alberta, noted that in those rural communities where church was held in the evening, the community dance and the summer evening baseball game were direct competition for the church, against which the church had no hope of winning. The Board of Social Service and Evangelism in 1913 wanted a group of movie theatres in Winnipeg charged with breaking the Lord's Day Act. The theatres had shown movies on a Sunday afternoon as a fundraiser for a charitable cause. The Board saw this as a blatant attempt to make Sunday movie-going a popular thing to do, and therefore to get the public to pressure the government to change the law. In a series of discussions surrounding the running of streetcars on Sunday, it was decided that in Edmonton and Calgary the streetcars could run to the city limits on Sunday, but no further. The purposes that lay behind the Lord's Day Act were for the good of humanity, but at times the rhetoric of the moral reformers sounded as though human beings were made for the Lord's day and not the Lord's day for human beings.[17]

TEMPERANCE

"The demon drink" was a roadblock to the coming of the Kingdom of God. It ruined the lives of those who drank in excess; they lost their jobs, they put their own lives at risk from being so intoxicated that they did not know what they were doing. It ruined the lives of everyone in the drinker's family; money that could have been put into feeding and clothing children was wasted in the saloon. Wives became not only caregiver but also bread-winner, putting extraordinary pressure on the family and in the case of the wife and mother who drank, the husband and father inherited the caregiving role along with his traditional breadwinning role. And "demon drink" cost society. Those charged with "drunk and disorderly conduct" were the larg-est group of accused persons to come before a judge during the early 1900's on the prairies. Those who drank to excess ate up court time, jails needed to be expanded to house them, and the police needed to find ways to make sure that they did not bother other people or harm themselves. Clergy on the prairies regularly saw the effects of alcohol on the lives of parishioners and community members; they had no trouble declaring that it was a blight on society that should be stamped out.

Attempts to bring in Canada-wide prohibition had failed, and tem-perance forces were left with the Scott Act which allowed local communi-ties to decide to become "dry." There were some variations on what "dry" meant. One option was to "ban the bar," closing all places where alcohol was sold for consumption on the premises, but allowing alcohol to be sold in a limited number of government licensed stores. Temperance advocates argued that the bar and the saloon increased drunkenness. The patron who on payday "treated everyone at the bar to a round," might actually only want one drink, but since they had treated everyone, others felt obligated to return the favour and so the one drink turned into many more. As well, the simple presence of the bar was a temptation to those whose willpower was in some way compromised. A second option was to ban the sale of any alcohol in the community. Most temperance advocates believed that the only way to eliminate the problems of drink was to cut off the supply entirely, and therefore they supported this second option. Some temper-ance advocates were so committed to the cause that they put their money where their mouths were. W.R. Motherwell funded the building of a tem-perance hotel in Abernethy; no alcohol was served in the hotel, even though the competition did serve alcohol.[18]

Presbyterians were leaders in the local campaigns to "ban the bar." It was in these efforts that the Women's Christian Temperance Union learned how to affect political decision-makers, and these women became leading advocates for granting women the right to vote, and in the struggle to have women recognized as "persons" under the law. In Manitoba, the struggle to get the local option legislation to work was a frustrating one. Those who sold liquor would challenge the validity of the referendum in the courts and have the referendum results overturned. Despite these problems, by the end of 1911, there were 44 municipalities where sale of alcohol was illegal and another 27 where no liquor licenses had been issued. Out of the 143 municipalities in the province, half were dry. Holding local option referendums in 1910, 73 voting districts in Saskatchewan put the question of "banning the bar" before the people; in 37 the bars were closed, in the other 36 the bars stayed open. However, the bar owners challenged the referendum results in court and had the ban on the bars overturned in most of those communities that had voted to go dry. In Alberta, General Secretary of the Temperance and Moral Reform League Rev. W.G.W. Fortune, a Presbyterian, was defamed as a way of discrediting the temperance movement. The Board of Moral and Social Reform reported to the Assembly that, "the plot was the work of liquor vendors." The provincial government demanded a $100 fee to hold a referendum in a voting area on the prohibition question; this was an impediment to the temperance forces. It was the coming of the war that sped the move toward prohibition in Canada and on the prairies. The argument went like this: winning the war would require all the resources that Canadians had and alcohol was a luxury that cost money and detracted from the war effort. It was a winning argument. On May 31, 1915, Manitoba went dry, as the result of a province-wide referendum, in which two-thirds of the voters were in favour of banning the sale of alcohol. Saskatchewan closed all bars and clubs on July 1, 1915, but left open 18 government-run stores where alcohol could be bought for "private home consumption." These stores were closed by January 1, 1917. Alberta, with two-third of the electorate voting in favour, went dry on July 1, 1916.[19]

The Board of Home Missions and Social Service joyfully reported the impact of prohibition as "working wonders." Broken families were being re-united now that alcohol was no longer a destructive force in their lives. People were saving money and paying off old debts, many stores reported increased sales. The jails were "empty or nearly so" and many police officers had been laid off since there was no need for them. Victoriously it was declared, "The bar-room and liquor shop have gone forever."[20]

But this claim was premature. In 1921, a group of voters with a third option had arisen, standing between the prohibitionists and the bar-owners: the Moderation League. This group advocated that the government operate liquor stores but maintain a ban on bars. Prohibitionists saw this as a retreat from their hard-won victory, a loss that would begin the slippery slide back to the problems of an earlier day. In Manitoba, the Rev. John

Cormie, district superintendent, was the chair of the Temperance Board of Manitoba, and he was given a leave of absence from his superintendency in 1923 to devote himself full time for five and half months to ensuring the continuation of prohibition. Prohibition was defeated. Cormie noted that those areas of the province where the Anglo-Saxon community or the Scandinavian community were in the majority prohibition was supported; whereas in Winnipeg and those rural areas where Anglo-Saxons were out-numbered, a majority voted against prohibition. In Alberta, also in 1923, the government-operated liquor store was approved by a province-wide referendum, much to the disgust of Southern Alberta District Superintendet Rev. J.T. Ferguson. Ferguson was particularly perplexed by the fact that women, who were allowed to vote in the referendum, voted against prohi-bition "for reasons which its difficult to define." The Presbyterian Church had brought in a number of heavy-weights to speak in favour of the con-tinuation of prohibition: John Shearer and the Rev. D.N. McLachlan, sec-retary for the Social Service Department of the Presbyterian Church. But even their intervention did not stop the defeat. Saskatchewan ended up at virtually the same place, only their referendum was delayed until 1924.[21]

The Social Service Department was also concerned about gambling, habit forming drugs, political corruption, and the city. And it is to that work in the city that we now turn.

The Church Responds to the City

In 1901, there was only one city on the prairies: Winnipeg with 42,300 residents. The next largest community had 5,600 people. Ten years later, there were seven communities with more than 10,000 people, and Winni-peg was now a city of 136,000. By 1921, there were nine prairie commu-nities with populations of more than 10,000, five of which had in excess of 25,000 inhabitants. Winnipeg was still by far the largest community having 179,000 people. In 1901, one out of every eight people on the prairies, or 52,000 individuals, could be said to be living in a city. By 1921, one in four prairie dwellers, or 450,000 people, were living in an urban centre of more than 5,000 people. This was remarkable urban growth, which confronted the church with a new challenge.[22]

The challenge of the city came at the church from two directions: the suburbs and the inner city. As cities grew, there was a need for more churches to minister to the increasing population. The Presbyterian Church responded to this need. In 1904, there were eight Presbyterian churches in Winnipeg; in 1914 there were 16 and by 1924 there were 24. The church had moved into the new neighbourhoods and suburbs to reach the people where they were. Knox Church, Winnipeg, proudly stated its missionary credentials when it described itself as "The Mother of Twenty-two Churches in Win-nipeg and Suburbs." A similar story can be told of Edmonton, where there were two Presbyterians congregations in 1904 and 10 in 1914. In Calgary, one congregation had grown to seven. Even in smaller centres like Brandon, Moose Jaw, and Medicine Hat, new churches had been started to meet the needs of the new arrivals. Each of these communities had three Presbyterian congregations by 1914, where there had been only a single congregation a decade earlier. In some communities the rapid expansion of churches did not happen until after 1914; there were three congregations in Port Arthur/Fort William, Ontario, that year, and in 1924 there were six. Between the head of Lake Superior and the Rockies in 1904 there were 20 Presbyterian congregations in the existing urban centres or the communities about to become urban centres; in 1914, there were 55 congregations in these communities; and by 1924, 74.[23]

Edmonton was in the middle of a economic boom in 1912 and 1913, and subdivisions were springing up all over the place. In these subdivisions labourers and tradespeople could afford to buy property and build their own homes, or barring that at least afford the rent. The Church Extension Committee of the Presbytery of Edmonton had seen the need for the church to follow these people into the new subdivisions. In the last part of 1912 and through 1913, the committee had purchased or received as gifts 14 parcels of land upon which to build churches. During 1913, six buildings had been constructed and on three sites a mission tent had been erected. The Committee had not gone to the Home Missions Board for the funding to purchase the land or to erect the buildings; rather the money had been raised through givings from the newly established congregations, an investment fund held in trust for the presbytery, and the generous contributions from First and Knox Churches in Edmonton which had caught the vision for the extension of the church into these new neighbourhoods.[24]

Providing the suburban dweller with a church in their neighbourhood, however, did not make them attend church. Church leaders complained that many suburbanites attended only one service on a Sunday, and this new attendance pattern was "accentuated by the use of automobiles." From Alberta the familiar lament of all clergy was heard, "The problem of how to get people out to church is a difficult one." The rising middle class, possessing all the freedom and resources that came with their new status, no longer saw the church as a source of entertainment or a place to socialize. Both of those could be found in other places, places that the car would take them. As consumerism became the dominant value of the middle class, the church was faced with a new challenge; how to attract and hold its membership in the face of competition not from other churches, but from sports, dances, and the beach. The great danger of the "rapid acquisition of wealth, with the increase of luxury and self-indulgence" was that people would lose their souls. The temptation to pursue material things was powerful; it was important to not be swept along that enticing road, but instead to carefully "keep thy soul." Few of the leaders who raised these concerns, understood how prophetic their insight was, and it was not until the end of World War I that the church would seek to address the profound challenge of middle class consumerism.[25]

The greater perceived threat that the city posed to the church, and society at large, was neatly summarized by S.C. Murray, district superintendent for Manitoba, in his 1920 report to the Assembly, his first report to be written after the Winnipeg General Strike,

> Urban centres are liable to be storm centres in the social and industrial world. The Church has a large part to play in clearing the atmosphere and in neutralizing destructive forces. She must play a large part in establishing and maintain principles of justice between the classes and the masses. Never was there greater need of intelligent and impartial study of social conditions, wise, strong and tactful leadership and vigorous prosecution of the Church's work, sanely adjusted to modern conditions.... Our cities are young, plastic and vigorous. It is easier to prevent the development of slums than to remove them after they have once formed. "Now is the accepted time."[26]

The church needed to become involved in the life of the city, finding ways to prevent the creation of slums and the rise of the radicalism that had so recently been seen in Winnipeg. The time to act was now; waiting might mean missing the opportunity to act altogether. The church needed to develop new ways of ministry if it was going to truly impact the city. The new patterns of ministry would arise from a careful, sociological study of the situation. Scientific methods would be brought to bear on the problem, and those methods would reveal a plan of action.

As early as 1910, the HMC had recognized that the church needed to do something different in the urban core of many cities. The temptation was for the churches "to follow their members and adherents to other and more desirable localities" in the suburbs. Such a departure, however, would be "disastrous" leaving "the densely populated districts in the heart of a city without the restraining and sanctifying influence of evangelical Christianity." Having rejected that option, it was equally clear that individual congregations remaining in the heart of the city were not properly equipped to address the "down town" adequately. The answer would be found in what became known as the Institutional Church, which was also called the Social Settlement.[27]

The leadership of the church had by 1916 come to conviction that the city was "the greatest challenge to the Church of Christ to be found in Canada." Solving the problem of the city was absolutely essential not only for the well-being of the church, but also for the country as a whole, because "the cities dominate the country and determine the trend of national life." The church would respond to the challenge in two ways. First, by working with government and business leaders to "right the wrong conditions under which these people labour." This co-operative effort, in which the church functioned as lobbyist and moral conscience, would seek to enhance the heart of the city's infrastructure by improving sanitation, housing, and recreational facilities, both by enforcement of existing laws and creation of new laws. Secondly, the church would minister to individuals and families, seeking to meet their physical, social, intellectual, and spiritual needs. This would include operating medical clinics, employing visiting nurses, offering life skills training, and finding the unemployed work. There would be opportunities for group gatherings as the mission house became a community centre. English would be taught, "free of cost—in the name of the Great Teacher." The good news about Jesus would be taught and the Word of God proclaimed, not through "preaching services," but "by His own methods which always combined what we call "Social Service" with "Evangelism.""[28] The motivation for this new venture in mission was clear:

> The Church must tackle this down-town problem as a *Church*. We are going into this work not merely inspired by a thin, sentimental humanism, but because we are Christian people who seek the advancement of Christ's Kingdom and the saving of men's lives. Any inspiration that we have for this work we draw from Jesus Christ, and we shall not hesitate to say whence we have received it; it is His Spirit. We must put Christ into the foreground and keep him there; and next to Him, His Church.... The work must all be correlated...to one great aim and purpose— to Christianize, definitely and consciously to put the Spirit of Christ into the lives of men, and to bring men into a conscious and confessed relationship to Him. [emphasis in original][29]

The great task of the 20th century would be solving the problem of the city. The solution would be found through acquiring accurate, first-hand, scientific data and then examining that data under the guidance of "the Spirit of Christ." The church was in desperate need of people who had the necessary scientific skills and who were guided by the Spirit; such a people would need to be specially trained for their great task.

While the Home Missions Committee and the Board of Moral and Social Reform were getting their plan together, the women of Winnipeg were getting on with the business of doing mission. In 1907, the Women's Presbyterial Union of Winnipeg was formed to respond to the pressing needs in the north end of Winnipeg. The area north of the CPR railyards was dominated by recent arrivals to Canada, and it was into the North End that those arriving by train would go looking for housing. By the end of the war only 10 percent of the North End's population was Anglo-Saxon and there were 16 newspapers being published in languages other than English and French. The Union found a building lot on Alfred Street, where they built the Alfred Street Mission. The focus of the mission was children, who were reached through a kindergarten programme. The kindergarten programme also drew in mothers, who became part of a mothers' club. Through these contacts, the deaconess at the mission heard about needs in the community at large and was able to use that information to visit people in need. There were Sunday evening youth services led in English by two students from Manitoba College, who used slides and a "steroptician" during the worship. By 1910, just as the HMC was beginning to talk seriously about city mission work, the programmes at the Alfred Street Mission had outgrown their facilities. In response to the pressing need for more space, the Presbytery of Winnipeg established the Winnipeg Presbyterian Association, which would oversee a bold new venture. The Presbytery had chosen the "energetic" Rev. Alexander McTaggart to lead the this settlement house. The mission congregation he served, Dufferin Street Church, would sell its newly-built building and move to a location where both a church and a mission building could be constructed. The agreed location was the intersection of McKenzie St. and Burrows Ave. The land was purchased and the church and mission were built on opposite sides of McKenzie St., south of Burrows Ave. The church and the mission would be called the Robertson Memorial Institute. One of the hopes of the Association was to bring the various Presbyterian mission efforts in the city of Winnipeg under one umbrella. The Robertson Memorial Institute formally opened its doors on November 19, 1911. In the basement there was a gymnasium and the boys' club rooms, on the first floor a hall that would seat 200 to 250 people, a kitchen, and meeting rooms. On the second floor was the kindergarten and the girls' club rooms.[30]

The Robertson Memorial Institute was in part staffed by deaconesses. Margaret Cameron began her work at Robertson in 1911. One of her primary responsibilities was visitation in the north end of Winnipeg. In the articles she wrote to the *Home Mission Pioneer* describing her work, she painted empathetic pictures of the women she met, wives and mothers who were the primary wage earners in theie households because their husbands were ill, who still managed to "keep their home and children sweet and clean." Cameron asked one such woman how much longer she would be able to stand the strain; the woman responded, "I do feel tired sometimes." There were other families who had been abandoned by husband and father or he was "intemperate" and again the wife was left to carry the entire household. For Cameron it was a "privilege" to be called to serve such "brave burden bearers." Cameron also met families in the most desperate of situations, helping them find affordable housing, using her contacts to get them a warm meal or sufficient funds to make it until the next pay day. Many individual Presbyterians provided her with clothing and furniture which she distributed as she thought best, but Cameron wanted something more than just clothing and furniture and money; she wished that those making these donations would "follow up their gifts by visiting the homes where their gifts are sent." It was only through personal contact that kindness and encouragement could flow to "restore self respect." Simply giving things to the needy would bring the poor "down to a still lower point of dependence and shame." Those requiring help needed to be treated with respect. There were many people in the churches who wanted to respond to the needs, Cameron believed; it was simply that they had no idea how to do it. Recognizing that she could not meet all the needs with which she came in contact, Cameron hoped to create relationships between giver and receiver and thereby expand the web of care. She was also in contact with a number of single, young women who had just arrived in Winnipeg, who were caught between their low salaries and the high cost of room and board. Cameron called on some of the "Christian women, who keep boarding and rooming houses" to charge these young women less than the going rate, so that they could get on their feet in a new city, and more importantly would have "one true friend." It was within the ability of ordinary church-goers to do something about the problem of the downtown. Responding to the downtown problem also meant carrying the good news of Jesus. Cameron read scripture and prayed with those she visited. She encouraged children to attend Sunday School, she established connections between the families she visited and nearby clergy, and she gave Bibles to those who did not have one in their home. Evangelism and social service were inseparable; they fed each other. Cameron could not conceive of doing one without the other.[31]

A wave of about 1,000 Russians came to live in the North End in 1911 and 1912. In name they were Russian Orthodox; however they had listened to enough socialist rhetoric to be disenchanted with all churches. In 1913, the Rev. A.S. Grant, now the general superintendent of Home Missions, who like Robertson was always on the lookout for capable leaders, met John Andreyevitch Schmidt, a Protestant school teacher from Russia, who was working in Manitoba and Saskatchewan as a colporteur for the Bible Society among New Canadians from Russia. Grant convinced Schmidt to join the Presbyterian work in Winnipeg. There Schmidt worked out of the reading room at the Robertson Institute, where he taught English as a second language. There was great opposition in the Russian community to his work, and for a while in 1914, his classes were boycotted. Over time, however, he was more trusted and his ability to act as translator, employment agent, and cultural interpreter made him a valued member of the Russian community. The goal of the outreach to the Russians was not to establish a Russian-speaking church in Winnipeg; rather those who were converted and wished to join a church were encouraged to become members at Robertson Memorial, which four did during Schmidt's time in Winnipeg. With the coming of the Russian Revolution a large number of the Russians in Winnipeg returned to their homeland and in August 1917 Schmidt returned with them, ending that part of the Robertson Memorial's ministry.[32]

One of the hallmarks of Robertson Memorial's ministry was the Fresh Air Camp at Gimli. In 1911, ten acres of land was purchased on Lake Winnipeg and the camping ministry began. The camp lodge had a dining room and a sitting room with a large fireplace, and a screened-in porch all on the main level; upstairs there were sleeping quarters. Mothers and their children came to camp for a week, sleeping in cabins. A team made up of staff from Robertson and volunteers from Presbyterian congregations prepared meals, organized programmes and games, planning "for every hour of the day, and every hour was supervised." The mothers had only two responsibilities at camp; to make their own beds and to bathe their babies. It was supposed to be as much a holiday for them as for their children. The day started at 7 a.m. with the wake-up bell, and almost immediately the call to breakfast. Following breakfast there were family devotions with everyone together and the programme for the day was announced. This included raising the flag and camp chores, after which there might be a walk to the lighthouse in Gimli, a hike through the woods, a visit with one of the local fishers, or a trip to a berry patch. Then there was lunch, followed by a rest time. The afternoon was spent on the beach. Following supper there might be games, an impromptu concert, or a bonfire. At 8:30 p.m. the day ended with "evening song and prayer." Mothers and children thrived in this environment; children who were constantly hungry at home ate as much as they wanted. In fact, five boys once finished off 19 large helpings of porridge between them, and another boy told the camp director he had let out his belt two notches during his week at camp. One mother, so moved by the generosity of the people who had paid her way to attend camp, insisted the last night of her week there that she was going to scrub the dining room floor as her token of thanks. Another mother, at her wit's end about how to discipline her two-year old, found support and help in talking to the staff and the other mothers at camp. The camp was also a place where people could hear the gospel message, away from the concerns of everyday life, and had an opportunity talk to staff about their lives and ask their questions about the Christian faith. During the nine week season in 1915, nearly 500 campers attended; in 1923, more than 800 campers came to the Fresh Air Camp programmes.[33]

The Robertson Memorial Institute, or Robertson House as it became known, was a very busy place. In 1923, it was estimated that 277 people came through the doors each day, attending a club or programme, picking up children, asking for assistance, or simply stopping by to socialize. There were seven full-time workers and one part-timer. The staff had contact with over 1,100 families, meaning mothers and children; only 6 percent of those attending programmes or seeking assistance were men. There were 41 different clubs, classes or programmes run out of the facility, including morning and afternoon kindergarten classes with a combined enrollment of 100. Seven different "nationalities" were represented among those using the services of Robertson House. In terms of religious affiliation, about 30 percent of those being helped were Jewish, a third were Protestant, approximately 20 percent were from Ukrainian backgrounds and the rest were Roman Catholics of various ethnicities. Robertson House had become the centre for the various cultural ministries the church had started in the North End. But the statistics do not give a sense of day-to-day ministry at Robertson House:

> Many unexpected calls come to us each day:—the Neckonetzna baby is 'fitting' (has a fit or convulsion and they run to the Institute;...Mrs. Eichorn has letters in English from some of her children which she wants read to her, and replied to; the Smiths have been turned out by the bailiff, and all come to spend the day in the warm Institute...; a child come with a note from a teacher in the big school across the way, asking if we can give the child something to eat as he has been crying with hunger;...the Fooderation boy can't go to school as he has no shoes; Mr. Haluszezak has been beating his wife and she comes for help; Mrs. Slobogac has a postal note from her husband who is working 'by a farmer,' and wants to be identified at the bank.[34]

Robertson House played an important role in the North End during the 1918 influenza epidemic. The building was turned over to the municipal authorities to use as a feeding and relief centre, with the Robertson staff providing the supervision and some of the labour. During the epidemic, 20,500 different individuals were fed at the City Diet Kitchen set up at Robertson House. Robertson House used sports to keep boys, in particular, out of the poolhalls and out of trouble. The Robertson Arrows Soccer team won the Manitoba senior boys championship on a number of occasions, and twice reached the national finals.[35]

Responding to people's material and emotional needs was as much part of gospel proclamation as was meeting their spiritual needs. However, by 1919, Robertson Church was in hibernation. When James Mutchmor arrived in early 1920 to become the pastor of Robertson Memorial, he found the Mission House functioning well under the leadership of Ruth Goldie, originally from Galt (now Cambridge), Ontario, but the session of the church had not met in over a year, and the congregation had disbanded. This was a state of affairs that Mutchmor found unacceptable. He believed social service and gospel preaching had to go hand in hand. He therefore went about rebuilding a congregation in the "polyglot" reality of north end Winnipeg. He began with the Sunday School, recruiting former Sunday School staff and using the Fresh Air camper lists to contact potential Sunday School students. Within a year and a half the Sunday school attendance was averaging 215 students a week, 30 percent of whom were New Canadians. From there Mutchmor turned to look at Sunday worship. He began by using the House Church model of "cottage prayer meetings and group discussions." The session was reconvened, and a number of key leaders returned. The congregation agreed to begin again, if Mutchmor would promise to stay with them. In the eight years since its opening, the Institute and Church had had three different clergy hold the position of superintendent and minister. Mutchmor gave his word that he would stay with them and the church re-opened with Sunday evening services. Average attendance grew to about 150, with 10 percent of the congregation being New Canadian. Building a multi-ethnic congregation was extremely difficult. What was more successful at bridging the cultural barriers was the interaction in the various mothers' clubs, Bible studies and other women's groups. Robertson House and Robertson Church had only one group in each of these categories between them; therefore Anglo-Saxon women and New Canadians rubbed shoulders in these small groups, getting to know each other and care for one another. Mutchmor described how the programmes at Robertson House related to Robertson Church in this way: "Though no pressure was exerted among members of the clubs and classes at Robertson House…every chance to show the link that should be made between week-day activity and Sunday worship and Sunday School, was used in a constructive way." The goal was to raise up "a Church House and a Neighbourhood Church."[36]

Robertson Memorial Institute was not the only Presbyterian city mission in the west, or even in Winnipeg. In 1920 a city mission was established at the Point Douglas church in Winnipeg. Through the first two decades of the 20th century Point Douglas had changed dramatically. Originally a residential area full of single family dwellings, it had been transformed because of its proximity to the CPR station into a community of rooming houses and houses converted into apartments owned by absentee landowners. Then in 1909, in the middle of the uproar over prostitution in Winnipeg, the city police determined that they would set up a segregated zone in Winnipeg where brothels would be allowed. The area chosen was two blocks in Point Douglas. The clerk of session for Point Douglas Church in 1923, William Duncan, lived a block a half from the "red light district." It was only natural that Point Douglas Church become the centre of a new city mission as the church sought "to meet the needs created by the change in population." Jessie Mackenzie was the deaconess in charge of the mission, helped by two students from Manitoba College. Mackenzie began the transformation of the church into a city mission through an intentional visitation programme in the neighbourhood to discover the needs and to help where it was possible to do so. She wrote, "In my visitation I have endeavoured to present the claims of Christ, the duty of man to His Church in order to produce a life worth while." Mackenzie was recognized as an integral part of the leadership at the Point Douglas church and she was invited to become a member of Session. This is one of the earliest references to a woman becoming a member of a session. As with all city missions, there was a focus on children's programming. By 1924, there were two full-time staff working at the mission with a need for three additional staff; 1,400 individuals took advantage of the programmes and services provided. Those coming to the mission represented 19 different nationalities; they were predominantly Protestant with only 30 percent of those coming through the doors identifying themselves as having a different religious affiliation. The Sunday school had 237 names on the roll, and there were eight mid-week programmes for teenagers. There was both morning and evening worship on Sundays. There were 191 households connected to the church, who may or may not have made use of the services provided by the mission.[37]

A third city mission was established in Edmonton in co-operation with the Methodists. Called the All Peoples Mission it opened its doors in 1921 in four different locations throughout the city. By 1923, it had six full-time staff whose work was expanded by 17 volunteers. There was a kindergarten programme and a mothers' meeting, along with a night school programme for men. Thirteen nationalities were represented among the 256 families who were involved in the mission. Sixty percent of those coming to the various locations were Ukrainian, another 20 percent were aligned with the Labour Church. There were three Sunday Schools and three Sunday worship services at which lantern slides were used. The focus of the spiritual part of the mission was on children and youth; it was taking time for adults to become part of the worship life of the mission. By 1924, William Simons, district superintendent for Northern Alberta, was convinced that that this mission was past the experimental stage and was starting to have a real impact on the lives of people.[38]

The All Peoples Mission was building on the work that Agnes Coutie, a deaconess, had been doing in Edmonton since 1913. She sought to befriend the single women working in the offices in downtown Edmonton, spending weekday lunch hours at First Church available to talk to anyone who might drop by. Visiting the sick, allowed Coutie into the lives of people who would never have attended church without her contact. She asked a man who was about to return to his home in China what he would tell people. The man replied, "I tell them God is good." Coutie ran a series of mother-and-child programmes around Edmonton, which gave mothers an opportunity to interact with each other, to receive assistance if they needed it, and to hear "the Gospel story." In 1919, Coutie led a combined Sunday School/Worship service at one of the new congregations that was being started in Edmonton.[39]

The Mission to the Jews in Winnipeg was in fact a fourth city mission on the prairies, although it was not recognized as such until 1920. On April 5, 1910, a group of leading Presbyterian clergy and lay people in Winnipeg gathered to hear the Rev. S. B. Rohold describe the mission work being done by the church among the Jews in Toronto. The result of the meeting was a resolution that the possibility of opening a Jewish Mission in Winnipeg be explored. Within a year, Mr. and Mrs. Hugo Spitzer and their three children were in Winnipeg to work among the estimated 13,000 Jews who lived in the city. The Spitzers were converts from Judaism who had worked for three years among their fellow Jews at the London City Mission in England before moving to Winnipeg. Almost immediately upon their arrival in Winnipeg and the setting up the mission, Spitzer faced opposition. One of the evangelistic meetings he led was so completely disrupted by a individual opposed to the work Spitzer had come to do that the police had to be called and the man removed. The Rev. J. McPherson Scott, one of the most committed mission executives in the Presbyterian Church, offered little support for Spitzer during this trying time, writing, "Certainly Mr. and Mrs. Spitzer are having a interesting time. It advertises the work and creates sympathy." In the late summer of 1911 the Spitzers were joined by Martha Smith, a trained nurse who was a veteran of the Mission to the Jews in Toronto. They were to form an effective team, establishing and expanding the mission over the next five years. In 1916, the Home Mission Board, which was at that time responsible for the mission to the Jews, made a significant decision about the philosophy of the mission. Only those people who already spoke Hebrew and Yiddish, or were willing to learn these languages, would be considered as candidates for ministry among the Jews. This was quite different than the approach being taken to the work in the Native community and among other non-English speaking groups.[40]

The mission work consisted of both social service and evangelism. Through the volunteer support of a doctor, a dispensary was opened to provide walk-in medical services on a twice-a-week basis. Through the dispensary people were met who would never have come to the mission for any other reason. There were also sewing classes and mothers' groups along with a kindergarten. The sewing classes were aimed at mothers of smaller children, and followed a fairly consistent pattern. There were classes for the children, so that their mothers could focus on sewing and the skills they were learning. Each week the women sewed something that they could take home. In addition to learning new sewing techniques and craft skills, there was a Bible lesson taken from the Old Testament which was "illustrated from the New Testament," emphasizing that the God of the Old Testament was also the God of the New Testament. The women would ask questions about the lesson, and this would be followed by a time for prayer during which the women were encouraged to pray one sentence prayers aloud. Through visiting in homes, the missionaries became aware of people's needs and found ways to address their material concerns. Home visiting included taking time to read a passage of scripture and to pray with the members of the household. The mission to the Jews also made use of the Fresh Air Camp at Gimli.[41]

There were more explicit evangelistic methods used by the mission to the Jews, the most dramatic of these being street preaching. In the summer of 1916, 22 outdoor services were held in Winnipeg on Saturday and Sunday evenings. Music would draw a crowd and then the preaching would begin in Hebrew, Yiddish, or English, depending on the speaker's skills and the crowd's make-up. The street meetings were "sometimes orderly, sometimes disorderly, but always interesting." Christian literature and gospel tracts were distributed at these meetings, and through other means as well. The missionaries used the half-hour a week that was set aside by the public schools for religious instruction, to visit schools where there were high concentrations of Jewish children and tell them about Jesus the Messiah. This last evangelistic method produced a reaction in the Jewish community in Winnipeg, who for a while pulled their children out of all church programming, both Presbyterian and Methodist, including the Fresh Air camps, and made plans to build a Jewish school.[42]

There were converts to Christianity as a result of this ministry. In 1916 a brother and sister, in the face of great opposition from their family, were baptized following their public profession of faith in Christ. Spitzer reported that there were others within the Jewish community in Winnipeg, who had become Christians but for fear of the social and economic consequences of a public profession of their faith, remained "secret believers."[43]

Following the Spitzers' departure from the mission in 1920, the work was re-organized under the umbrella of Robertson House and moved into larger quarters nearer the Institute on Burrows Ave. Violet Burt remained the deaconess in charge of the Jewish Mission. This amalgamation was part of a new policy to join missions focused on the Jews with missions that sought to reach all racial groups, making the Jewish mission "a department of the larger mission." Finally in 1923, the Jewish department moved into Robertson House.[44]

204 / PETER BUSH

THE YEAR OF THE STUDY

The Board of Moral and Social Reform had argued that it was not enough to just dive into ministry; it was necessary to properly study the context in which the ministry was going to take place. Such a study should include an examination of the sociological, economic, and political realities of the particular context. In the year following the 1913 Pre-Assembly Congress, no less than six substantial studies of this kind were done in various parts of Canada, funded by the Methodist and Presbyterian churches. Four of the studies were done within the geographical area covered by this book.

The studies done of Fort William and Port Arthur in 1913 emphasized the rapid growth of these communities. Fort William, which had enjoyed steady growth between 1891 and 1905, tripled in size between 1905 and 1912, as 15,000 new people called it their home. This runaway growth had put a strain on all aspects of the community's life. Most obviously there was a housing shortage. The surveyors found one five-room house in which 18 people were living. In fact, the surveyors estimated that in the city core, on average four people slept in each room. One of the city blocks they surveyed had 238 people, including 51 children, living in 35 dwellings, which shared 23 outhouses. There was not a single bathtub or indoor toilet in the block, and only 23 houses had water taps. The residents complained that the city either rarely or never collected garbage on their block. The survey team studied three other blocks in Port Arthur and Fort William that revealed similar problems. This, for all intents and purposes, was a slum. Among the concerns raised by the surveyors were the public health issues of providing clean drinking water, the prevention of infectious diseases like tuberculosis, and the general improvement of living conditions. The surveyors re-published an article on "How to avoid slum conditions," that had appeared in the Port Arthur *Daily News* in March of 1912. Among the suggestions were rigorous enforcement of the building code, giving low interest or no interest loans to working class people to build their own houses, build more playgrounds for children, and appoint women, along with men, as health inspection and school attendance officers.[45]

The surveyors drew a link between the ease people had in acquiring liquor and the crime rate. There was concern that the opportunity to bring in some form of prohibition was rapidly vanishing, as the "foreign population is easily manipulated in the voting by liquor dealers and this population is steadily growing." The time to have a prohibition referendum was now, before the non-Anglo-Saxons, many of whom had a different culturally relationship with alcohol than did the Anglo-Saxon community, became the dominant voice in the community. They also noted the rise in socialist ideas in the Lakehead community, particularly among the Finnish-speaking population. Remarkably these Preliminary and General Social Surveys done of Fort William and Port Arthur, funded by the Methodists and Presbyterians, contained no study of the churches in the communities, and gave no suggestions as to what the churches as churches could do about the challenges outlined. Even when the discussion turned to the role charitable organizations might play, the churches were not included in the discussion. This would certainly have been an incomplete study in the mind of the Presbyterian Board of Moral and Social Reform, which had envisioned studies informed by the Spirit of Christ and showing the church how to be a church in a particular situation.[46]

The rural surveys done in the summer of 1914 of the Turtle Mountain and Swan River Valley districts of Manitoba did include detailed discussion of the role the church did play, and what role it should play. Spurred on by declining church attendance and the flight of young people to the city, these studies sought to determine what had changed in the rural community to lead to this state of affairs. These studies, each over 70 pages long, had the explicit goal of outlining for rural congregations how they could become "more and more the social centre of community life." The two areas for study were chosen because Turtle Mountain was one of the longest settled areas in the province, and the Swan River Valley was one of the most recently settled areas. If the timing and pattern of settlement had any impact, it was expected to show up when these two communities were compared. Both surveys outlined in detail the farming practices used, the educational patterns, and the community organizations in the area. Both reports were adamant that consolidated multiroom schools were more effective at teaching children than were one-room schools. In some of the one-room schools surveyed, only a quarter of students entering grade 1 remained in school long enough to enter grade 7, and only one in every 14 students starting school would finish grade 8. While consolidated schools still had challenges—for example, low attendance rates—the education outcomes were better than those experienced in one-room schools. For the purposes of the present study the most interesting material was the survey results related church life.[47]

The Turtle Mountain District Survey studied the area near the present-day Turtle Mountain Provincial Park, the region defined by Boissevain, Deloraine, and Minto. Strikingly, one quarter of all resident farmers were tenants, not owning the land they farmed. When this was combined with the 15 percent of rural dwellers who were hired help, that meant that only 60 percent of people living in the region were living in families that actually owned the farm they were working. The enlarging of farms so that by 1914, almost half of all farms were three-quarters of a section or larger, had not reduced the rural population; rather, the population had changed. The long-time farmers had sold their land and moved to the nearby towns, and they were replaced by tenants and hired help who had fewer connections to the land and the community. The tenant, the crop-payment buyer, and the hired help were strangers to the rural church and no one reached out to them to encourage them to become part of the church community. About a third of tenant farmers had never been visited by a clergy person, and another 45 percent had been visited only once or twice. The church was ignoring 80 percent of the new economic class that was arising within the community. Not surprisingly then, only half of tenant farmers became members of a local church. Hired help faced an additional problem; they often did not own a means of transportation and had to depend on their employer providing them with a way of getting to church. Less than half of those employing hired help were willing or able to give them access to transportation. These factors had led to a crisis in church attendance in Turtle Mountain. While the overall population of the area had risen by 8 percent between 1904 and 1914, church membership had risen by just over 2 percent in the same 10 years. In fact, only a third of the congregations in the region had grown in the past 10 years, and nearly 45 percent of them were losing members. Evangelistic meetings had been held in about a quarter of the congregations in the district, and half of the new members in area churches had made a profession of faith during the evangelistic meetings. The surveyors did not believe it mattered whether the leader of the evangelistic meetings was from within the local group of ministers or was a full-time evangelist brought in from outside. Most of the evangelistic campaigns were two weeks in length.

One of the central findings of the Turtle Mountain Survey was that clergy were being spread too thinly, as pastoral charges were amalgamated into ever larger groupings. Using a farming analogy, the surveyors wrote,

> The Church is to-day apparently following the "lead" of the land farmers in joining circuit to circuit and mission field to mission field. The wisdom of this policy is doubtful.... Opposed to this tendency the farmers in both Turtle Mountain and Swan River are rapidly becoming more intensive in their methods of agriculture. They are plowing twice where they used to plow once. With few exceptions they tell you their farms are more profitable than they used to be. The churches are becoming less intensive in their methods. They are often putting one man where they used to put two. In many places it must be acknowledged that it has not been more profitable.[48]

The time had come for the church to also use more intensive methods, to work the mission fields as hard as they could be worked. The study concluded that those congregations that were growing were those "which have the longer pastorates and where the parishes have been relatively small (in area)." It was through intensive work over the long haul that the church would become a central part of the community's life.

The most effective way for that to happen, the surveyors concluded, would be to end the overlapping and competition between churches. Instead of one minister trying to provide leadership to four struggling congregations of one denomination, while a clergy colleague of another denomination tried to provide leadership to congregations located almost exactly the same places, the eight congregations should be joined to become four, and each clergyperson could then take responsibility for two congregations, giving them the intensive work for which the surveyors were calling. Not surprisingly then, the surveyors supported church union.[49]

The Swan River Valley survey studied the area around Swan River, Manitoba, covering from Minitonas in southeast to Kenville and Benito in the southwest, and north through Bowsman to Roaring River. This area being more recently settled than Turtle Mountain, the congregations were still receiving grants from their respective home missions board and were using the stewardship methods of the pioneers. An open collection was taken each week, without the use of offering envelopes. Then in the fall, as the harvest was just being completed, a small group of church leaders would divide up to visit every household in the congregation asking for money to pay the rest of the missionary's salary. Not only did this approach make financial planning extremely difficult, it led some givers to believe that they had bought a portion of the minister's time and the right to see the minister more often that those who had not contributed as much to the work of the church. One church member told the surveyors, "We give $20.00 of hard-earned money to the minister's salary and we have a right to a lot of his time." This "donation" was about 2 percent of the minister's stipend. With this attitude widespread it is not surprising to learn that the surveyors found that the most well-to-do households received the most pastoral visits and those who were struggling financially, either due to misfortune or just starting out in farming, or who were new to the community received the fewest visits, if any at all. The surveyors were blunt,

> Let our church membership once realize that both they and their pastors are banded together primarily to minister to the community, then, if it should be impossible to minister fully to all, they will see readily that the best pastor is he who goes where the need is greatest—to the marginal people of the community.[50]

In this more newly settled area there was a higher level of co-operation among the population than there was in the Turtle Mountain District. Co-operative enterprises of all sorts flourished: co-op stores, farmer-owned grain elevators, consolidated schools, boys' and girls' clubs, and union Sunday schools. Half of the Sunday schools in the district were union schools.

In fact, in many small communities the Sunday school drew a more diverse, broad-based group of people together than any other community organization. The surveyors challenged the clergy in the area to see the co-operative movement that was evident everywhere as a powerful tool in the advance of the church. "Those ministers who are broadminded and who can work together will achieve the most." This co-operation between churches, should include "organized athletic and social affairs" for adolescents. The young people needed to be given the opportunity to serve the local community in some way, one suggestion being the funding of a "free" bed at the Swan River Hospital.[51]

Both the Turtle Mountain and Swan River Surveys ended with a descriptive outline of what a country church at work should have in programming and physical facilities. The church had five functions. First, there was "shepherding the flock," which consisted of public worship, pastoral visiting, and religious education. The religious education was to include: a Sunday school, with teacher-training programmes; adult Bible classes for both men and women; and a young people's society. The second function was evangelism, which was to be exercised by making direct appeals to people in regular worship services to decide to follow Christ; by the minister, elders, Sunday school teachers, and everyone in the church making a personal effort in this area; and through special evangelistic services. "Special attention should be given to neglected or marginal folk, such as the poor, hired help, adopted child-help, drunkards, people of shady reputation. Jesus never passed such by. He *sought the lost*."" (emphasis in original) The third programme aspect of the church at work was social service; this meant encouraging the full range of moral, social, and economic reforms that might be indicated by a careful study of the local conditions. The church should seek to right wrongs, to engage in philanthropic work in the community, and act to prevent "rural depletion and degeneration." This was too large a task for one congregation to accomplish on its own; it needed the co-operation of a group of churches to bring about the effective change that was envisioned. The church also needed to find ways to attract men to church, through working together on projects, enjoying good fellowship, and participating in church sponsored athletic events, men would be drawn into the life of the congregation. Fourth, the country church needed to learn about and be involved in "missionary endeavour" outside of the parish boundaries. Through preaching, lantern (slide) presentations, and the distribution of literature the broader mission of the church needed to be brought before the congregation. Congregations were encouraged take on a mission project, to support a particular person or ministry, thereby creating a deeper connection between the local church and its mission in another place. The fifth church programme was "local church finances," or, stewardship. Church finances needed to operate "upon a business basis." There was to be systematic teaching and preaching about proportionate giving for all aspects of the church's work, which should include an annual stewardship visit of every member's home and encouraging people to use weekly offering envelopes. The physical plant a country church needed was: a suitable room for preaching and worship; appropriate space for the Sunday school; a place for social gatherings and if possible a playing field and/or gymnasium; and comfortable sheds for horses to stay while their owners were at worship or attending a church function.[52]

The two rural surveys show how closely linked were evangelism and social service in the minds of many within the church. Those who advocated for social reform also believed that the church should be intentionally involved in evangelism both on a personal level and through preaching missions. The great divide between these two was to take place at a later date. Through their study and interviews the surveyors used scientific methods to reveal the ways in which the church could more effectively accomplish its mission in the rural west. This was exactly the kind of study that the Board of Moral and Social Reform had had in mind.

THE WINNIPEG GENERAL STRIKE

The Board of Home Missions and Social Service had for a number of years been bringing the complex issues of "wealth, industry, and commerce" to the attention of the Assembly. In 1919, just in time for the General Assembly, the Board released a wide ranging statement about the economy and social conditions. The Board, sensing the friction that existed within the country wrote, "today in Canada the only alternatives are revolution or radical reform." Preferring reform to revolution, the Board outlined its vision for the "new social order" "organized on the principles of the Kingdom of God." Natural wealth was all undeveloped resources, and natural wealth was a gift from God given to all people, and should not be held in private hands. Natural wealth that was already in private hands, and which was not being used for the good of all, should be expropriated. The development of public utilities for the public good were strongly supported. In fact, all industry and commerce was to be operated for the service of the people. No one should be allowed to make excessive profits from selling "the necessaries of life." The church should make it one of its goals to end poverty and to ensure that all people would enjoy a minimum standard of life, including: comfortable, sanitary housing; sufficient food and clothing; education; and leisure time and activities. A system of social insurance should be put in place to deliver people from the "tormenting fear" of being laid off, injured on the job, getting sick, or being too old to do the job but not having a pension. To achieve these goals would require "frequent, frank and free discussion" where all parties could express their views and get past the prejudices that divided labour from capital and industry from community.[53]

The Rev. William R. Wood, a minister in the Presbyterian Church and an elected member of the Legislative Assembly in Manitoba from 1915 to 1919, having run as a farmer's candidate, wondered in print whether the church would actually support a politician who in the public called for this kind of radical change. "Recognizing that it will mean requiring wealthy corporations to disgorge to a degree unheard of the wealth they have filched from the common people, and to loosen the grip they still hold upon millions of acres of the public domain, will the Church have the courage to interpret these principles in terms of the actualities of the time?" Wood was not convinced that the Church was prepared to face the task.[54]

The friction between labour and capital that had been festering through the winter and spring of 1919 reached its climax in May and June of 1919, with the Winnipeg General Strike. The strike, as historian Richard Allen has noted, did not divide one church from another; rather it split congregations right down the middle, with some members and clergy being in support of the strike and others opposed. Cormie, district superintendent for Manitoba, spoke about the strike at a meeting held in late May 1919 in the Presbyterian Church in Dauphin. He said,

> If we were inclined to fret under the inconvenience of the strike, let it be remembered that labour has had to fight for everything that it has, and that it has had to use what weapons were available. Labour has been faced from the earliest ages by a class which has had many weapons, which have been used without mercy and without scruple. The strike has shown the principle of social solidarity in operation. We are all involved, we all have to help to settle it.

The Presbyterian *Record* on the other hand, called for caution; it did not matter to the editor whether the strike was justified or not, what mattered was that cool heads would prevail so that the ship was not wrecked. The *Presbyterian and Westminster* was concerned about the talk of "class control," fearing that the radical elements would lead the strikers into socialism or worse. In fact, the weekly quoted The Hon. Gideon Robertson, minister of Labour, who had stated that he believed that one of the goals of the strike leaders was to bring about the overthrow of Canada's constitutional government. Even at the end of the strike, the paper showed little understanding of the goals of the strike, saying of Winnipeg, "The city is slowly returning to normal conditions, and it is fully expected that all traces of the six weeks' upheaval will soon disappear."[55]

The Winnipeg Strike was in full swing when the General Assembly of the Presbyterian Church met in Hamilton in June 1919. During the afternoon of the sixth day of Assembly, the Board of Home Missions and Social

Service came with a lengthy resolution regarding Social Unrest, an indirect way of talking about the Winnipeg Strike and the other strikes that were taking place across the country. That entire evening was given over to the discussion of the resolution and the social situation across the country in general. Ephraim Scott, editor of the *Record,* said that it was one of the liveliest discussions he had witnessed at Assembly: "the benefit of the evening consisted more in relaxation than information, giving some pent-up feeling opportunity for expression." The resolution was very balanced, asking both labour and capital to act for the good of the public. Both capital and labour were to function in service to the community as a whole. Complementing those industries that were giving workers a voice in decision making, providing a living wage and enough time off, and working with labour and government to develop insurance against unemployment and accident, and a pension plan, the Assembly made clear the kind of relationship they believed should exist between labour and capital. The right of workers to organize and negotiate as a block was upheld, but the contracts negotiated should not be violated by sympathy walkouts as were being experienced in Winnipeg. The Assembly was also deeply concerned about the "present tendency to organize in groups and classes." While recognizing that sometimes such class activity was necessary, "the spirit of faction and mutual suspicion can be avoided only by the different classes subordinating their particular aims in devotion to the common good." Finally, the Assembly affirmed "its belief that the only permanent cure for the evils of our time is the practical application of Christian principles to the whole conduct of life."[56]

THE FORWARD MOVEMENT

An overture came to the 1918 General Assembly which contained a profound indictment of the church, "…the conviction is deepening that the witness of the Church has been too feeble and too much permeated with the spirit of the world rightly to interpret to the world the spirit of Jesus Christ." The church had become captive to the cultural values of the day, and was no longer living by the "spirit of Jesus Christ." The overture called for united prayer and practical efforts to move the church forward, out of its feeble state to one of "fuller witness to the power of Christ to heal the wounds of humanity, meet the immeasurable need of hungry souls, and regenerate the world." The General Assembly, in true Presbyterian fashion, established a committee to inaugurate a Forward Movement within the church, which had three purposes: placing before the church the mission challenges of the moment; organizing a recruitment plan ministry candidates; and raising the necessary funds to advance the mission of the church. A committee of 50 eminent Presbyterians was struck to guide the Forward Movement. Most historians who have written about the Forward Movement agree with John Moir's analysis that it was primarily a fundraising scheme that by 1923 had run out of steam. Moir does acknowledge that it was "a programme of evangelism, service, stewardship, missionary education, and social concern," but he does not explore how the Forward Movement went about advancing its mandate beyond saying that it did not meet all of its financial objectives.[57]

The plan was that each Presbyterian congregation in the country would set aside a full week, Sunday to Sunday, to focus on the claims of the Forward Movement. That week was to have nightly congregational meetings along with daytime events with women's groups, children and youth programming, and small group discussions. The central theme of the Forward Movement was that the world's only hope lay "in the awakening of a Christian consciousness powerful enough to dominate all other forces and enlist them in the service of humanity." The material promoting the movement began with a call for personal spiritual awakening and a deepening of the church's spiritual life. This was to be advanced first and foremost through prayer. "Comrades of Intercession" were sought who would pray for "the salvation of souls," "the Christianizing of our social, industrial, national, and international relationships," and "the coming of Christ to the whole world." This voice of prayer was to rise not just from individuals and congregations, but also from families who committed themselves to prayer and study of the Bible at the "family altar."[58]

Secondly, Christian consciousness was to be awakened through personal evangelism and intentional Christian education. Half of those who started in a Sunday school programme left before they reached the age of 21, the age of adulthood at the time. Even more disturbing was that three-quarters of those who began in a Presbyterian Sunday school did not attend church on a regular basis in adult years, and never joined the church. The answer to this problem was two-fold. There were at least 400,000 Canadians who had a Presbyterian heritage who had not made a public profession of their faith in Jesus Christ; they would be reached through evangelism "wisely and sympathetically planned as to bring every person face to face with Jesus Christ." Second, the church's work among children and youth needed to be examined so that this drop-out rate did not continue.[59]

A third focus of the Forward Movement was mission and service. Young people, male and female, needed to be confronted with the opportunities for service in the church. The denomination was looking for 700 young people to be ministers and deaconesses in Canada, and another 300 to be missionaries overseas. The committee hoped that during one service in the week of meetings young people would be given an opportunity to re-dedicate their lives to the service of Jesus Christ, even if they were not going to be entering full-time ministry in the church. For people of all ages there was a call to become more committed to the mission of the church, taking up their role in the church's mission in their local community and in their knowledgeable financial and prayer support of the broader mission of the church in Canada and internationally.[60]

The fourth focus was money and stewardship. With the ending of the war in November 1918, the Committee of Fifty came to the Assembly in June 1919, proposing a Peace Thank-Offering, with the goal of raising four million dollars for mission programmes and capital projects. During a one week canvass, in November 1919, $5,138,000 was pledged, and by 1923 more than four million dollars actually had been received. The second goal of doubling the funds given to the boards and committees of the church by 1924 was not realized.[61]

On the prairies the Forward Movement had a number of impacts. First, a large number of clergy took the opportunity to make use of the Presbyterian evangelistic teams that were in the area, or to lead their own evangelistic services without using the teams. It is no coincidence that there were seven evangelistic teams working across the country at the time when the Forward Movement was at its peak. At Manyberries, south of Medicine Hat, Alberta, the missionary held a three-week preaching campaign, which showed few results at the beginning, but in the end 35 people made public profession of their faith, including 13 on one night in the third week. Even the Ukrainian-speaking clergy took the opportunity to hold special meetings in their congregations. Although not every church had evangelistic services, "The gospel of Salvation, through Christ, was preached to the people with a new passion." It was in the wake of the Forward Movement that Gipsy Smith and G. Campbell Morgan did their Canadian tours.[62]

Second, the broad mission focus of the Forward movement called people into a deeper involvement in the mission of the church, for everyone could find something in which to participate. From the intentional family devotional times through to the host of material produced about the various missions of the church, there was something to be read. The stories of how congregations were responding to the Forward Movement stimulated other congregations to find mission projects in which to become involved. In particular, mission charges in the prairie provinces anticipated benefiting from this new focus on mission, being the recipients of some of the money raised. The funds showed that the rest of the church was concerned about the challenges of the church in the West, just as the funds showed that the church was seeking to meet the needs of the inner city.

By talking explicitly about money, the leadership of the church was attempting to tap into the rapidly growing affluence of the middle class. Following Jesus meant following with one's money; sacrifice was also about sacrificial giving. But the church was largely unable to help the rising middle class deal with its newly minted consumer mentality.

The rise of evangelism and social service as tools of the church were driven by a realization that many members of the church were apathetic in their commitment and that the church as an institution was having little impact on the moral reform of society. The clear proclamation of the gospel and the claims of Christ challenged individuals to make a choice to follow Jesus, and many accepted the challenge. The church's involvement in the reformation of society and in providing physical and social support to those in need, broadened the church's impact in the society, bringing people who had never heard the good news about Jesus into contact with the gospel message. Some church leaders were clear-eyed enough to recognize that the church needed to flee from dominant social values of the day, or it would simply be swept along in the rising tide of materialism. These leaders sought to use evangelism and social service to recapture the mission passion that had driven the church in a earlier day. These leaders were seeking to keep the mission of the church alive in a new day, in the face of a new challenge.

Kindergarten at Robertson Memorial Institute, pledging allegiance to Union Jack.
(United Church of Canada/Victoria University Archives, 93.049P/3272)

Three sisters at Robertson Memorial Institute/House.
(United Church of Canada/Victoria University Archives, 93.049P/3271)

Presbyterian Fresh Air Camp at Gimli, MB.
(United Church of Canada/Victoria University Archives, 93.049P/3165)

CHAPTER 7

"By their fruits ye shall know them"[1]
Church United/Church Divided

At the Methodist General Conference held in Winnipeg in 1902, Principal William Patrick of Manitoba College, brought greetings to the Conference on behalf of the General Assembly of the Presbyterian Church in Canada. It was to be the regular greetings that one branch of the Christian church brings to another branch of the church at such gatherings, wishes for God's blessings and encouragement to continue the good work of the church. But instead of such pleasantries, Patrick took this opportunity to propose the organic union of the Protestant churches in Canada, as a way of meeting the problems he saw confronting the Canadian church. By organic union, Patrick envisioned a number of existing denominations coming together to create a new denomination, and in the process the previously existing denominations would cease to exist. It was to be a marriage of two, three, or maybe more denominations. With Patrick's proposal began the 20 year battle over church union, a battle which would culminate on June 10, 1925 in dividing the Presbyterian Church, as approximately two-thirds of the church's membership joined with the Methodists and most of the Congregationalists to form the United Church of Canada and the other third remained members of the continuing Presbyterian Church in Canada.

In the period from 1923 to 1933, three books were written about the Church Union Movement in Canada. Both E. Lloyd Morrow, author of *Church Union in Canada*, and Ephraim Scott, longtime editor of the *Presbyterian Record* and writer of *"Church Union" and The Presbyterian Church in Canada*, were opposed to church union. On the other hand, C. E. Silcox, a Congregationalist and author of *Church Union in Canada: Its Causes and Consequences*, was a supporter. These three books quite effectively outline the chain of events leading up to June 1925, from two very different perspectives. Writing in 1985, 60 years after the climax of the battle, N. Keith Clifford gave an account in *The Resistance to Church Union in Canada, 1904-1939* of why those who were opposed to church union resisted it, and the methods they used to make their opposition known. It is impossible to tell the story of the Presbyterian Church on the prairies without making explicit reference to the ways in which that 20-year debate impacted the mission and ministry of the church in the West. By using the broad history of the movement towards church union as a framework, this chapter explores the ways church union affected the Presbyterian Church on the prairies, asking which Presbyterian congregations, clusters of congregations and leaders were resistant to union. In particular, this chapter will examine what role members of the Presbyterian Church Association, the group organized to oppose church union, had in congregations that remained part of the Presbyterian Church. Readers who are interested in greater detail about the moves and counter-moves made by the various parties during the debate and controversy can turn to Morrow, Scott, Silcox, and Clifford.[2]

It has become commonplace in many circles to make three claims about the drive toward church union. First, union was accomplished in response to a crisis among the churches in western Canada, where the presence of so many denominations in a single community meant that each congregation was too small to be viable either in economic terms or in their ability to meet the needs of their community. Church union would, it was argued, eliminate this problem by ending the dreaded problem of "overlapping." Overlapping was defined "as the evil of multiplying religious services within a given area by different denominations to minister to the Protestant population." The reality of the west, it was argued, demanded the removal of this "evil" through the creation of larger, and therefore more stable, congregations in small towns and rural areas. The second claim, often stated, is that church union was done for mission purposes. By amalgamating denominations there would in total be fewer church buildings to maintain and heat, lowering costs; there would be fewer congregations to manage, freeing up people's energy and personnel. These resources of energy, money, and clergy, it was argued, could be poured into the mission work of the church both in the local area and further afield. A third claim is that the opposition to union was largely to be found among large established urban congregations, and it was these congregations that remained Presbyterian. In describing how the movement towards church union affected the mission of the church on the prairies, this chapter will also explore the validity of these claims.[3]

THE OVERLAPPING DEBATE PRIOR TO 1902

The issue of overlapping was being raised in the secular press as early as the 1890's. There were too many congregations in western Canada, it was argued, for the small number of people who actually lived on the prairies. It needs to be remembered that by the early 1890's population growth had slowed dramatically and many observers wondered if the west would ever reach the potential that had been originally imagined for it. The west was in the minds of many eastern Canadians, a bane rather then a benefit. In this environment it was easy to criticize the churches for pouring too much of their limited resources into a small number of people. Surely, the argument went, there must be some way for the denominations to co-operate to save money and use their limited personnel more effectively. The press had few concrete ideas of what such co-operation would actually look like. One proposal they did have was that the west be divided up in the same way that the foreign mission fields had been divided up; where this community or region would be served by the Presbyterian church, the next one by the Methodists, and the third by the Anglicans, and so on.

James Robertson, who was not only aware of what was being said in the secular press, but also knew that the views expressed there were present in the thinking of the donors whose support the home mission enterprise so desperately needed, responded to the gauntlet that had been thrown down. First, with whom, he wondered, were the Presbyterians to co-operate? Neither the Anglicans nor the Baptists were willing to co-operate with other denominations, and Robertson was none too sure that he wanted to co-operate with the Anglicans and their system of bishops. There were a few small denominational groupings present in the west by the 1890's but they were too small to make co-operation with them worthwhile. That left only the Methodists. Robertson noted a number of ways in which these two denominations were already co-operating. Local Presbyterian and Methodist congregations ensured that they did not have services at the same time in the same community. As well, when both denominations were using circuits that were traveled on a two week rotation, on week one, the Presbyterian missionary would travel the circuit north of the railway preaching in two or three places, while the Methodist went to the circuit south of the railway, then on week two they would switch.[4]

Robertson believed that in many communities where there were both Presbyterian and Methodist missionaries, the work was too great for one person to cover effectively the work that the two were doing; therefore there would need to be two clergy present working out of one amalgamated church. Robertson recognized that many of the settlers came with deeply rooted denominational ties, and that while they were willing to attend worship services of a denomination that was not their own if that was their only choice, as soon as a congregation with their denominational label came along they would move to the newly started congregation. Therefore, if the work level demanded two missionaries, Robertson argued they would be better supported if they carried two different denominational labels than if they carried the same label.[5]

Robertson's third argument against further co-operation was that the financial burden of Presbyterian home mission work was not that significant; all that was needed in the mid-1890's was for each communicant member of the Presbyterian Church in Canada to give 78 cents a year to the work and all the financial needs would be met. Robertson was also worried about what might happen if Church of Scotland donors to the home mission work in Canada became aware that Presbyterians immigrating to Canada from the Old Country were being forced to become Methodists and that the Presbyterian Church in Canada had no intention of ever ministering to them because the community they were living in had been declared "Methodist." He feared funds and personnel support from Scotland would dry up. Robertson firmly believed that the west would reach the potential he dreamed of, and therefore the prairie was big enough and its spiritual needs great enough for all the denominations to do their ministry without crowding each other. Robertson did not live to hear Principal Patrick propose organic church union to the Methodists; if he had lived, Patrick and the other pro-unionists would have found Robertson an articulate and highly committed opponent.[6]

THE RESPONSE TO THE UNION PROPOSAL, 1902-1912

A story, which is most likely apocryphal, is often told to illustrate the competition that existed between the Methodists and the Presbyterians on the prairies. There was an unwritten rule that the first clergyperson to a town could claim the town for their denomination. The story goes like this: The Methodist Superintendent of Mission was getting on the train to travel to a town on the line that had just been started. He recognized the Presbyterian Superintendent of Mission getting on the same train, presumably heading to do the same thing. To ensure that he would be to the town first, the Methodist Superintendent arranged with the conductor to be able to ride in the baggage car, which was immediately behind the engine and coal car. But much to his shock, when he arrived at the platform in the new town the Presbyterian Superintendent was already there to greet him. The Presbyterian, realizing what was happening, had hitched a ride on the cowcatcher on the front of the engine.[7]

In direct response to Patrick's proposal to the Methodist General Conference, a small group of duly appointed Presbyterians and Methodists came together to deal with "the matter of overlapping in the Mission field." This group made up of the general secretaries for Home Mission, superintendents of Mission, and their equivalents, met three times between September 1902 and April 1903. The result of their work was a four-point plan. First, identical letters were sent to all Methodist and Presbyterian ministers on mission fields asserting "the expectation that they will co-operate in all practicable ways to promote" the end of overlapping. To meet this expectation, mission superintendents of the two denominations, whose regions of responsibility were substantially the same, were to meet regularly "in the spirit of mutual helpfulness, and ready concession, respecting the opening of new fields, or the possible readjustment of fields already occupied." The ready concession was to include, that wherever one of the denominations had occupied a mission field for at least one year, the other denomination would act "as far as possible on the principle of non-intrusion." And finally, missionaries of the churches whose fields covered the same area were to meet to discuss if a readjustment of the charges could be done to "mutual advantage." It is important to note that this was essentially the approach that some of the secular press had been advocating 10 years earlier. It was a far cry from the organic union for which Patrick had called.[8]

It was not until 1904 that a proposal for church union came before the Presbyterian General Assembly. That fall, a number of presbyteries discussed the proposal. J.C. Herdman, superintendent of mission for Alberta and British Columbia, reported that five of the eight presbyteries in his region had discussed the topic. He summarized the views expressed as being, "a pronounced one in favour of ultimate union" but it was "almost unanimously" agreed by those participating the discussion "that as yet the time was not ripe for such a consummation." Herdman noted that the level of co-operation between the Methodists and Presbyterians had increased markedly, and it was "pleasing to see that the churches are working together in more unity and kindliness that formerly." But in the middle of all this goodwill, he wished that there were some guidelines to help "simplify and advance" the discussions that were taking place around co-operation at the local level. Co-operation was generally viewed as a good thing, and simply by having raised the possibility of organic union Patrick had stimulated a greater level of "unity and kindliness" between the two denominations. The feeling among those actually doing home mission work in late 1904, however, was that the time was not right for union.[9]

A response to Herdman's request for guidelines to lead the co-operation discussions was not to appear at the General Assembly level until 1911. The Home Missions Committee of the Assembly had recognized the need for such guidelines, and therefore in 1908 had asked the Assembly to appoint representatives to a joint Congregationalist, Methodist, and Presbyterian Committee to work on them. But it took the Joint Committee on Co-operation in Home Mission three years of deliberations to develop their plan. By then Alberta had its own guidelines in place. In 1910, Alexander Forbes had gone to the Peace River; a little later that same year the Methodist Charles Hopkins also arrived there. The two clergy, recognizing the vastness of the territory and their need to co-operate, divided the Peace into two parts. It was a local decision, that received the stamp of approval from the Methodist and Presbyterian Joint Committee on Co-operation in 1913, three years after it had become the basis for the Presbyterian and

Methodist action in the Peace. The slowness of the national joint committee to come up with a process for working through the complex questions
of co-operation caused the Methodists and Presbyterians in Alberta to begin meeting in 1910, and by January of 1911 they had completed their
task. Again it was those in the actual trenches of mission work, for Alberta
was still a growing region with new areas being settled and new mission
fields presenting themselves each year, who were able to quickly develop a
plan to eliminate overlapping and unseemly competition.[10]

The national Joint Committee's report also sought to put an end to
such harmful competition. The report dealt with three areas: overlapping
occurring on already existing fields, the dividing up of new mission fields
among the three denominations, and ending competition in the work among
"non-English-speaking races." The model suggested by the Joint Committee
for dealing with existing fields was very similar to the one being used in
Alberta. In communities where there was overlap, a local committee made
up of equal representation from each denomination in question would
work together to determine which denomination would be given the field.
There were four things to be considered in this process: which denomination
had been the first to occupy the mission field; what was the relative strength
of each denomination in terms of both membership and givings; how
quickly could each denomination put in place the personnel needed to
minister "effectively" in the field; and last, but certainly not least, for it was
the factor which was to be given the greatest weight in the decision, what
was the denominational preference of the majority of the people in the
district. The results of the local committee's work were to be noted on
specially designed forms and sent to the Co-operating Committee of their
Synod (in the Methodist Church this was the Conference level) for their
approval. Once approved, the re-alignment could implemented.[11]

With new mission fields, each denomination annually submitted a report as to its expansion plans for the coming year. If there were areas of
conflict, the denomination that had experienced the greatest "disadvan-
tage," that is, greatest number of mission fields lost to the other denomination, in the previous year, would be given the new field. The committee
had been unable to decide how to divide up the work among the non-
English speaking peoples, and contented itself with agreeing to combine
their resources to carry on united work, where that was the preferable
option.[12]

As noted above the Alberta model was virtually identical to the one
developed by the committee working at the national level. In Alberta, the
model that had moved beyond being simply a piece of paper and was
actually being used, was called a federation of the Methodist and Presbyterian
churches in the province. In most cases all the parties involved exercised
the discipline necessary to make the model work. In 1913, the Methodists

withdrew from the town of Langdon in the Presbytery of Calgary, leaving it to the Presbyterians. That same year in the Presbytery of Lacombe, the Presbyterians withdrew from Merna leaving it to the Methodists. The effectiveness of this model in eliminating overlapping raised the hopes of many people who were opposed to organic union, but saw the value in co-operation among the churches.[13]

THE FEDERATION OPTION

Since 1906, a group within the Presbyterian Church that was resistant to church union had being advocating for some form of federation between the Presbyterians and the Methodists. By federation, the advocates meant a model where each denomination maintained its distinct identity, heritage, and traditions, while at the same time being part of the larger church body which acted in unity, a unity built on the diversity of the federation's members. If organic union was like a marriage, federation was like a partnership in which individual identities were maintained. When Robert Campbell, the senior clerk of the General Assembly, first proposed federation in 1906 as an alternative to organic union, it was attacked by unionists because there were no examples of effective church federations. By the time of the 1911 Assembly, the advocates of federation had two Canadian Presbyterian examples to which they could point.

The first example was noted by John Mackay, the first principal of Westminster Hall, the Presbyterian college in Vancouver and a spokesperson for the cause of federation. It was the Presbyterian experience with the Independent Greek Church. The relationship between the two churches addressed one of the prominent concerns raised by the unionists; the need for an effective response to the non-Anglo-Saxon immigrants who were coming into Canada. The members of the Independent Greek Church may not have become Presbyterians, but, it was argued, the church had aided the Ukrainians in becoming Canadians. In fact, if the Methodists and Presbyterians could form a federation which recognized the distinct characteristics of each denomination, and celebrated those distinctives, while at the same time working together, it would be possible for other denominational groupings like the Independent Greek Church to become part of a larger Canadian church while not losing their distinct culture. Mackay argued, "we ought to look forward to a number of such churches organized from within and federated with some of the stronger denominations, instead of trying to impose the same deadening uniformity upon all peoples."[14] It is ironic that the ardent unionists, Principal Patrick and C.W. Gordon, were the among leading players in the negotiations to have the Independent Greek Church "federated" with the Presbyterian Church in Canada.

The second example of an effective federation was the Alberta model for the elimination of overlapping. This example of a federation was brought to the attention of the denomination as a whole by W.G. Brown, another anti-unionist and the minister at Knox Church in Red Deer, Alberta. He had played a leading role in negotiating the terms of the Alberta plan to eliminate overlapping. Brown's article outlining the Alberta plan was published in the *Presbyterian* on Feb. 2, 1911, a full four months before the report of the national Joint Committee on Co-operation in Home Mission presented its report to the General Assembly. Following the publication of this article Brown was quickly recognized as a leader among those in the west who were resistant to union. Brown knew well the challenges faced by mission field charges, for he was the long-time convenor of his presbytery's home mission committee. In that capacity he dealt with the ups and downs of planting churches on the prairies, and the struggles of small membership churches.[15]

Even though the advocates of federation now had two Canadian examples from within the Presbyterian Church on the prairies, their approach was rejected by the unionist forces because it did not bring about the unity of the church that should be the hallmark of the Body of Christ in the world. The unionists also felt that it would not bring about the resource saving that they anticipated coming from organic union. The almost out-of-hand rejection of the federation alternative left many who were resistant to union convinced that the unionists forces were unwilling to consider anything but union.[16]

THE 1912 VOTE

The 1911 Assembly agreed to the members of the Presbyterian Church in Canada being asked their opinion on church union. The ballot had three questions:

1. Are you in favour of Organic Union with the Methodist and Congregational Churches?

2. Do you approve the proposed Basis of Union?

3. Have you any suggestions or alternatives to offer?

The ballot was perforated. The first two questions were on the left hand portion of the ballot, which also asked the voter to give the name of the presbytery they were in, the name of the congregation, and to sign the ballot. The tear-off section had the third question and a place for the voter to sign. Frustratingly, from a researcher's perspective, the tear-off section of the ballot did not ask for where the voter was located, making it impossible to determine what type of suggestions or alternatives were offered by voters on the prairies. The ballots to be used by elders, members, and adherents were identical except that under the signature line on each portion of the ballot was the word indicating whether this was an elder's, member's, or adherent's ballot.[17]

There were problems getting ballots to congregations in rural Saskatchewan, either because ballots were not sent to some of the small preaching points, or because on some of the mission fields it had been impossible to get the names of "responsible men...who would look after the vote." Those voting problems aside, Presbyterian congregations in the west voted overwhelmingly in favour of organic union with the Methodist and Congregational churches. Nationally, 69 percent of voters were in favour of church union and 31 percent were opposed, but only 55 percent of Presbyterian membership had bothered to vote. The unionist forces agreed that this was not a sufficient mandate to go ahead with church union. The bitter irony confronting the unionists was that for the organic union they dreamed of to take place, the Presbyterian Church would end up being divided. Church union would only come about through church division. Between this harsh reality and the low number of voting congregations church union was put on hold.

On the prairies, in only 35 of the more than 400 pastoral charges that voted did the membership oppose union; seven in Manitoba and northwestern Ontario, 13 from Saskatchewan, and 15 from Alberta. In only five of these charges did a majority of the elders vote in favour of church union and the congregation vote against union. There were 14 other charges where the elders voted "No" to union, while the congregational membership voted "Yes." In about five percent of voting charges, the elders and the members of the congregation reached different conclusions about union. Not surprisingly then, the elders' voting pattern was an accurate predictor of how the congregation would vote. The Crofter congregation at Bellafield, Manitoba, refused to vote by ballot, "but agreed to remain united as a congregation and voted unanimously against the proposed union." The Crofter congregation at Dunleath, Saskatchewan, did use the ballots, voting unanimously against union. Another ethnically distinct congregation, the predominantly Hungarian church at Esterhazy, voted 36 to one against union. The Presbytery of Glenboro, Manitoba, collected the various suggestion that were made in response to question 3 on the ballot and sent them in together. Among the suggestions they submitted was that the name "elder" be maintained to designate lay leaders within the congregations of the new united church and that the words "the Word of God" be inserted into the Basis of Union.[18] Only a handful of Presbyterian congregations on the prairies voted against union in 1912, and they were not on the whole large urban or even stable town churches. The future for those westerners who were opposed to union was bleak.

The 1915 Vote
In order to show that Canada needed a united Protestant church, the Joint Committee on Church Union conducted a national survey of church

conditions in the first months of 1914. The committee produced an impressive 52 page document which, it was argued, showed clearly the need for union. The problems with the study were three-fold: it was done very quickly, in fewer than four months, and therefore the authors did not have the time for careful analysis; a number of presbyteries, including six from the prairies, sent in no responses of any kind; and the study was led by pro-unionist personnel and their biases appear. Having said that, the study did reveal a number of noteworthy things.

Overlapping was identified as a problem in a number of Manitoba's rural areas and through northwestern Ontario. This were the result either of denominations misjudging how large communities would become and planting more churches than the town ended up needing, or through the impacts of rural de-population the number of prospective church attendees was in decline. The introduction of modern machinery, it was argued, meant that one family could manage a larger farm than had been previously possible. Where there had once been a family on every quarter-section, now there was a family and a hired hand farming, in some cases, a full section. The other three families had left the area, going to the cities, British Columbia, or the newly opening areas of the west. The shrinking of the rural population meant fewer people were available to keep the many community organizations, including the churches, going. As we saw in the last chapter this analysis was inaccurate, at least for the Turtle Mountain District of Manitoba, where the size the rural population was unchanged, although its socio-economic make-up had changed.[19]

The report clearly recognized the work that had been done particularly in Saskatchewan and Alberta through "co-operation and delimitation of territory," which had "promoted a Christian spirit…conserved men and money, and…rendered the work of both denominations more effective." One of the out-growths of this co-operative effort in Saskatchewan had been the rise in Union congregations. These were independent congregations, un-affiliated with any of the denominations negotiating union. In addition to those congregations, which had already formed such unions, there were other communities who were waiting in the wings to establish such churches. While the unionist authors of the 1914 study were pleased that there was such a grassroots movement towards union, they were concerned that these congregations had no larger body to give them support or to which they were accountable, and they found disturbing the lack of mission giving among these grassroots churches. One of the great hopes was that the ending of overlapping through the creation of a united church would free up people and money to engage in the mission of the church. In particular that meant mission to "the non-English-speaking immigrants who have flocked in upon us in recent years," who the Protestant churches in Canada had "as yet scarcely touched." From Saskatchewan the question was bluntly put, "would the new [united] church be in a position to attack the task of giving the Gospel to the foreigners of this province?"[20]

The authors of the study saw a new thing beginning to happen in Canada, particularly in the urban centres and in the west as hundreds of thousands of immigrants poured into the country. The new realities called for a new vision and a new model of church. Quoting at length from the report for Manitoba, the study noted,

> It is to be recognized that the growing diversity of population in newer districts is breaking up the old simple denominational unit, such as Presbyterians, Methodists, Anglicans, etc., so that in few districts are there a sufficient number of any denomination to form a congregation. Any church under such conditions must be composite in its membership. Generally speaking, in the West, so far as Protestants are concerned, the denominational spirit is secondary to the community interest. It is impossible to exaggerate the importance to the church of such an alliance with the community spirit as is only possible in a union church...the Church in western Canada should seek to ally with herself the vigorous and almost universal community spirit so dominant in our rapidly expanding towns and cities.[21]

The only way for the church to effectively connect with this community spirit was to become a community church, and that meant union. With this study supportive of union in their hands, the unionists arrived at the June 1914 Assembly pushing for another denomination wide vote on union, this time to be held in the fall of 1915, following that year's General Assembly. No one knew that the events of the late summer of 1914 in far away Sarejevo would set in motion a chain of events that would lead to World War I.

The early stages of the war did not put an end to the drive towards union, and the 1915 vote was held as planned. This time the voter turn out was better, with a staggering 96 percent of the ruling elders across the church casting ballots. Over 500 of the nearly 800 pastoral charges on the prairies voted this time round. Nationally, 60 percent of the membership voted for church union. In the western part of the country (from Lake Superior to the Pacific Ocean), the vote was 78 percent in favour of union. In only five of the 76 presbyteries across the country did a majority of the ruling elders vote against church union. Three of those presbyteries were on the prairies: Weyburn, Saskatchewan, Red Deer, and Castor, Alberta. In 11 of the presbyteries a majority of the communicant members voted against union. Two of those were in the West: Red Deer and Medicine Hat. This time in a total of 62 charges in the three prairie provinces, a majority of the members voted against union: seven were in Manitoba; 24 were in Saskatchewan; and 31 were in Alberta. Again the voting pattern of the ruling elders of a congregation was indicative of how the congregation as a whole would vote; this time in less than four percent of pastoral charges did elders and congregational members reach different conclusions about church union. Again, few large urban congregations voted against union. Only eight of the congregations who voted against union were from urban centres, of which only five could be described as large churches. In Winnipeg, the largest urban centre on the prairies, only one congregation voted against union in any of the three votes held between 1912 and 1925. Calvin Church was the smallest Presbyterian congregation in the city, and its membership was made up of railway workers and their families. In Regina and Saskatoon, not a single congregation voted against union in any of the three votes. The comparative strength of the anti-union forces was in some rural and small town prairie congregations. This challenges the view commonly espoused that the resistance to union in the west was from well-established, urban congregations.[22]

Eighteen of the charges that had voted against union in 1912 did so again in 1915. Clear pockets of resistance were being established throughout the prairies. Again some ethnically based congregations voted against union: the Crofter churches in Hilton, Manitoba and Dunleath, Saskatchewan and this time the Finnish mission in the Alberta foothills near Rocky Mountain House. A number of congregations in the southwest corner of Manitoba and the southeast corner of Saskatchewan (including Melita, Hartney, Elkhorn, Redvers, and Moosomin) consistently voted against union or had large minority groups that were opposed to union. Ruling elders like Judge A. Farrell of Moosomin (he later moved to Regina), James Duncan of Melita, and James Duthie of Hartney exercised great influence in their congregations. But the presence of those strong lay leaders does not explain why other congregations in that area, in which Farrell, Duncan, and Duthie were not elders, voted against union. Other areas of consistent resistance to union in Saskatchewan included the Qu'Appelle Valley and the towns of Moose Jaw and Weyburn. In Alberta consistent opposition to union was found in Edmonton, where Dr. McQueen, the first Presbyterian minister in the city, was the minister of First Presbyterian Church. McQueen was an advocate of denominational co-operation, but he was an opponent of church union. In McQueen the opponents of church union in Edmonton had a role model; therefore the opposition at North Edmonton and Robertson Memorial is in part attributable to McQueen's presence in the city. The region south and west of Lloydminster, Alberta, the western half of the Presbytery of Vermilion, was another pocket of resistance. In this area, in addition to the four congregations which voted "No," there were three congregations where the elders opposed union while the congregational membership voted in favour of union. This dissent from union, was supported by the longtime convenor of the presbytery's home missions committee, William Simons, who in 1912 was appointed district superintendent of Mission for Northern Alberta. After 1925, Simons was to return to the area south of Lloydminster, ministering to one of the continuing Presbyterian congregations in the area. Two urban congregations that showed great tenacity in their opposition to union were: Grace Church in Calgary and St. John's in Medicine Hat. The resistance in Medicine Hat is attributable in part to the long-term ministry of J.W. Morrow at St. John's Church, who was an opponent of union.[23]

Historians have, for a long time, been interested in pinpointing what led some congregations to vote in favour of union while others opposed it. It is beyond the scope of this present study to explore those questions in any detail, so only the most general of comments can be made about the local factors that led these various areas to be so opposed. It is hoped that some future researcher will explore that question. The largest pocket of resistance to union on the prairies was to be found in the area around Red Deer, Alberta, and heading west to Rocky Mountain House. That resistance owed much to the work of W.G. Brown.

W.G. BROWN

Walter George Brown was by far the most effective opponent to church union in the west. Brown was born in the province of Quebec and attended McGill before taking his theological training at Presbyterian College, Montreal. He graduated in 1902. Turning down a number of attractive calls, he became a missionary in the lumber camps of northern Ontario and the mining camps of British Columbia. He and his family knew something of the struggles faced by the pioneers. While living in New Denver, B.C., one of the Browns' children died. In 1907, he accepted a call to Red Deer, where he kept his hand in the home mission enterprise as the long time convenor of the presbytery's committee and as one of the key players in the negotiations leading to the Alberta model for the elimination of overlapping.[24]

Brown was an able orator and quick with his rejoinder in debate, which stood him in good stead during the heated discussions that took place around church union. In one such confrontation, Dr. Samuel Lyle of Hamilton, Ontario, demanded to know of Brown, "Would you dare to resist the will of God?" To which Brown replied, "No, but I would dare to resist your interpretation of it." Brown was a commissioner to the 1923 General Assembly, which was held in Port Arthur, Ontario. It was the Assembly at which it became clear that the unionists were going to force through organic union even if it split the Presbyterian Church. C.W. Gordon, better known by his pen-name as the novelist Ralph Connor, a staunch unionist had spoken in passionate terms about the need for union. Brown in his rebuttal wondered aloud where Gordon had been "in the last seven years, living in the land of fiction?"[25]

Brown was a brilliant organizer who mobilized dozens of groups resistant to union across the prairies. He was able to raise up enough leaders opposed to union within the Presbytery of Red Deer that he was freed up to move further afield. He became a much sought after speaker among those opposed to union, becoming an expert on the financial implication of union. He advocated that those opposed to union stop contributing to the Budget of the Church. This campaign was so effective that from 1922 on, the Home and Foreign Mission Boards of the church were in a constant state of crisis, unable to fund the work to which they were committed. By 1923 he was so well-known across the church that Thomas McMillan, the president of the Presbyterian Church Association, and Principal Daniel Fraser, of Presbyterian College, Montreal, offered him the position of dominion organizer for the Association. Brown turned down the opportunity to become the national spokesperson for the opponents to union, saying,

> The great principles at stake, the soundness and justice of our cause made a very strong appeal to me. Over against this was the West, the work that I have tried to build up and the Home Mission fields that I have tried to develop through much labour. The present is such a serious time in the future of the church. It is most important that the church shall retain its national character and therefore that we ought to retain every field in the west where a fair presentation of the case will lead the people to stay with the Presbyterian Church. By staying in Alberta I believe that I can be of more service to our cause in the west.[26]

With a vision that the Presbyterian Church needed to be a national church after the split that was about to take place, and with a heart for the mission field of the west, Brown said, "No," to the opportunity to play on the national stage. His willingness to accept new challenges was evident, when shortly after union was completed, Brown accepted a call to pastor the Presbyterians in Saskatoon. None of the Presbyterian congregations had retained their building and therefore had been meeting in a dance hall when Brown came to be their minister.

The Truce and its Aftermath on the Prairies

The unionists, having won the congregational vote in the fall of 1915 and the Assembly vote in 1916, prepared for the 1917 Assembly arguing that union should now be accomplished. That the pain of dividing the

Presbyterian Church would be more than compensated for by the joy that would be experienced when the union with the Methodists and Congregationalists was consummated. The anti-union forces came to the 1917 Assembly asking that any moves towards union be put on hold so that the whole energy of the church could be focused on the national crisis of the war. This was not the time to bring about union; there were more important things to worry about. This call for a truce won the day and all plans to move towards union were shelved.

But the shelving of church union at the national level did not mean that church union at the local level was postponed. In fact, the truce at the national level seemed to increase the interest in co-operation across the prairies.[27] There were, however, two fundamentally different models of co-operation at work on the prairies.

Arising first in Saskatchewan and then moving on to Manitoba was the union charge movement. The pattern followed by these union churches was that the congregations cut all denominational ties creating community churches, which were essentially independent bodies. These unions were the result of local people coming together "entirely on their own initiative." Denominational leaders were hard pressed to encourage these independent churches to affiliate with a larger denomination, fearing that they were witnessing the rise of a new denomination with whom they would need to negotiate a new union agreement. There were in fact three distinct kinds of union charges. First, there were the independent ones, which had no ties to any denomination and were organized around the principles and doctrine laid out in the proposed Basis of Union. As independent churches they gave or did not give to the mission work of the larger denominations, as the local congregation saw fit. By 1924, there were 15 such independent union charges, involving 31 preaching points, in southern Saskatchewan. The second kind of union charge were the double affiliation charges. These were locally driven unions where the Methodists and the Presbyterians in the community maintained their denominational linkages, but worshipped together and the congregation had one communion roll, one Sunday school, one missionary society, and so on. The minister of the charge would be Methodist for four years; that minister would then leave and a Presbyterian would come for four years. These congregations, as well, were organized around the proposed Basis of Union. There were 33 of these double affiliation charges involving 86 preaching points in southern Saskatchewan by 1924, most of which had been formed since 1920. By 1923, there were about 80 such double affiliation charges in rural Manitoba, most of which had been formed following World War I. The third kind of union charge was the single affiliation charge, which was like the double affiliation charge, but the minister did not flip denominations every four years. Rather the charge had decided to call their ministers from one denomination. There were five such union charges in southern Saskatchewan, involving 12 preaching points, and two or three single affiliation charges in Manitoba by 1924.[28]

The double affiliation system addressed the often-expressed concern that, "neither side wants to become members of the other, especially is this true of the Presbyterians." While maintaining their denominational labels, local Presbyterians and Methodists had found a way to work together to build a stable congregation that was able to address the needs of the local community more effectively and which, and this was the important factor in the minds of many denominational leaders, was self-supporting. By the end of 1922 there were 84 self-sustaining double affiliation charges in Manitoba. This freed up home mission funds to go into other projects.[29] It seems that this was the only way that local church unions could take place in those areas of the prairies that had been settled for a generation or more. The emotional and spiritual ties to a name and a heritage were too deeply engrained to be given up easily. The corporate memory of years of relationship between the denominations in the community meant that joining the other side was impossible. Local communities at their own initiative found the way to balance the question of economics and the reality of heritage, and in the process developed a ministry model that made sense for them.

The situation in Alberta was markedly different, where there were only three union charges in the entire province. As a more recently settled territory, Alberta's residents did not have deep roots in their local communities of faith. As new arrivals in a new land, the settlers were prepared to do things differently than they had back in their town or country of origin. This meant they were willing to attend a church that did not have the name of their preferred denomination on the door. Therefore the Alberta model for the elimination of overlapping worked well. William Shearer, district superintendent for central Alberta, told of a Methodist and a Presbyterian missionary who each had the same two-point charge: Spring Bank and South Calgary. The points were 25 kilometers apart. The two missionaries met one another each Sunday, traveling to lead worship in the community where the other missionary had just finished leading worship. The missionaries were able to get the Methodists and Presbyterians in each community to sit down together to determine how to address this problem. The result was that the two congregations in Spring Bank joined together to become a Methodist church, and the two congregations in South Calgary joined under the Presbyterian banner. This pattern for dealing with overlapping was firmly in place by the end of the war. By that time, in the four central Alberta presbyteries alone, the Methodists had withdrawn from ten mission fields leaving them to the Presbyterians, while the Presbyterians had withdrawn from eight. By the spring of 1918 from both the northern and central Alberta District Superintendents, the refrain was heard, "There is absolutely no overlapping in the country missions." The story was somewhat different in the towns and villages where the various denominations had invested in buildings; this was particularly a problem central Alberta. Although the presence of property complicated the situation, the co-operation committees were not shying away from facing the challenge head-on.[30]

The Presbyterians and Methodists on the prairies had developed local patterns for the ending of overlapping and competition between the denominations. While the Board of Home Mission and the District Superintendents supported these "co-operation movements" providing advice if asked, it was the policy of the Board and the Superintendents "not to *initiate* these movements" (emphasis in original.)[31] The locally initiated movements had virtually eliminated overlapping on the prairies by 1924; the financial and personnel savings that were to be achieved by organic union had almost entirely already been realized. It is true that the 20-year debate about union had encouraged local congregations of different denominations to explore ways in which they could co-operate; without the church union proposal being before the church some of this co-operation might not have taken place. But that does not change the fact that by 1924, church union was no longer something that the west demanded, for the west had already completed union in a patchwork quilt of federation approaches.

CHURCH UNION/CHURCH DIVISION

In 1920, Principal Alfred Gandier of Knox College wrote to the General Assembly asking whether the question of church union would ever be brought down from the shelf where it had been placed in 1917. And so with the General Assembly of 1921, which was held in Winnipeg, the proponents and opponents of church union were again preparing for battle. The Presbyterian Church Association, which had gone into hibernation in 1917 with the announcement of the truce, was now re-activated. This time round, it was clear that the unionists would stop at nothing short of consummating the union that had been in the works for 20 years, even if that meant splitting the Presbyterian Church in the process. At the 1923 Assembly, held in Port Arthur (now Thunder Bay), Ontario, C. W. Gordon expressed the unionists' commitment to victory when he said, "We will force you rebels in by an act of parliament, whether you like it or not." Following this assembly the issues in debate were the actual process by which congregations would decide if they would be entering the United Church or not and what the legislation to be passed by the provincial and federal governments would say. While the opponents of union kept up a gallant fight trying to stop union, most leaders of the resistance movement shifted their energy to keeping as many congregations as possible part of the continuing Presbyterian Church in Canada.[32]

An examination of the Presbyterian Church Association's mailing list for the prairies provides insight into some of the general factors that lead congregations to remain Presbyterian. It is important to recognize that this was not a membership list; rather it was a list of people to whom brochures and other material could be mailed for further distribution by the recipient. This, then, was a list of people who had enough commitment to the cause to be identified in their home communities as people who were opposed to union.

The mailing list for Manitoba included 28 names. There were only five clergy on the list, none of whom were from Winnipeg. In fact, there were only seven people on the list who had Winnipeg mailing addresses, one being the lawyer H.A. Robson, who was a member of the Board of Trustees of the Presbyterian Church Association. Robert Paterson, whose name was also on the list, was the minister at St. Andrew's Church in Brandon. In 1912, St. Andrews had voted 49 to three in favour of union, but in 1925 it voted 67 to five to remain Presbyterian. One of the things that was different in 1925 was the presence of Paterson, who was a strong voice in opposition to union. C.K. Nicoll, who had been the last minister at the church in White Horse and had been a military chaplain during World War I, was the minister in Carberry, Manitoba, and his opposition to union would have helped swing the congregation towards remaining Presbyterian. A further factor was that the ministers in the nearby communities of Wellwood and Neepawa were also opposed to union, and were able to keep the congregations they served out of union as well. But congregations did not always vote the way the minister thought they should. R.G. Stewart, at Vista, although resistant to union, was not able to convince a majority of the members of the charge to vote against it. And in both Selkirk and Hartney the minister supported union, but the representative elder, who was an influential voice within the congregation, was opposed to union, and his opposition would have encouraged those congregational members who were also opposed to maintain the struggle to keep the congregation Presbyterian. The tiny congregation at Winnipegosis remained Presbyterian on a five to nothing vote. In 1913 the community had been assigned to the Methodists in a co-operation agreement so that there was no specifically Presbyterian worship for a period of time. When given the opportunity, however, to voice their preference, the congregation of Knox Church wished to be Presbyterian.

There were in some Winnipeg congregations and in other congregations around Manitoba large minority groups who were resistant to union. These were Presbyterians who had been on the short end of the vote in their home congregation, and so the congregation and the building had gone into the United Church. Many of those who were on the losing end of the vote had no intention of attending worship in the United Church and therefore these minority groups, if they believed their numbers were large enough, started new Presbyterian congregations. In Winnipeg, four such congregations were started in the year following church union: First, Norwood, St. James, and St. John's. Congregations with similar histories were: First Church, Brandon and First Church, Portage la Prairie.[33]

There were 35 names on the Presbyterian Church Association's mailing list for Saskatchewan, 17 of whom were the names of clergy. Again in the urban centres of Regina and Saskatoon, there was little support for the Association's work; only four of the people on the list lived in those cities. Of the clergy, eight were in active parish ministry, and five of the charges served by those eight clergy remained Presbyterian after 1925. In the cases of Dunleath and the charges in the Qu'Appelle Valley, however, these congregations had been consistently opposed to union, and the presence of a minister who was also opposed to union simply strengthened the already existing resistance. As in Manitoba, the simple presence of a minister who was actively opposed to union did not guarantee that the church would remain Presbyterian. The charges at Expanse, Balcarres, and Lashburn had all been ministered to by activists for the Presbyterian Church Association, but each of these charges went into union. St. Paul's Church, Moose Jaw remained Presbyterian in part because Moose Jaw was a hotbed of opposition to union. Three of the individuals on the mailing list lived in Moose Jaw including a minister who was not in active parish ministry and two lay people. Together these three received 600 copies of each brochure the Association produced, which was more than a quarter of the brochures that were distributed in Saskatchewan. It was to St. Paul's that the minority groups from the other two Presbyterian churches in town would eventually go. At Prince Albert, three prominent lay people, Lieutenant-Colonel Lindsay; Lieutenant-Colonel Laurie, the post master; and James Stewart, a pharmacist, were actively opposed to union, and together they would have encouraged each other and the congregation to resist union even though the minister, R.J. McDonald, favoured union. The congregations at Weyburn and at Melfort stayed Presbyterian, but in a move that looked like they were saying, "A plague on both of your houses," became Independent Presbyterian in the year following church union. They did return to the fold of the Presbyterian Church in Canada later. Until late 1924, W.W. Bryden, who would go on to become the professor of systematic theology at Knox College, Toronto, was the minister at Melfort, and his presence would have influenced the decision of this congregation to remain Presbyterian. In both Regina and Saskatoon, minority groups came together to form new congregations.[34]

There were 55 names on the Presbyterian Church Association's Alberta mailing list. Thirteen of the individuals lived in communities within the boundaries of the Presbytery of Red Deer; nine of these were clergy. It is not surprising then to discover that 16 charges made up of 21 preaching points in this presbytery voted to remain Presbyterian. This was, as we have seen, W.G. Brown's stomping grounds. Given Brown's longevity in Red Deer (18 years by 1925) and his role convening the home missions committee of the presbytery, it is easy to speculate that he played a role in selecting ministers for vacant charges in the presbytery who were also opposed to union. Or it may been simply that his well-known opposition to union attracted clergy of a similar persuasion to the presbytery. In any case Brown's influence would have been felt throughout the presbytery. The congregation Brown served, Knox Church, Red Deer, voted 70 to four to stay out of union. Having a cluster of clergy within a presbytery who were opposed to union was no guarantee that congregations would remain Presbyterian. The Presbytery of Castor, located to the east of Red Deer including the communities of Settler, Consort, and Castor, was made up of eight pastoral charges and an equal number of mission charges which were covered by students or catechists. In 1923, four of the clergy in the presbytery, including the Rev. Angus Sutherland, were opposed to union and were active in the Presbyterian Church Association. Following union in 1925, not a single preaching point from the former presbytery remained Presbyterian. The difference between the presbyteries of Castor and Red Deer could be due in part to the later settlement of region covered by Castor presbytery. The charges were younger, more flexible, and less rooted in the Presbyterian traditions. Overlapping had been eliminated years earlier in both presbyteries so that would not have been a factor. A similar pattern was seen in the Peace River country. There congregations not much younger than those in Castor Presbytery all voted to go into union, even though Alexander Forbes, the pioneer of the Peace who was still in active ministry in Grande Prairie, opposed union and distributed material outlining why union should be resisted. In the Peace River region, there never had been a problem with overlapping. So the savings that were anticipated by ending the "evil" of multiplying "religious services" would not be realized.[35]

There was a marked difference between how Presbyterians in the major urban centres of Alberta reacted to union and how those in Winnipeg, Regina, and Saskatoon responded. As noted earlier, D.G. McQueen's resistance to union would have rallied the other opposition forces in Edmonton. There were five clergy and three lay people in Edmonton who distributed materials on behalf of the Association. Six congregations in Edmonton, including First Church with its over 800 members, remained Presbyterian. In Calgary, there were five lay people, including two women, who were actively engaged promoting the Presbyterian cause through the distribution of Association materials. After the dust had settled in 1925, there were three Presbyterian congregations in Calgary that had retained their buildings. These included Grace Church, which with its 1,100 members, challenged Knox Church to be the largest Presbyterian church in Calgary. Smaller urban centres showed resistance to union as well. St. John's Church, Medicine Hat, maintained its long history of opposition to union, voting "No" once again. In Lethbridge and Wetaskiwin minority groups were strong enough to start new Presbyterian congregations. Consistent with their persistent dissent to union through the votes of 1912 and 1915, a number of congregations south and west of Lloydminster remained Presbyterian. An ironic twist took place as Banff, under the ministry of Presbyterian Church Association activist, J.B. Thompson, voted "No" to church union. Banff had been where C.W. Gordon, avid supporter of union, had begun his career in ministry.[36]

It is a truism to say that congregations staying out of union needed leaders, either clergy or ruling elders, who were clearly opposed to becoming part of the United Church of Canada. Interestingly, the way the ruling elders of a congregation chose to vote was a more accurate indicator of how the congregation would vote, than was the way the minister voted. Leaders who were resistant to union were not enough; knowing that there were neighbouring congregations that also were opposed to union, provided moral support and further solidified the opposition. While there were some outstanding exceptions, on the whole, congregations who became part of the continuing Presbyterian Church in Canada had been consistent in their opposition to union throughout the years of voting and heated debate.

The consummation of church union left the continuing Presbyterian Church in Canada with pastoral charges consisting of 154 preaching points. Three-quarters of the pastoral charges, that is 69, were in rural areas or small towns. This roughly was the ratio between rural and urban pastoral charges prior to union. These figures indicate that the relative strength of the opposition to union in rural and small-town western Canada was similar to its relative strength in urban centres. This once more challenges the view that the opposition to union was almost completely an urban phenomenon on the prairies. While the continuing Presbyterian church had been decimated by union, it had not been wiped out in either the rural or the urban areas.

In reading the names of those clergy who were opposed to organic union, one is struck by how many of them are the names of leaders in the Presbyterian Church's home mission enterprise: D.G. McQueen, the first Presbyterian minister in Edmonton; Alexander Forbes, "the apostle to the Peace" (as he was sometimes called); A.S. Grant, minister-doctor in Dawson City and later General Superintendent of Home Mission; R.B. Heron, long-time missionary among the Native people in Saskatchewan; W.D. Reid, W.S. Simons, and W.A. Cameron, district superintendents of Missions after

1910; and W.G. Brown, missionary to the mining communities of British Columbia and long time home mission committee convenor. Brown himself recognized this fact, listing an additional 13 clergy "who have been in Home Mission work on the frontier for the last quarter of a century and more, all of whom are opposed to the present Organic Union Movement."[37] This list begs the question of what exactly was the purpose of church union; clearly many of those most intimately involved with the mission work of the church on the prairies did not believe that organic union was necessary or beneficial to the advance of the gospel. As we have already seen, overlapping was essentially eliminated by 1923, and the hoped-for financial and personnel savings that were to flow to other mission projects would already have been realized. Church union was being pursued not as an aid to the mission of the church, but as an end in itself. The advocates of church union had accepted the business models of the day, which called for larger and more efficient organizational structures.

The mission passion that had driven the Presbyterian Church in Canada into the work on the prairies did not go in its entirety into the United Church; neither did the creativity and ingenuity of those missionaries. Through their resistance to union, a number of pioneer missionaries on the prairies ensured that the continuing Presbyterian Church in Canada was also heir to the mission passion and creativity that had made the church the largest denomination on the prairies through the first quarter of the 20th century.

AFTERWORD

The Presbyterian Church in Canada saw the prairies as a mission field and as a great challenge. The challenge of the land and the wide open spaces became the challenge of the new Canadians and the urban centres. It was those people who were at the edge of the mission enterprise who reminded the church of the fact that it had a message about Jesus Christ to proclaim. The temptation to turn the church's message into the proclamation of "Canadianism" was very real and a number of Presbyterians traded in the gospel of Jesus for the gospel of Canadian social religion. Those individuals at the frontier of mission called the church back, recasting for the church what its real purpose was: to proclaim the good news about Jesus Christ in word and deed. The frontier of mission was sometimes the geographical frontier as well; the passionate commitment to the gospel seen in the lives of those working in the Yukon and the Peace River country reminded the whole church of what its mission was. But the frontier of mission was also found in the city, where James Mutchmor and Agnes Coutie clearly articulated the gospel while caring for people's physical needs. The frontier of mission was found by people like James Thomson and hundreds of unnamed lay people who reached across cultural barriers to bring the good news of Jesus to people who were strangers. The frontier of mission was also found by people like the Dakota missionaries and the clergy of the Independent Greek Church and the D'Augustinos in Winnipeg, who found their lives changed by Jesus and took that message back to their own culture and community. The mission frontier forced the creation of new ministry models within the church as lay people and women stepped into new roles and took on new responsibilities. The mission frontier forced the church to do new things, to try out some new wineskins, like evangelistic crusades and city missions. In each of these and in a myriad other ways, individuals and the church as a whole were called to risk, to step out in faith in proclaiming the good news about Jesus. As they stepped out in faith, people were calling into question the values of the dominant culture. They were proselytizing when all around them people said that was inappropriate behaviour; they were caring for the stranger when all around them people said let "those people" manage on their own; and they were giving sacrificially in an increasingly consumer-dominated world. The real frontier of mission is found when people step out in faith, and choose to defy the dominant culture and trust God instead. When the church was no longer willing to be different than the culture around it, when it had become comfortable with the values and worldview of the society at large, that is when the edge of mission vanished, and the church became the purveyor of middle class social religion.

J.H. Edmison described the mission frontier in this way:

> It is the high privilege of those who share in Home Mission work to join with Jesus in His Church-Building enterprise. And what finer privilege could there be than that! It is a sacred task to erect a building—of boards or brick or stone—in which some Church may meet and minister to the souls of men. As a Board of Home Missions, we have the joy of such labour. But finer far is the privilege of acting with Christ in building the Church itself—that spiritual body of men and women, young men and maidens, boys and girls, who have seen in Jesus what Peter saw in Him, whose minds are filled with His ideas, whose hearts are steeped in His spirit, and who will go out to permeate the whole of human life with His influence. To have even the humblest part in a task such as that is the highest sort of privilege. And that is the task of Home Missions.[1]

It is exactly that "finer far" privilege to which the Presbyterian Church on the prairies was called. A calling not just for the clergy to hear, but rather for all the members of the church to hear, to take the risk of becoming involved in the proclamation of the gospel. Here was an invitation to step out in faith and move to the mission frontier.

END NOTES

Introduction

1   *Census of Canada*, 1891, 1901, 1911, 1921.

2   James Marnoch, *Western Witness:The Presbyterians in the Area of the Synod of Manitoba, 1700-1885* (Winnipeg,Watson & Dwyer Publishing, 1994).

3   E.H. Oliver,"The Religious History of Saskatchewan to 1935," (unpub. history in United Church Archives, St.Andrew's College, Saskatoon); C.A. Dawson and EvaYounge, *Pioneering in the Prairie Provinces:The Social Side of the Settlement Process* (Toronto, MacMillan Company, 1940); Charles Gordon, *The Life of James Robertson: Missionary Superintendent in Western Canada* (Toronto,The Westminster Company, Ltd., 1908); Hugh McKellar, *Presbyterian Pioneer Missionaries in Manitoba, Saskatchewan, Alberta and British Columbia* (Toronto, Murray Printing Company Ltd., 1924).

4   Royden Loewen,"On the Margin or In the Lead: Canadian Prairie Historiography," *Agricultural History*,Vol. 71, #1,Winter 1999, pp. 27-45. See Loewen, *Family, Church and Market: A Mennonite Community in the Old and New Worlds, 1850-1930* (Toronto, University of Toronto Press, 1995).

5   Frank Peake,"From the Red River to the Arctic: Essays on Anglican Missionary Expansion in the Nineteenth Century," *Journal of the Canadian Church Historical Society*,Vol. 31, #2, October 1989, pp. 1-169; Robert Choquette, *The Oblate Assault on Canada's Northwest* (Ottawa, University of Ottawa Press, 1995); Marnoch, *Western Witness.*

6   Dennis L. Butcher, Catherine Macdonald, Margaret E. McPherson, Raymond Smith, A. McKibbin Watts, eds., *Prairie Spirit: Perspectives on the Heritage of the United Church of Canada in the West* (Winnipeg, University of Manitoba Press, 1985); Barry Ferguson, ed., *The Anglican Church and the World of Western Canada* (Regina, University of Regina Press, 1991).

7   John Moir, *Enduring Witness: A History of the Presbyterian Church in Canada*, (Toronto, Presbyterian Publications, 1975); Neil Semple, *The Lord's Dominion: The History of Canadian Methodism*, (Montreal & Kingston, McGill-Queen's University Press, 1996); Richard Allen Morton,"'Means of Grace': Directions in Presbyterian Home Mission Work, 1870-1885," *American Presbyterians*, vol. 72, #2, Spring 1994, pp. 123-34.

8   Richard Allen, *The Social Passion: Religion and Social Reform in Canada, 1914-1928*, (Toronto, University of Toronto Press, 1971); Michael Owen, "'Keeping Canada God's Country:' Presbyterian Perspectives on Selected Social Issues, 1900-1915," (Unpub. Ph. D. Thesis, University of Toronto, 1984); Marilyn Barber, "Nationalism, Nativism and the Social Gospel: The Protestant Church Response to Foreign Immigrants in Western Canada, 1897-1914," in Richard Allen, ed, *The Social Gospel in Canada*, Papers of the Inter-disciplinary Conference on the Social Gospel in Canada, 1973 (Ottawa, National Museums of Canada, 1975), pp. 186-226; Brian Fraser, *The Social Uplifters: Presbyterian Progressives and the Social Gospel in Canada, 1875-1915* (Waterloo, ON:Wilfrid Laurier University Press, 1988); Nancy Christie and Michael Gauvreau, *A Full-Orbed Christianity:The Protestant Churches and Social Welfare in Canada, 1900-1940* (Montreal & Kingston, McGill-Queen's, 1996).

Chapter 1

1   James Robertson, *Acts and Proceedings of the General Assembly of The Presbyterian Church in Canada*, 1887, App. #1, p. xii.

2   McMicken," *Dictionary of Canadian Biography*, vol. 14 (Toronto: University of Toronto Press), pp. 727-9; *A&P*, 1882, App. p. xiv.; 1883, App. p. xiv.

3   Smith attended St. Paul's Church in Montreal, Alexander Reford, "Donald Alexander Smith," *DCB*, vol. 14, pp. 939-47; *PCA*, Special Committee for Aids for Social Worship, *Aids of Social Worship*, p. 2.

4   A.A. den Otter, "Sir William Whyte," *DCB*, vol. 14, pp. 1062-3; David Neufeld, "Donald Alexander Stewart," *DCB*, vol. 12, p. 989; John Patrick Day, "Donald McLeod," *DCB*, vol. 12, pp. 671-2.

5   Roger Graham, *Arthur Meighan: The Door of Opportunity* (Toronto: Clarke, Irwin and Co. Ltd., 1960), pp. 222-229, 245-272.

6   R.C. Macleod, "James Farquharson Macleod," *DCB*, vol. 12, pp. 672-675; David Crawford, *Blue Flame in the Foothills: Presbyterian Activities in the Calgary Region* (Calgary: Century Calgary Publications, 1975), pp. 27-29.

7   Morris Mott, "John B. Mather," *DCB*, Vol. 12, pp. 711-712; Charles W. Anderson, "Stephen Nairn," *DCB*, vol. 12, pp. 777-778.

8   Anderson, "Nairn," *DCB*, vol. 12, p. 777.

9   A lot has been written about Riel and the Rebellion, one of the best is Bob Beal and Rod Macleod, *Prairie Fire: The 1885 North-West Rebellion* (Toronto: McClelland and Stewart, 1994). *Presbyterian Record*, Vol. 10: #3, March 1885, pp. 58-9; #5, May 1885, p. 121, #6, June 1885, pp. 149-150.

10   UCA, PCC, Mission to Aboriginal Peoples in Manitoba and the Northwest (MAPMNW), Box 1, File 5, Report of Hugh McKay, April 13, 1885.

11   *Record* UCA, Robertson Papers, *DCB*, vol. 12, pp. 147-148.

12   *Record*, vol. 10 #5, May 1885, p. 121.

13   UCA, PCC, MAPMWN, Box 1, File 5, MacWilliam to Wardrope, May 5, 1885; *Record*, Vol. 10 #5, May 1885, p. 121; #6, June 1885, p. 150.

14   Charles Gordon (Ralph Connor), *The Life of James Robertson: Missionary Superintendent in Western Canada* (Toronto: The Westminster Company, Ltd., 1908), pp. 313-315 (Quoted from Hansard.)

15   John Chalmers, *Laird of the West*, (Calgary, Detselig Enterprises Ltd., 1981), pp. 203-258; E. Brian Titley, "W.M. Graham: Indian Agent Extraordinaire," *Prairie Forum*, 1983, Vol. 8, #1, pp. 25-41.

16   Chalmers, *Laird*, pp. 203-258.

17   Lewis Herbert Thomas, *The Struggle for Responsible Government in the North-West Territories, 1870-1897* (Toronto: University of Toronto Press, 1956), pp. 111-135, quote on p. 123.

18   L.J. Roy Wilson, "Thomas Andrew Tweed," *DCB*, vol. 13, pp. 1043-4.

19   J.J. Harrold Morris, "David George McQueen: Pioneer of Western Canada," in Stanford Reid, ed., *Called to Witness*, vol. 1 (Toronto: Presbyterian Publications, 1975), pp. 194-195.

20   The material for the following section is derived from the *Census of Canada*, 1891, 1901, 1911, 1921; and David J. Hall, ""The Pole Star of Duty": A.M. Burgess and the Department of the Interior," *Prairie Forum*, Spring 1991, Vol. 16, #1, pp. 32.

21   Richard Willie, "Colin H. Campbell," in *DCB*, vol. 14, pp. 173-176.

22   *A&P*, 1915, App. p. 35.

23   Much of this following discussion comes from two sources: Louis Aubrey Wood, *A History of Farmer's Movements in Canada* (Toronto: University of Toronto Press, 1975, reprint of 1924 edition by Ryerson Press), pp. 159-327; Harald S. Patton, *Grain Growers Co-operation in Western Canada* (New York: AMS Press, Inc., 1969, reprint of 1928 edition, Cambridge, Mass.), passim.

24   Allan R. Turner, "W.R. Motherwell: The Emergence of a Farm Leader," *Saskatchewan History*, Autumn 1958, Vol. 11, #3, pp. 94-103.

25   W.L. Morton, *The Progressive Party in Canada*: (Toronto: University of Toronto Press, 1950), pp. 41, 46; Richard Allen, *The Social Passion: Religion and Social Reform in Canada, 1914-1928* (Toronto: University of Toronto Press, 1973), pp. 16, 203, 210-11.

26   Max Foran, "George Murdoch," in *DCB*, vol. 13, pp. 747-748.

27   Wilson, "Tweed," *DCB*, vol. 13, pp. 1043-4; L.J. Roy Wilson, "William Thomas Finlay," *DCB*, vol. 14, pp. 356-7.

28   Maggie Siggins, *Revenge of the Land: A Century of Greed, Tragedy, and Murder on a Saskatchewan Farm* (Toronto: McClelland and Stewart, Inc., 1991), pp. 262-311.

29   A.A. den Otter, "Lethbridge: Outpost of a Commercial Empire, 1885-1906," in Alan Artibise, ed. *Town and City: Aspects of Western Canadian Urban Development* (Regina: Canadian Plains Research Center, 1981), pp. 171-202; den Otter, *Civilizing the West: The Galts and the Development of Western Canada* (Edmonton: University of Alberta Press, 1982), p. 39.

30   den Otter, "Lethbridge," pp. 171-202.

31   *Ibid.*; Hall, "The Pole Star of Duty," *Prairie Forum*, Spring 1991, Vol. 16, #1, pp. 30-31.

32   John Patrick Day, "Donald McLeod," *DCB*, vol. 12, pp. 671-672.

33   Ruben Bellan, *Winnipeg First Century: An Economic History* (Winnipeg, 1978), pp. 115n, 124.

34   Vera K. Fast, "Charlotte Whitehead (Ross)," *DCB*, vol. 14, pp. 1054-5.

35   Vera K. Fast, "Jessie Turnbull (McEwen)," *DCB*, vol. 14, pp. 1023-4.

36   Siggins, *Revenge of the Land*, pp. 263, 278, 292.

37   Willie, "Campbell," *DCB*, vol. 14, p. 175.

38   Charles Gordon, *Postscript to Adventure: The Autobiography of Ralph Connor* (Toronto: McClelland and Stewart, Ltd., reprint of 1937 edition), p. 206-7.

39   Duff Crerar, *Padres in No Man's Land: Canadian Chaplains and the Great War* (Montreal and Kingston: McGill-Queen's University Press, 1993) pp. 235-247; Maureen K. Lux, "'The Bitter Flats': The 1918 Influenza Epidemic in Saskatchewan," *Saskatchewan History*, Spring 1997, p. 5.

40   Gordon C. Church, "Alfred Frank Mantle," *DCB*, vol. 14, pp. 742-3.

41   Lux, "The Bitter Flats," *Saskatchewan History*, Spring 1997, pp. 3-13; *A&P*, 1919, App. p. 33.

42   Lux, "The Bitter Flats," *Saskatchewan History*, Spring 1997, p. 5; *A&P*, 1919, App. p. 38.

43   Siggins, *Revenge of the Land*, p. 288.

44   Walter Young, *Democracy and Discontent: Progressiveism, Socialism and Social Credit in the Canadian West*, 2nd ed. (Toronto: McGraw-Hill Ryerson Ltd., 1978), pp. 17-23.

45   Graham, *Meighan*, pp. 229-244.

46   Ralph Connor, *To Him that Hath: A Novel of the West of Today* (Toronto: McClelland and Stewart, 1921).

47   Christine MacDonald, "Pioneer Church Life in Saskatchewan," in D.H. Bocking, ed., *Pages from the Past: Essays on Saskatchewan History* (Saskatoon: Western Producer Prairie Books, 1979), pp. 123, 132-3; and Choquette, *Oblate Assault*, p. 180.

Chapter 2

1   *Knox College Monthly*, Feb. 1886, pp. 171-2.

2   *Knox Monthly*, Jan. 1888, p. 168.

3   *A&P*, 1892, App. p. xv; 1880, App. p. xi; 1881, Minutes, pp. 20, 21. Quoted in Allan Farris, "Presbyterianism and the Office of Superintendent," unpub., n.d., a copy is in the possession of Peter Bush.

4   Charles W. Gordon (Ralph Connor), *The Life of James Robertson: Missionary Superintendent in Western Canada* (Toronto: The Westminster Press, 1908), pp. 13-75.

5   *Ibid.*, pp. 94-152.

6   UCA, Robertson Papers, Reel 2, Robertson to wife, June 16, 1881.

7   *A&P*, 1882, Minutes, pp. 19-20; See PCA, Robertson Letters (1986.5001). This is a small collection of correspondence (24 letters) between Robertson and Robert Crawford an elder at Indian Head, Saskatchewan. Written over the course of seven years, the letters give an insight into the administrative aspects of Robertson's work and the pastoral role he played in the lives of not just ministers but also lay people.

8   UCA, Robertson Papers, Reel 4, Sermon Notes, Matthew 20:1-16.

9   Toronto *Mail*, March 23, 1883, p. 2.

10   UCA, Robertson Papers, Reel 2, Robertson to wife, March 30, 1883.

11   *A&P*, 1886, Minutes, pp. 17, 27-29; University of Manitoba, Archives and Special Collections, Papers of Charles William Gordon, Box 36, File 5, "Home Mission Superintendence" by A.B. Baird.

12   *A&P*, 1884, app., p. xviii, Robertson's Report.

13   Gordon Harland, "James Robertson," *DCB*, vol 13, pp. 880-881.

14   See Peter Bush, ""Sending the Gospel": The Development of the Knox College Student Missionary Society, 1845-1925", *The Canadian Society of Presbyterian History Papers*, 1987, pp. 49-70.

15   *A&P*, 1898, App. p.27; 1891, App. p. xxiii; 1913, App. pp. 12-13; 1887, App., p. xv.

16   *A&P*, 1885-1925, Augmentation Committee Reports; Catherine Macdonald, "James Robertson and Presbyterian Church extension in Manitoba and the North West, 1866-1902," in *Prairie Spirit: Perspectives on the Heritage of the United Church of Canada in the West*, ed., Dennis Butcher, et. al. (Winnipeg: University of Manitoba Press, 1985), pp. 91-95.

17   Gordon, *Robertson*, p. 181.

18   *A&P*, 1891, App. #1, p. xxiv; 1894, App. #1, p. xv. See also Peter Bush, "'Sending the Gospel': The Development of the Knox College Student Missionary Society, 1845-1925," *The Canadian Society of Presbyterian History Papers*, 1987, pp. 49-70.

19   *A&P*, 1891, App. #1, p. xxiv, Robertson Report; 1893, App. #1, p. xiv, Robertson Report; 1903, App. p. 7.

20   UCA, Robertson Papers, Reel 2, Robertson to student, June 4, 1889.

21   *A&P*, 1898, app., p. 26; *Record*, Sept. 1898, Vol. 23, #9, p. 232.

22   UCA, Robertson Papers, Reel 4, Tributes to Robertson, 1902.

23   U of M, Archives, Gordon Papers, Box 37, File 1, "The Personal Side of the Superintendent."

24   UCA, Robertson Papers, Reel 3, Robertson to wife, Nov. 19, 1892.

25   U of M, Archives, Gordon Papers, Box 8, File 6, Robertson to Gordon, Nov. 15, 1897.

26   UCA, Robertson Papers, Reel 2, J. Robertson to Tina Robertson, Oct. 31, 1885.

27   U of M, Archives, Gordon Papers, Box 8, File 6, Robertson to Gordon, Nov. 15, 1897.

28   *A&P*, 1903, App., p. 3-4; 1904, App., p.3.

29   *A&P*, 1903, App. p. 3.

30   *A&P*, 1913, App. p. 64-65, 1914, App. p. 59-62.

31   *A&P*, 1912, App. p. 3.

32   *A&P*, 1912, App., p. 3; 1913, App., p. 3.

33   *Pre-Assembly Congress* (Toronto: The Presbyterian Church in Canada, 1913), Appendix of Charts, "Get in, Brother." See Bush, "Sending the Gospel" on how this bureaucratization and centralized control affected the Knox College Student Missionary Society.

34   Bush, "Sending the Gospel," pp. 64, 70.

35   *A&P*, 1893, App. pp. xv-xvi.

36   *A&P*, 1893, App., pp. xv-xvi; 1906, App., p. 4; 1907, App. p. 7-8; 1909, App., p. 5; 1917, App., p. 18; *Mission Pioneer*, Jan. 1911, Vol. 7 #11, p. 155; Oct. 1913, Vol. 10, #7, p. 102-3.

37   *A&P*, 1913, app., p. 43; 1915, App. p. 42; Christine MacDonald, "Pioneer Church Life in Saskatchewan," in D.H. Bocking, ed., *Pages from the Past: Essays on Saskatchewan History* (Saskatoon: Western Producer Prairie Books, 1979), p. 124.

38   *A&P*, 1903, App., p. 7; 1906, app., p. 8.

39   *A&P*, 1913, App. p. 12-13; 1915, App. pp. 43, 47.

40   *A&P*, 1918, App. p. 188; 1919, App., pp. 28-29, 37, 192.

41   *A&P*, 1923, app., pp. 14, 30; 1924, App. p. 402.

42   PCA, Special Committee for Aids for Social Worship, *Aids for Social Worship*, 1900, passim; *A&P*, 1923, App. p. 37.

43   *A&P*, 1912, App. p. 22-23.

44   *A&P*, 1890, App. #1, p. xix; 1891, App. #1, p. xxiii; 1912, App. p. 5.

45   W.A. Cameron, "Home Missions Fifty Years Ago: Sermon delivered at Jubilee Synod of Saskatchewan, 1955" a printed copy of the sermon is in the possession of Peter Bush.

46   *Knox Monthly*, Jan. 1888, p. 168

47   Cameron, "Home Missions"; U of M, Archives, Gordon Papers, Box 37, File 3, Notes for *Life of Robertson*.

48   UCA, MAPMNW, FMC, WS, Box 7, File 119, F.A. Clare to R.P. Mackay, March 23, 1909.

49   *A&P*, 1891, App. #1, p. xxiii.

50   *The Home Mission Pioneer*, Oct., 1912, Vol. 9 #8, pp. 97-98.

51   *A&P*, 1891, App. #1, xxiii.

52   UCA, Synod of Manitoba and the Northwest Territories, Home Missions Committee, Minutes, vol. 1, March 17, 1886, "Instructions and Regulations for the guidance of Missionaries;" *A&P*, 1896, App. #1, p. xxvii., Robertson; Quote from A.T. Murray, quoted in Lyle Dick, *Farmers "Making Good": The Development of Abernethy District, Saskatchewan, 1880-1920* (Ottawa: Studies in Archaeology, Architecture and History, 1989), pp. 156-7.

53   *A&P*, 1896, App. #1, p. xxviii.

54   Cameron, "Home Missions"; *Mission Pioneer*, vol. 8, #8, Oct. 1911, pp. 105-106.

55   Cameron, "Home Missions."

56   *Mission Pioneer*, vol. 8, #8, Oct. 1911, p. 106; vol. 9, #8, Oct. 1912, pp. 99-101.

57 A&P, 1912, App. p. 301; 1919, App. p. 35; 1915, App. p. 47.

58 *Mission Pioneer*, Oct. 1912, vol. 9, #8, p. 100; A&P, 1918, App., p. 36-37. A similar story can be found in Ralph Connor's *The Sky Pilot: A Tale of the Foothills* (Toronto,: The Westminster Company, 1899) only this time it is the minister's playing for the home team in a baseball game that leads to the break-through (p. 69-75).

59 *Mission Pioneer*, Feb. 1911, vol. 7, #12, pp. 174-176; Oct. 1911, vol. 8, #8, p. 106; Cameron, "Home Missions."

Chapter 3

1   UCA, PCC, Mission to the Aboriginal People in Manitoba and the Northwest (hereafter MAPMWN), Box 1, File 5, Report by H. McKay, March 17, 1885.

2   Robert Choquette, *The Oblate Assault on Canada's Northwest* (Ottawa: University of Ottawa Press, 1995); Frank Peake, "From the Red River to the Arctic," *Journal of the Canadian Church Historical Society*, Vol. 31, #2, October 1989; John Webster Grant, *Moon of Wintertime: Missionaries and the Indians of Canada in Encounter since 1534* (Toronto: University of Toronto Press, 1984); James Marnoch, *Western Witness: The Presbyterians in the area of the Synod of Manitoba, 1700-1885* (Winnipeg, Watson and Dwyer Publishing, 1994), pp. 57-70.

3   Darcee McLaren, "Living the Middle Ground: Four Native Presbyterian Missionaries, 1866-1912," unpub Ph.D. Thesis, McMaster University, 1997, pp. 87-88.

4   UCA, MAPMNW, Box 1, File 5, Report by H. McKay, March 17, 1885.

5   A&P, 1916, App. p. 63.

6   A&P, 1911, App. pp.132-3; 1912, App. pp. 139-40, 156.

7   John Webster Grant, "Two-thirds of the Revenue: Presbyterian Women and Native Indian Missions," in Elizabeth Gillan Muir and Marilyn Fardig Whiteley, eds., *Changing Roles of Women with the Christian Church in Canada* (Toronto: University of Toronto Press, 1995), pp. 99-116.

8   UCA, MAPMNW, Box 1, File 5, Report of Hugh McKay, April 13, 1885.

9   *Record*, Vol. 10, #10, Oct. 1885, p. 239.

10 *Record*, Vol. 11, #7, July 1886, p. 192.

11 *Record*, vol. 12, #9, Sept. 1887, p. 236.

12 Peter Lorenz Neufeld, "Keeseekoowenin," *DCB*, vol. 13, pp. 537-8.

13 McLaren, "Living the Middle Ground," pp. 61-66, 71-81.

14 McLaren, "Living the Middle Ground," pp. 66-71, 81-88; A&P, 1916, App. p. 49.

15 UCA, MAPMNW, Box 7, File 119, McLaren to MacKay, March 31, 1909; A&P, 1920, App. p. 51; 1908, App. p. 185; 1912, App. p. 139.

16 cf. Peter Bush, "The Dakota Missionaries of The Presbyterian Church in Canada, 1877-1903," *Presbyterian History*, vol. 40, #2, October 1996.

17 UCA, MAPMNW, Box 1, File 1, Extract Minute from Presbytery of Manitoba, May 17, 1876. Interestingly The Foreign Mission Committee (Western Section), PCC, had been considering a mission to "the Sioux Indians in British Territory," they had a motion on their books from Oct. 5, 1875 to explore the possibility of such work. (*Minutes of the FMC (WD), PCC*, vol. 2, Oct. 5, 1875).

18 Peter Douglas Elias, *The Dakota of the Canadian Northwest: Lessons for Survival* (Winnipeg: University of Manitoba Press, 1988).

19 *Ibid.*, pp. 180-210.

20 *Ibid.*, p. 229, fn. 14. All Presbyterian sources spell Solomon's last name Tunkasiuciye, this reference from Elias' book is the only place I have seen it spelt Tookanshaecheye. Given the description that Elias gives, there is no doubt that this is the same Solomon T. of Presbyterian Church's records.

21 *A&P*, 1880, App., p. lxxxiii; 1881, App. p. lxxxi; UCA, MIPMNW, PCC, WS, Box 1, File 3, Hart to MacLaren, May 20, 1882.

22 UCA, MAPMNW, Box 1, File 20, W. Hodnett to T. Wardrope, Oct. 17, 1887.

23 UCA, MAPMNW, Box 1, File 18, Report of Hugh MacKay, March 15, 1885; *A&P*, 1888, App. p. xvii.

24 *A&P*, 1893, p. xliv; *A&P*, 1894, p. xxxi.

25 McLaren, "Living the Middle Ground," pp. 103-105.

26 UCA, 79.199, Box 2, File 9, Baird to McKay, June 3, 1895; *A&P*, 1895, xxvii.

27 *A&P*, 1897, p. 167.

28 UCA, Board of Home Mission and Social Service, PCC, Box 1, File 7, May 7, 1888.

29 *A&P*, 1898, p. 180; *A&P*, 1899, p. 142.

30 UCA, PCC, Board of Home Mission and Social Service, (hereafter BHMSS), Box 3, File 29, Thunder to McKay, Sept. 9, 1901; Box 3, File 32, Thunder to McKay, Dec. 21, 1901; *A&P*, 1902, p. 177.

31 UCA, BHMSS, Box 3, File 36, Hanska to McKay, April 16, 1902.

32 McLaren, "Living the Middle Ground", pp. 102-103.

33 *Ibid.*

34 *A&P*, 1907, App. p. 169; 1908, App. p. 193.

35 *A&P*, 1908, App. p. 186; 1912, App. p. 142.

36 *A&P*, 1908, App. p. 185.

37 UCA, MAPMNW, Box 7, File 117, R.B. Heron to R.P. McKay, Jan. 19, 1909.

38 UCA, MAPMNW, Box 7, File 117, F.A. Clare to R.P. MacKay, Jan. 29, 1909; File 119, Clare to MacKay, March 23, 1909

39 UCA, MAPMNW, Box 7, File 119, McLaren to MacKay, March 16, 1909.

40 *A&P*, 1916, App. p. 41.

41 UCA, BHMSS, Box 1, File 3, Response from Pitts to Heron's "Paper Read Before Regina Presbytery," 1923.

42 Grant, "Presbyterian Women and Native Indian Missions," pp. 107-8; Priscilla Lee Reid, "Lucy Baker: Missionary to Canada's North West," in Stanford Reid, ed. *Called to Witness*, vol. 1 (Toronto: Presbyterian Publications, 1975), pp. 67-82; *A&P*, 1912, App. p. 139; 1921, App. p. 42 reports the death of one of the Bruce sisters, Christina, who at the time was living in Lethbridge.

43 PAC, RG10, Vol. 6040, File 160-4, part 1, Kate Gillespie to Frank Pedley, Deputy Super. Gen. of Indian Affairs, May 1908.

44 *A&P*, 1908, App. p. 184.

45 UCA, MAPMNW, Box 7, File 117, "Resolution of the Indian Worker's Association of the Presbyterian Church for Saskatchewan and Manitoba," 1909 (undated); cf. PAC, RG10, Vol. 6040, file 160-4, part 1, "Resolution of the Indian Workers Association of Presbyterian Church for Saskatchewan and Manitoba," May 1909.

46 UCA, MAPMNW, Box 8, File 154, McLaren to McKay, April 16, 1913.

47 UCA, MAPMNW, Box 7, File 119, McLaren to McKay, March 16, 1909.

48 *A&P*, 1911, App. pp. 133, 234.

49 UCA, MAPMNW, Box 8, File 145, McKay to Pedley, May 29, 1912; File 151, McKay to McKay, Oct. 4, 1912.

50 UCA, MAPMNW, Box 8, File 154, McLaren to McKay, April 16, 1913.

51 UCA, BHMSS, Box 1, File 3, Heron, "Paper read before Regina Presbytery," May, 1923; and J.R. Miller, *Shingwauk's Vision: A History of Native Residential Schools* (Toronto: University of Toronto Press, 1996), p. 157.

52 UCA, BHMSS, Box 1, File 3, Clarke to Edmison, Aug. 7, 1923; Pitts to Edmison, 1923 (no date); Clark to Edmison, Aug. 7, 1923.

53 Maggie Siggins, *Revenge of the Land: A Century of Greed, Tragedy, and Murder on a Saskatchewan Farm* (Toronto: McClelland & Stewart, 1991), pp. 97-98.

54 UCA, MAPMNW, Box 7, File 117, Agnes Sibbald to Rev. Dr. Farquharson, Jan. 30, 1909; Box 6, File 99, J.D. McLean to R.P. Mackay, July 18, 1907; Rev. Dr. Farquharson to A.E. Armstrong, July 29, 1907; Box 8, File 151, H. Mackay to R.P. Mackay, Oct. 1, 1912.

55 UCA, BHMSS, Box 1, File 4, Report by RNWMP written by Sgt. C. Richardson; H. McKay to E. Taylor, Aug. 27, 1919; Inspector Christianson, "Report on the Round Lake Boarding School," n.d. (circa 1920).

56 UCA, MAPMNW, Box 8, File 151, H. Mackay to R.P. Mackay, Oct. 1, 1912; Box 7, file 131, P.W. Gibson Ponton to R.P. MacKay, Feb. 1, 1911.

57 Miller, *Shingwauk*, p. 341, cf. 337-339.

58 UCA, MAPMNW, Box 7, File 124, Jennie Cunningham to R.P. MacKay, Aug. 28, 1909; Miller, *Shingwauk's Vision*, p. 238.

59 *A&P*, 1908, App. p. 182; 1924, App. p. 27.

60 UCA, MAPMNW, box 7, file 122, McLaren to Mackay, June 22, 1909; Mackay to McLaren, June 30, 1909.

61 PAC, RG10, vol. 6253, File 575-9 part 1, Grant to Scott, July 30, 1914.

62 *Ibid.*, Keon to Scott, Dec. 9, 1914.

63 *Ibid.*, Grant to McLean, Jan. 2, 1914 (the letter is misdated, the correct date is Jan. 2, 1915).

64 *Ibid.*, Scott to Scott, July 20, 1915.

65 *A&P*, 1908, App. pp. 183-184.

66 UCA, BHMSS, Box 1, File 3, J.D. McLean to Edmison, April 7, 1922.

67 *A&P*, 1905, App. p. 165; UCA, MAPMNW, Box 7, File 123, Farquharson to MacKay, July 26, 1909; File 124, MacKay to Farquharson, Aug. 12, 1909.

68 *A&P*, 1905, App. p. 166; 1908, App. p. 185-186.

69 *A&P*, 1904, App. p. 183; 1906 App. p. 221; E. Brian Titley, "W.M. Graham: Indian Agent Extrordinaire," *Prairie Forum*, 1983, Vol. 8, #1; Sarah Carter, *Lost Harvests: Prairie Indian Reserve Farmers and Government Policy* (Montreal and Kingston: McGill-Queen's University Press, 1990), pp. 239-244.

70 *A&P*, 1923, App. p. 30; 1924, App. p. 26.

71 *A&P*, 1916, App. p. 51; 1914, App. p. 5-6, 24; 1917, App. p. 37.

72 UCA, PCC, MAPMNW, Box 7, file 117, Jonathan Beverly to R.P. MacKay, Jan. 2, 1909.

73 UCA, PCC, BHMSS, Box 1, file 9, "Memo Re: Board Schools," 1920.

Chapter 4

1   *Pre-Assembly Congress*, Appendix of Charts shown at the Congress; Census of Canada, 1921.

2   *Record*, Feb. 1919, Vol. 44, #2, p. 38-39.

3   *A&P*, 1888, Appendix 1, p. xi.

4   *A&P*, 1889, App. #1, p. xv; 1891, App. #1, p. xxvii; 1894, App. #1, p. xii.

5   *A&P*, 1892, App. #1, p. xxiii; 1893, App. #1, p. xviii; 1895, App. #1, p. xix.

6   A "Homogeneous Unit" is defined as "a section of society in which all the members have some characteristic in common." On the prairies the various ethnic groups among whom the Presbyterian church sought to do ministry were homogeneous units—the Presbyterian church sought to establish congregations where people shared a common ethnic background—making them a homogeneous unit. See Donald McGavran, *Understanding Church Growth* (Grand Rapids, Michigan: Wm. B. Eerdmans, 1970); and C. Peter Wagner, ed., *Church Growth: State of the Art* (Wheaton, Illinois: Tyndale House Pub., Inc., 1986).

7   *A&P*, 1895, App. #1, pp. xviii, xix.

8   *A&P*, 1901, App. p. 18.

9   *A&P*, 1892, App. #1, p. xiv.

10   *A&P*, 1889, App. #1, p. xiv.

11   *A&P*, 1893, App. #1, p. xv.

12   *A&P*, 1892, App. #1, p. xv.

13   *A&P*, 1900, App. p. 11.

14   *A&P*, 1896, App. 1, p. xxxi; 1891, App. 1, p. xix.

15   *A&P*, 1891, App. #1, p. xix.

16   *The Home Mission Pioneer*, Jan. 1912, Vol. 8, #11, pp. 148-9; Oct. 1912, Vol. 9 #8, pp. 105-6; *A&P*, 1913, App. p. 293.

17   *A&P*, 1903, App. p. 22; 1905, App. p. 24.

18   *A&P*, 1903, App. p. 26; 1909, App. p. 36; *Pioneer*, April 1910, Vol. 7, #2, pp. 20-21.

19   *A&P*, 1906, App. p. 27.

20   *A&P*, 1904, App. p. 27; 1905, App. pp. 27-28.

21   *A&P*, 1910, App. p. 41; 1906, App., p. 32.

22   *A&P*, 1908, App. p. 38; 1909, App. p. 43; 1912, App. p. 19.

23   UCA, PCC, Board of Home Missions and Social Service (hereafter BHMSS), Box 2, File 2 [n.d. circa 1914].

24   *Ibid.*

25   *Ibid.*

26   *Ibid.*, and UCA, PCC, BHMSS, Box 2, File 21, William Simons Report to A.S. Grant, [n.d. circa 1914].

27   UCA, PCC, BHMSS, Box 2, File 21, Simons Report to Grant, [n.d. most likely 1914].

28   *A&P*, 1904, App. p. 13; 1905, App. p. 9; "The Story of the Anna Turnbull Hospital at Wakaw," compiled by Douglas Fraser and Miss Carmichael, WHMS, n.d.

29   *A&P*, 1906, App. p. 13; 1908, App. p. 11; 1916, App. p. 52.

30   UCA, PCC, BHMSS, Box 2, File 15: "Hungarian Work," Oct. 6, 1910; A. Anthony, et. al. to Presbyterian Home Mission Committee, Mar. 27, 1911; Kovachy to Farquharson, Mar. 30, 1911; Kovach to James Frazer, Oct. 25, 1911.

31   *A&P*, 1914, App. pp. 548-9, 566-7, 570-1; 1924, App. pp. 406-7. 1918, App. p. 32.

32   *A&P*, 1916, App. pp. 40, 52; 1918, App. p. 32.

33   *A&P*, 1921, App. p. 17; 1923, App. p. 14; 1924, App. p. 10; J. Leishman, "The Hungarians," *Pioneer*, Dec. 1910, Vol. 7, #10, p. 132.

34   Norman Macdonald, *Canada: Immigration and Colonization, 1841-1903* (Toronto,:Macmillan of Canada, 1966), pp. 230-231.

35   *A&P*, 1904, App. p. 13; 1903, App. pp.12, 14.

36   *A&P*, 1915, App. p. 36; 1918, App. p. 30; 1921, App. p. 18; 1924, App. p. 30.

37   *A&P*, 1903, App. p. 5; 1924, App. p. 36; cf. James Ballantyne, "The Doukhobors" (sic), The Home Mission *Pioneer*, April 1911, Vol. 8 #2, pp. 21-23.

38   *A&P*, 1908, App. p. 33; 1906, App. p. 34.

39   *A&P*, 1914, App. p. 41; 1919, App. p. 37-8; 1923, App. p. 38.

40   *A&P*, 1921, App. p. 22; 1924, App. p. 9-10.

41   *A&P*, 1915, App. p. 41.

42   *A&P*, 1916, App. p. 55; 1917, App. p. 15; 1918, App. pp. 35, 48; 1919, App. p. 35; 1920, App. p. 42; 1921, App. p. 31; 1923, App. p. 35; 1924, App. p. 32.

43   *A&P*, 1905, App. p. 9; 1924, App. p. 450; 1913, App. p. 27.

44   *A&P*, 1918, App. p. 31; 1921, App. p. 18; J. Leishman, "The Bohemians," *The Home Mission Pioneer*, April 1911, Vol. 8 #2, pp. 19-20.

45   *Census of Canada*, 1900-1901, vol. 1 (Ottawa, 1902).

46   John Bodrug, *Independent Orthodox Church: Memoirs pertaining to the history of a Ukrainian Canadian Church in the years 1903 to 1913*, trans. Lydia Biddle and Edward Bodrug (Toronto: Ukrainian Canadian Research Foundation, 1980), pp. 9-12, 24, 25, 39; *A&P*, 1901, App. p. 17.

47   *A&P*, 1904, App., p. 28.

48   *A&P*, 1903, App. p. 22; 1904, App., p. 27; PCA, Jean Kipp, "Our Medical Missions," pamphlet published by Women's Home Missionary Society, PCC, 1913.

49   Kipp, "Medical Missions;" *A&P*, 1922, App. p. 50. See Raymond R. Smith, "A heritage of healing: Church hospital and medical work in Manitoba, 1900-1977," in Butcher, et. al., *Prairie Spirit*, pp. 265-282.

50   UCA, PCC, WHMS, Minutes; *Pioneer*, June 1910, Seventh Annual Report of the WHMS, pp. 16-18.

51   *Pioneer*, Aug. 1910, Vol. 7 #6, p. 67. The WHMS was so serious about this, that often they would recruit a minister who was interested in work among the Ukrainians and would then send him to medical school after his commitment to the mission principles was assured. An example of this is the Rev. R.G. Scott, who became the Medical Missionary at Wakaw. (*Pioneer*, June 1910, Seventh Annual Report, p. 17.)

52   Bodrug, *Independent Orthodox Church*, p. 91.

53   Bodrug, *Independent Orthodox Church*, pp. 41-45.

54   PCA, WHMS, Pamphlet, "The Story of the Anna Turnbull Hospital at Wakaw," p. 10.

55   See for example: Milos Mladenovic, "Canadian Orthodoxy and the Union of Churches," in John Webster Grant, ed., *The Churches and the Canadian Experience: A Faith and Order Study of The Christian Tradition* (Toronto: The Ryerson Press, 1963), pp. 111-113; Vivian Olender, "The Reaction of the Canadian Presbyterian Church towards Ukrainian Immigrants (1900-1925): Rural Home Missions as agencies of Assimilation," unpub. Ph.D. thesis,

(University of St. Michael's College, Toronto School of Theology), 1984, passim; Paul Yuzyk "Religious Life" in Manoly Lupul, ed., *A Heritage in Transition: Essays in the History of Ukrainians in Canada* (Toronto, McClelland and Stewart, 1982), pp. 150-152. UCA, PCC, BHMSS, Box 2, File 13, Minutes of HMC of the General Assembly, May 29, 1912.

56   UCA, PCC, BHMSS, Box 2, File 18, "Celibacy" by M. Glora, *Ranok*, translation by A.J. Hunter.

57   UCA, PCC, BHMSS, Box 2, File 13, Farquharson to Grant, July 6, 1912; File 17, "Report of the Editors of Canadian Ranok," 1923.

58   *A&P*, 1905, App. pp. 9-11; 1907, App., p. 15; Bodrug, *Independent Orthodox Church*, p. 119.

59   UCA, PCC, BHMSS, Box 2, File 13, Bodrug to Farquharson, March 2, 1912; Box 3, File 34, Zalizniak to Farquharson, May 29, 1912.

60   UCA, PCC, BHMSS, Box 2, File 14, Grant to Farquharson, Aug. 10, 1911; *A&P*, 1913, HMC Report, App. p. 7. cf. "any further extension of the work among the Ruthenian people should be under Presbyterian supervision, and that in general closer supervision of work among the Ruthenians is desirable." UCA, PCC, BHMSS, Box 2, File 13, Minutes of HMC of the General Assembly, May 29, 1912. A.J. Hunter, *A Friendly Adventure: The Story of the United Church Mission among New Canadians at Teulon, Manitoba* (Toronto: The United Church of Canada, 1929), pp. 34, 37.

61   UCA, PCC, BHMSS, Minutes of Sub-Committee on The Reception of Ministers of the Independent Greek Church into the Presbyterian Church, Oct. 24, 28, 1912.

62   Bodrug, *Independent Orthodox Church*, p. 119.

63   *A&P*, 1921, App., p. 45; 1922, App., p. 49; App. p. 44-45. There were two schools in Edmonton (primarily French-Canadian), two school in Vegreville, one in Ethelbert, one in Sifton, two in Teulon, one in Battleford, SK, one in Canora, one in Prince Alberta, and new in 1923 one in Assiniboia, SK. See Michael Owen, "'Keeping Canada God's Country': Presbyterian school-homes for Ruthenian children," in Butcher, et. al, *Prairie Spirit*, pp. 184-201.

64   Michael Owen, "'Keeping Canada God's Country': Presbyterian Perspectives on Selected social Issues, 1900-1915," unpub. Ph.D. Thesis, Department of Education, University of Toronto, 1984, p. 77.

65   *Pioneer*, July-August, 1913, Vol. 10, #5, p. 70.

66   *Census of Canada*, 1911, vol. 1, (Ottawa, 1912).

67   *A&P*, 1909, App., p. 109; 1910, App. p. 140; 1911, App., p. 122; 1914, App. p. 141-142; 1916, App., p. 145.

68   *A&P*, 1914, App. p. 23; 1915, App. p. 26.

69   *A&P*, 1913, App. p. 45; 1914, App. p. 40; 1915, App. p. 43.

70   *A&P*, 1913, App. p. 61; 1914, App. p. 62.

71   Ralph Connor (Charles Gordon), *The Foreigner: A Tale of Saskatchewan* (Toronto: The Westminster Company, Ltd., 1909), p. 253.

72   *Ibid.*, p. 275.

73   *Ibid.*, p. 372-3.

74   *Pioneer*, July-August 1913, Vol. 10 #5, p. 70.

75   *A&P*, 1916, App. p. 50.

76   UCA, PCC, BHMSS, Box 3, File 22, Oliver to Ramsay, April 15, 1916; *A&P*, 1921, App. p. 20.

77   *A&P*, 1923, App. pp. 14, 36.

78   John Webster Grant, "The Reaction of WASP Churches to Non-WASP Immigrants," in *Canadian Society of Church History Papers, 1968*, Part 1, pp. 1-15.

Chapter 5

1   Charles Gordon (Ralph Connor), *The Life of James Robertson: Missionary Superintendent in Western Canada* (Toronto: The Westminster Company, Ltd., 1908), p. 347.

2   UCA, Robertson Papers, microfilm, Roll 3, John Pringle to Robertson, n.d. (almost certainly late 1898).

3   Suzanne Zeller and Gale Avrith-Wakeam, "George Mercer Dawson," *DCB*, vol. 13, pp.260.

4   Morris Zaslow, *The Opening of the Canadian North, 1970-1914* (Toronto: McClelland and Stewart, 1971), pp. 101-103; and Thora McIlroy Mills, *The Contribution of the Presbyterian Church to the Yukon During the Gold Rush, 1897-1910* (Toronto: United Church Publishing House, 1977), p. 65-67.

5   Gordon, *Robertson*, p. 347.

6   *Ibid.*, pp. 353-354, 357-359.

7   *Record*, Dec. 1897, vol. 22 #12 through Oct. 1899, vol. 24 #10; quote from Feb. 1898, Vol. 23, #2, p. 31.

8   *The Westminster*, April 2, 1898, quoted in Gordon, *Robertson*, p. 362; also see Gordon, *Robertson*, pp. 350-351, 361-362; *A&P*, 1898, App., p. 32; 1899, App., p. 21.

9   Mills, *Contribution of Presbyterian Church*, p. 12-16.

10   *Ibid.*, p. 42, 71.

11   UCA, Robertson Papers, microfilm, Reel 3, A.S. Grant to Robertson, Feb. 28, 1898.

12   Hall Young, "A Letter from Klondike," (dated Dec. 1, 1897), *The Presbyterian Record*, April 1898, pp. 86-89. Young added a P.S. to his letter, "Sixty degrees below zero today; I stood it well."

13   UCA, PCC, WMS (WD), Box 14, File 8, "The History of the Women's Home Missionary Society," n.d., p. 1.

14   UCA, Robertson Papers, Reel 3, Grant to Robertson, Dec. 1898.

15   *A&P*, 1904, app., p. 4.

16   UCA, Robertson Papers, Reel 3, Grant to Robertson, Dec. 1898; Grant to Robertson, Jan. 13, 1899.

17   *Record*, Oct. 1899, vol. 24, #10, p. 295.

18   *A&P*, 1902, app., p. 28.

19   *Record*, March 1898, vol. 23, #3, p. 59.

20   PCA, Andrew Shaw Grant Papers, Box 2, File 14, Grant to Laurier, March 19, 1901.

21   Morris Zaslow, *The Opening of the Canadian North, 1870-1914* (Toronto McClelland and Stewart, 1971), p. 137-138. Quotation from Mills, *Contribution*, p. 78.

22   *A&P*, 1902, app., p. 28.

23   James M. Sinclair, *Mission Klondike* (Vancouver: Mitchell Press Ltd., 1978), p. 207-210; *A&P*, 1902, app., 28, 1903, app., p. 6; 1909, app., p. 19; 1914, app., p. 624-625.

24   *A&P*, 1908, app., p. 14; 1909, app., 19; 1910, app. p. 24; 1924, App. p. 38.

25   Mills, *Contribution*, p. 77; *Record*, Sept. 1898, p. 232.

26   *Record*, Feb. 1899, vol. 24, #2, p. 41.

27 UCA, Robertson Papers, Reel 3, Pringle to Robertson, n.d., almost certainly late 1898.

28 *Record*, Feb. 1899, vol. 24, #2, p. 42.

29 UCA, PCC, WMS (WD), Box 14, File 8, "The History of the Women's Home Missionary Society," n.d.

30 *Record*, Oct. 1899, vol. 24, #10, p. 294.

31 Catherine Calkin, "The Hospital Mission in Atlin, 1899 to 1909," (unpub. paper, Knox College, 1989), p. 6-8

32 *Ibid.*; *A&P*, 1913, App. p. 15; 1924, App. p. 47.

33 *A&P*, 1924, App. p. 47.

34 *A&P*, 1903, app., p. 16; *A&P*, 1904, app., p. 466-467.

35 *The Home Mission Pioneer*, vol. 7, #1, March 1910, p. 7.

36 Minutes, Presbytery of Edmonton, p. 251, 1908 quoted in J. J. Harrold Morris, "The Presbyterian Church in Edmonton, Northern Alberta, and the Klondike, 1881-1925, largely according to Official Documents," (unpub., M.Th. Thesis, 1974), p. 75.

37 Harold M. Troper, *Only Farmers Need Apply: Official Canadian Government Encouragement of Immigration from the United States, 1896-1911* (Toronto: Griffin House, 1972), p. 6.

38 *Mission Pioneer*, vol. 7 #1, pp. 4-9; #2, pp 21-22.

39 Morris, "Presbyterian Church," pp. 76-77.

40 Morris, "Presbyterian Church," pp. 78-80 and *A&P*, 1914, app., pp. 36-38.

41 *Mission Pioneer*, vol. 8, #8, Oct. 1911, pp. 100-102; *A&P*, App. p. 47.

42 Morris, "Presbyterian Church," pp. 82-84; and *A&P*, 1925, app., pp. 440-441.

43 *A&P*, 1921, app., p. 35.

44 *A&P*, 1923, app., p. 35.

45 *A&P*, 1912, app., p. 15.

46 *A&P*, 1915, app. p. 23.

47 *A&P*, 1919, app., p. 26; 1921, app. p. 31; 1922, app., p. 26-27.

48 *A&P*, 1924, app., pp. 23, 392-393.

49 *A&P*, 1923, app., p. 27; 1924, app., p. 23.

Chapter 6

1 *A&P*, 1916, App. p. 18.

2 *A&P*, 1914, App. p. 296; 1916, App. p. 8; Brian Fraser, *The Social Uplifters: Presbyterian Progressives and the Social Gospel in Canada, 1875-1915* (Waterloo, ON: Wilfrid Laurier University Press, 1988), p. 35.

3 *A&P*, 1909, App. p. 257.

4 *A&P*, 1909, App. pp. 258-9; Fraser, *Presbyterian Progressives*, pp. 34, 108.

5 *A&P*, 1911, App. pp. 247-248.

6 *A&P*, 1921, App. p. 14.

7 *A&P*, 1919, App. pp. 15-17.

8 *A&P*, 1921, App. p. 14.

9 *A&P*, 1920, App. pp. 12-13.

10   *A&P*, 1914, App. p. 301.

11   Eric Crouse, "They 'left us pretty much as we were': American Saloon/Factory Evangelists and Canadian Working Men in the Early-Twentieth Century," *Historical Papers 1999: The Canadian Society of Church History*, pp. 51-71; *A&P*, 1924, App. p. .

12   John G. Shearer, "The Redemption of the City," in *Pre-Assembly Congress* (Toronto,: The Presbyterian Church in Canada, 1913), p. 172; Richard Allen, *The Social Passion*.

13   UCA, PCC, Board of Moral and Social Reform (BMSR), Box 1, File 2, Minutes of Executive, Jan. 31, 1910.

14   *A&P*, 1916, App. pp. 15-16, 57-58; 1917, App. pp. 31-32; 1919, App. p. 15; 1920, App. p. 7; 1921, App. p. 11; 1924, App. pp. 8-9, 25.

15   PCA, PCC, Board of Social Service and Evangelism, pamphlet by Charles W. Eliot, "The Double Standard of Morals and The Social Diseases," pp. 6-7; *A&P*, 1916, App. pp. 15-16.

16   *A&P*, 1915, App. p. 31.

17   Compare this to Mark 2:27, 28. *A&P*, 1909, App. p. 248; 1913, App. p. 38, 44, 278; 1914, App. p. 42; 1916, App. p. 46.

18   Lyle Dick, *Farmers "Making Good": The Development of Abernethy District, Saskatchewan, 1880-1920* (Ottawa: Environment Canada, 1989), p. 157.

19   *A&P*, 1911, App. pp. 255.

20   *A&P*, 1917, App. p. 25.

21   *A&P*, 1923, App. pp. 25, 27, 34.

22   *Census of Canada*, 1921

23   *A&P*, 1904, App. pp. 426-67; 1914, App. pp. 544-617; 1924, App. pp. 376-455; PCA, PCC, James Robertson Memorial Fund Committee, pamphlet, "Our Non-English Speaking Canadians," 1918, backcover.

24   *A&P*, 1914, App. p. 36.

25   UCA, Church Union Collection, Joint Committee on Church Union, Box 2, File 30, "Survey of Church Conditions," p. 16; *A&P*, 1913, App. p. 44; *Pioneer*, April 1912, Vol. 9 #2, A.S. Grant's Address, p. 20.

26   *A&P*, 1920, App. p. 29.

27   *A&P*, 1911, App. p. 8, 9; UCA, PCC, Board of Moral and Social Reform (BMSR), Box 1, File 2, Minutes of the Board, Sept. 6, 1910.

28   *A&P*, 1916, App. p. 18.

29   UCA, PCC, Board of Moral and Social Reform (BMSR), Box 1, File 2, Minutes of the Executive, Nov. 16, 1910.

30   *Pioneer*, March 1912, vol. 9 #1, pp. 3-4; UCA, PCC, BHMSS, Box 2, File 19, "Institutional Work among the Foreigners of Western Canada," n.d., almost certainly 1909 or 1910; UCA, PCC, WMS, Department of the Stranger, Box 2, File 21, opening words "Sunday, July 30th" marked "Winnipeg, n.d." circa 1911.

31   *Pioneer*, Sept. 1911, Vol. 8 #7, pp. 85-6; Jan. 1912, Vol. 8 #11, pp. 149-50; March 1913, Vol. 10 #1, pp. 6-7; May 1914, Vol. 11 #3, pp. 216-7.

32   *A&P*, 1915, App. p. 26; 1916, App. p. 40-1; PCA, PCC, Robertson Memorial Fund, "Our Non-English Speaking Canadians," p. 31.

33   *A&P*, 1916, App. pp. 20-21; *Pioneer*, Sept. 1913, Vol. 10 #6, Martha Smith, "The Jew, The Gentile and the Church in Camp," pp. 84-85; UCA, PCC, BHMSS, Box 3, File 36, "Community Centres, Annual Report, 1923."

34   *A&P*, 1916, App. p. 19-20.

35   *A&P*, 1919, App. p. 14; 1920, App. pp. 8-9; 1921, App. p. 7; 1923, App. p. 8; 1924, App. p. 8; UCA, PCC, BHMSS, Box 3, File 36, "Community Centres, Annual Report, 1923;" UCA, James Ralph Mutchmor Papers, Box 17, File 213, Memoirs, pp. 63-78.

36   *A&P*, 1919, App. p. 14; 1920, App. pp. 8-9; 1921, App. p. 7; 1923, App. p. 8; 1924, App. p. 8; UCA, Mutchmor Papers, Box 1, File 1, McLachlan to Mutchmor, May 13, 1922; Box 17, File 213, Memoirs, pp. 63-78.

37   Alan F.J. Artibise, *Winnipeg: A Social History of Urban Growth, 1874-1914*, (Montreal, McGill-Queen's Press, 1975), pp 254-263; *A&P*, 1916, App. pp. 6, 7; 1921, App. p. 30, 45; UCA, PCC, BHMSS, Box 3, File 36, "Community Centres, Annual Report, 1923;" UCA, PCC, WMS, Department of the Stranger, Box 2, File 21, "Report of Deaconess Work—Point Douglas Presbyterian Church, Winnipeg, 1923."

38   *A&P*, 1923, App. p. 13, 36; 1924, App. p. 11, 32; UCA, PCC, BHMSS, Box 3, File 36, "Community Centres, Annual Report, 1923."

39   *A&P*, 1919, App. p. 56; 1920, App. p. 55; 1921, App. p. 44; Agnes Coutie, "Only a Home Missionary," *Pioneer*, May 1914, vol. 11 #3, pp. 213-214.

40   UCA, PCC, Board of Foreign Missions, Missions to Jews, Box 1, File 22, Baird to Mackay, April 6, 1910; Scott to Mackay, Mar. 14, 1911; Scott to Baird, April 24, 1911; Baird to Mackay, May 25, 1911.

41   *A&P*, 1917, App. p. 19-21, 40.

42   *A&P*, 1917, App. p. 19-21; UCA, PCC, Foreign Missions, Missions to Jews, Box 1, File 22, Baird to Mackay, May 25, 1911.

43   *A&P*, 1917, App. p. 21.

44   *A&P*, 1919, App. p. 11.

45   PCA, Board of Social Service and Evangelism, Box 1, File 1, "Report of a Preliminary and General Social Survey of Fort William, March 1913;" Box 1 File 2, "Report of a Preliminary and General Social Survey of Port Arthur, March 1913."

46   *Ibid.*

47   UCA, *Report on a Rural Survey, Turtle Mountain District, Manitoba*, June-July, 1914; *Report on a Rural Survey, Swan River Valley, Manitoba*, August-September.

48   *Rural Survey, Turtle Mountain*, p. 55.

49   *Ibid.*, pp. 48-71.

50   *Rural Survey, Swan River*, pp. 50-67, indented quotation on p. 59.

51   *Ibid.*, pp. 50-67.

52   *Rural Survey, Turtle Mountain*, pp. 72-74; Rural Survey, Swan River, p. 67-69.

53   *Presbyterian and Westminster*, April 10, 1919, p. 351. The Methodist Church of Canada made a similar statement in 1918.

54   *Ibid.*, May 8, 1919, p. 457.

55   From *Dauphin Herald*, May 29, 1919 quoted in David P. Yeo, "Rural Manitoba Views the 1919 Winnipeg General Strike," *Prairie Forum*, vol. 14 #1, Spring 1989, p. 28; Allen, *The Social Passion*, p. 115; *Presbyterian and Westminster*, May 29, 1919, pp. 518-9; June 5, 1919, pp. 548-9; June 26, 1919, pp. 628-9.

56   *Record*, Vol. 44, #7, July 1919, pp. 198, 203-4.

57   *A&P*, 1918, Minutes, p. 68; Moir, *Enduring Witness*, pp. 216-217.

58   *A&P*, 1918, Minutes, p. 68; The Forward Movement, Box 1, File 1, pamphlets, "What is the Forward Movement?" and "The Forward Movement in the Local Congregation."

59   *Ibid.*

60   *Ibid.*

61   *Ibid.*; Moir, *Enduring Witness*, p. 217.

62   *A&P*, 1920, p. 33, 39, 42; *Record*, Fred Robertson, "Evangelism on the Prairie," July, 1919, vol. 44, #7, p. 213.

Chapter 7

1   PCA, Presbyterian Church Association Collection, 1982-1003, Box 5, File 32, Red Deer Branch, "Presbyterian Duty and Responsibility," circa 1924, no author is named but most likely was written by W.G. Brown.

2   See E. Lloyd Morrow, *Church Union in Canada: Its History, Motives, Doctrine, and Government*, (Toronto, Thomas Allen, Pub., 1923); Ephraim Scott, *"Church Union" and The Presbyterian Church in Canada*, (Montreal, John Lovell & Son, Ltd., Pub., 1928); Claris Edwin Silcox, *Church Union in Canada: Its Causes and Consequences*, (New York, Institute of Social and Religious Research, 1933); and N. Keith Clifford, *The Resistance to Church Union in Canada, 1904-1939* (Vancouver, University of British Columbia Press, 1985).

3   UCA, *Turtle Mountain District, Manitoba, Rural Survey* (Departments of Social Service and Evangelism of the Presbyterian and Methodist Church, June-July 1914), p. 63. See for example the pamphlet by John McNab, "Why We Remained as a Presbyterian Church in Canada," (n.d., circa 1936), pp. 10-11, photocopy in the possession of Peter Bush and Neil Semple, *The Lord's Dominion: The History of Canadian Methodism*, (Montreal & Kingston, McGill-Queen's University Press, 1996), pp. 434-439.

4   *A&P*, 1893, App. pp. xii-xiii; 1894, App. pp. xii-xiii.

5   *Ibid.*

6   *Ibid.*

7   I have heard a couple of variations on the story, the most obvious one being that it was the Methodist who rode the cow catcher and the Presbyterian came second. See B.G. Smillie, "Conclusion," in *Visions of The New Jerusalem: Religious settlement on the prairies*, ed., Benjamin G. Smillie, (Edmonton, NeWest Press, 1983), p. 183.

8   *A&P*, 1903, App. pp. 8-9.

9   *A&P*, 1905, App. p. 12.

10   Morris, "The Presbyterian Church in Edmonton," p. 78; J.J. Harrold Morris, "David George McQueen: Pioneer of Western Canada, 1887-1930," in *Called to Witness: Profiles of Canadian Presbyterians*, vol. 1, (Toronto, Presbyterian Publications, 1975), p. 196; *A&P*, 1911, App. p. 4-5.

11   *A&P*, 1911, App. p. 6.

12   *Ibid.*

13   *A&P*, 1912, App., p. 19; 1914, App. p. 40, 41.

14   Clifford, *Resistance*, p. 45.

15   *The Presbyterian*, Feb. 2, 1911, pp. 158-59.

16   Clifford, *Resistance*, pp. 51-52.

17   UCA, Church Union Collection, Box 6, File 134, Ballot for 1912 Vote on Church Union.

18   *Ibid.*, Box 6, files 134, 135, Results of the 1912 Vote in Manitoba, Saskatchewan, and Alberta.

19   *Ibid.*, Box 2, File 30, "Survey of Church Conditions in the Dominion of Canada made by a Joint Committee of the Methodist, Congregational, and Presbyterian Churches," 1914, p. 18-21.

20   *Ibid.*, pp. 31, 46-47.

21   *Ibid.*, pp. 48-49.

22   *Ibid.*, Box 7, Files 148, 149, Results of the 1915 Vote in Manitoba, Saskatchewan, and Alberta.

23   *Ibid.*

24   J.M. Pitsula, "W.G. Brown: "Righteousness Exalteth A Nation," in *Saskatchewan History*, vol. 33 #2, Spring, 1980, p. 56; *A&P*, 1907, App. p. 23.

25   W.G. Brown, "Why I Remained with the Presbyterian Church in Canada," *Sermons in Answer to Questions* (Saskatoon: Saskatoon Printers, 1937); and PCA, Presbyterian Church Association Collection, 1973-1003, Box 5, File 3, R.G. Stewart to Brown, Aug. 20, 1923.

26   PCA, PCA Collection, 1973-1003, Box 5, File 3, Brown to MacMillan, June 25, 1923.

27   *A&P*, 1918, App. p. 6-8.

28   PCA, PCA Collection, 1982-1003, Box 3, File 13, Peter Strang, "Union in Southern Saskatchewan," May 29, 1924; *A&P*, 1923, App. p. 27.

29   *A&P*, 1915, App. p. 33; 1923, App. p. 27.

30   *A&P*, 1919, App. p. 38; 1918, App. p. 7-8.

31   *A&P*, 1918, App. p. 9.

32   Stanford Reid, "The Quebec Trio: W.D., A.S., A.D. Reid," in Stanford Reid, *Called to Witness*, vol. 2 (Toronto,: The Presbyterian Church in Canada, 1980), p. 100.

33   PCA, PC Association, 1973-1003, Box 19, File 10, Mailing List; *A&P*, 1914, App. p. 22; 1925, Part 2, App. pp. 32-35, 1926, App. pp. 176-189.

34   PCA, PC Association, Mailing List; *A&P*, 1925, Part 2, App. pp. 32-35, 1926, App. pp. 176-189.

35   PCA, PC Association, Mailing List; *A&P*, 1925, Part 2, App. pp. 32-35, 1926, App. pp. 176-189.

36   PCA, PC Association, Mailing List; *A&P*, 1925, Part 2, App. pp. 32-35, 1926, App. pp. 176-189.

37   PCA, PC Assoc., 1973-1003, Box 5, File 3, W.G. Brown File, 1922-1924, untitled, undated document beginning "If the Unionists wanted..." The names Brown adds are: "Fisher of Innisfail...Morrow of Medicine Hat...White of Canmore, Short of Olds, Kennedy of McLeod, Allan of Coleman, Lang of Vegreville, MacAfee of Indian Head, Farquharson of Pilot Mound, Stewart of Neepawa, Oliver of Moosomin, Munro of Battleford, Reeves of Qu'Appelle."

Afterword

1   *A&P*, 1923, App. p. 3.

Selected Bibliography

Primary Sources

Manuscript Materials

National Archives of Canada RG10—Records of the Department of Indian Affairs

Presbyterian Church Archives (PCA)
    Andrew Shaw Grant Papers
    James Robertson Papers
    Presbyterian Church in Canada:
        Board of Moral and Social Reform, 1908-1912
        Board of Social Service and Evangelism, 1912-1914
        Forward Movement Collection
        James Robertson Memorial Fund Committee
        Presbyterian Church Association Collection
        Women's Home Missionary Society Collection

United Church Archives (UCA)
    James Ralph Mutchmor Papers
    James Robertson Papers
    Presbyterian Church in Canada:
        Mission to Aboriginal Peoples on Manitoba and the North-West Collection
        Board of Moral and Social Reform
        Board of Home Mission and Social Service
        Mission to the Jews
        Church Union Collection
        Women's Missionary Society (WD) Collection
        Women's Missionary Society—Department of the Stranger

University of Manitoba, Department of Archives and Special Collections Charles W. Gordon Papers

Printed Primary Material

Acts and Proceedings of the General Assembly of The Presbyterian Church in Canada, 1876-1926

Aids for Social Worship (Toronto, The Westminster Co., Ltd, 1900).

Bodrug, John, "Independent Orthodox Church: Memoirs pertaining to the history of a Ukrainian Canadian church in the years 1903-1913," (Toronto: Ukrainian Canadian Research Foundation, 1980).

Gordon, Charles (Ralph Connor), *The Foreigner: A Story of Saskatchewan* (Toronto: The Westminster Co. Ltd., 1909).

_____, *The Sky Pilot: A Tale of the Foothills* (Toronto: The Westminster Co. Ltd., 1899).

_____, *To Him That Hath: A Novel of the West of Today* (Toronto, McClelland and Stewart, 1921).

Home Missionary Pioneer, 1903-1925

Hunter, A.J., *A Friendly Adventure: The Story of the United Church Mission among the New Canadians at Teulon, Manitoba* (Toronto: United Church of Canada, 1929)

Pre-Assembly Congress, 1913 (Toronto: Board of Foreign Missions, Presbyterian Church in Canada)

Presbyterian Record, 1885-1925

Swan River Valley, Manitoba: Report on a Rural Survey, Methodist and Presbyterian Churches, Aug-Sept., 1914. (Copy at UCA)

Turtle Mountain District, Manitoba: Report on a Rural Survey, Methodist and Presbyterian Churches, June-July, 1914. (Copy at UCA)

Secondary Materials

Allen, Richard, *The Social Passion: Religion and Social Reform in Canada*, 1914-1928 (Toronto: University of Toronto Press, 1973).

Artibise, Alan F.J., *Winnipeg: A Social History of Urban Growth, 1874-1914*, (Montreal: McGill-Queen's University Press, 1975).

Barber, Marilyn, "Nationalism, Nativism and the Social Gospel: The Protestant Church Response to Foreign Immigrants in Western Canada, 1897-1914," in Richard Allen, ed., *The Social Gospel in Canada*, Papers of the Inter-Disciplinary Conference on the Social Gospel in Canada (Ottawa: National Museums of Canada, 1975), pp. 186-226.

Bocking, D.H., *Pages from the Past: Essays on Saskatchewan History* (Saskatoon: Western Producer Prairie Books, 1979)

Brass, Eleanor, *I Walk in Two Worlds* (Calgary, AB: Glenbow Museum, 1987).

Butcher, Dennis, et. al., *Prairie Spirit: Perspectives on the Heritage of the United Church of Canada in the West* (Winnipeg: University of Manitoba, 1985)

Calkin, Catherine, "The Hospital Mission in Atlin, 1899-1909," (unpub. paper: Knox College, Toronto, 1989).

Campbell, Jean, ed., *A Lively Story!: Historical Sketches of the Women's Missionary Society (Western Division) of The Presbyterian Church in Canada, 1864-1989* (Toronto: Women's Missionary Society (Western Division, 1989).

Carter, Sarah, *Lost Harvests: Prairie Indian Reserve Farmers and Government Policy* (Montreal & Kingston: McGill-Queen's Press, 1990).

Clifford, N. Keith, *Resistance to Church Union in Canada, 1904-1939* (Vancouver: University of British Columbia Press, 1985).

Crawford, David, *Blue Flame in the Foothills: Presbyterian Activities in the Calgary Region* (Calgary: Century Calgary Publications, 1975).

den Otter, A.A., "Lethbridge: Outpost of a Commercial Empire, 1885-1906," in Alan F.J. Artibise, *Town and City: Aspects of Western Canadian Urban Development* (Regina: Canadian Plains Research Center, 1981).

Dick, Lyle, *Farmers "Making Good": The Development of Abernethy District, Saskatchewan, 1880-1920* (Ottawa: Canadian Parks Service, 1989).

Dictionary of Canadian Biography, vols. 12-14 (Toronto: University of Toronto Press).

Elias, Peter Douglas, *The Dakota of the Canadian Northwest: Lessons for Survival* (Winnipeg: University of Manitoba Press, 1988)

Fraser, Brian, *The Social Uplifters: Presbyterian Progressives and the Social Gospel in Canada, 1875-1915* (Waterloo, ON: Wilfrid Laurier University Press, 1988).

Friesen, Gerald, *The Canadian Prairies: A History* (Toronto: University of Toronto Press, 1984).

Gordon, Charles, *The Life of James Robertson: Missionary Superintendent in Western Canada* (Toronto: The Westminster Company, 1908).

Grant, John W., "The Reaction of WASP Churches to Non-WASP Immigrants," *Canadian Society of Church History Papers*, 1968, part 1, pp. 1-15.

Loewen, Royden, "On the Margin or In the Lead: Canadian Prairie Historiography," *Agricultural History*, vol. 73, #1, Winter 1999, pp. 27-45.

Lux, Maureen, "'The Bitter Flats': The 1918 Influenza Epidemic in Saskatchewan," *Saskatchewan History*, Spring 1997, pp. 3-13.

McKellar, Hugh, *Presbyterian Pioneer Missionaries in Manitoba, Saskatchewan, Alberta and British Columbia* (Toronto: Murray Printing Co. Ltd., 1924).

McLaren, Darcee, "Living the Middle Ground: Four Native Presbyterian Missionaries, 1866-1912," (unpub. Ph. D. Thesis, McMaster University, 1997).

Marnoch, James, *Western Witness: The Presbyterians in the Area of the Synod of Manitoba, 1700-1885* (Winnipeg: Watson and Dwyer Publishing, 1994).

Miller, J.R., *Shingwauk's Vision: A History of Native Residential Schools* (Toronto, University of Toronto Press, 1996).

Mills, Thora McIlroy, *The Contribution of the Presbyterian Church to the Yukon During the Gold Rush, 1897-1910* (Toronto: United Church Publishing House, 1977).

Moir, John, *Enduring Witness: A History of the Presbyterian Church in Canada* (Toronto: Presbyterian Publications, 1975).

Morris, J.J. Harrold, "The Presbyterian Church in Edmonton, Northern Alberta, and the Klondike, 1881-1925, Largely according to Official Documents," (unpub. M. Th. Thesis, Vancouver School of Theology, 1974).

Morton, Richard Allen, "'Means of Grace': Directions in Presbyterian Home Mission Work, 1870-1885," *American Presbyterians*, Vol. 72, #2, Summer 1994, pp. 123-134.

Owen, Michael, "'Keeping Canada God's Country': Presbyterian Perspectives on Selected Social Issues, 1900-1915," (unpub, Ph.D. Thesis, University of Toronto, 1984).

Patton, Harald S., *Grain Growers Cooperation in Western Canada* (New York: AMS Press, 1969) reprint of 1928 edition published in Cambridge, Mass.

Smillie, Benjamin, *Visions of the New Jerusalem: Religious settlement on the Prairies* (Edmonton: NeWest Press, 1983).

Strang, Peter, *History of Missions in Southern Saskatchewan*, (Regina, 1929).

Troper, Harold Martin, *Only Farmers Need Apply: Official Canadian Government Encouragement of Immigration from the United States, 1896-1911* (Toronto: Griffin House, 1972).

Valverde, Mariana, *The Age of Light, Soap, and Water: Moral Reform in English Canada, 1885-1925* (Toronto: McClelland and Stewart, 1991).

Wood, Louis Aubrey, *A History of Farmer's Movements in Canada* (Toronto, University of Toronto Press, 1975) reprint of 1924 edition printed by Ryerson Press.

Zaslow, Morris, *The Opening of the Canadian North: 1870-1914* (Toronto: McClelland and Stewart, 1971).

INDEX